SOMETHING WENT WRONG

Works by

LEWIS BROWNE

Histories, etc.

Stranger Than Fiction
This Believing World
The Graphic Bible
Since Calvary
How Odd of God
Something Went Wrong

Biographies

That Man Heine
Blessèd Spinoza

Novels

All Things Are Possible
Oh, Say, Can You See!

SOMETHING WENT WRONG

A Summation of Modern History

By
LEWIS BROWNE

With Decorations and Maps by
Myna and Lewis Browne

New York · 1942

THE MACMILLAN COMPANY

FIRST PRINTING.

PRINTED IN THE UNITED STATES OF AMERICA
AMERICAN BOOK–STRATFORD PRESS, INC., NEW YORK

For

BOB AND DICK LISSNER

Who Asked for a True Mystery Story

"It has never been established that any author ever wrote a strictly objective history—perhaps because there has never been any reader equal to the exertion of wading through so dull a work."

EGON FRIEDELL,
A Cultural History of the Modern Age.

CONTENTS

MAPS AND CHARTS

SOMETHING WENT WRONG

I. CAME THE REVOLUTION

F YOU should ask what happened in 1776, you would probably be told it was the year when the Declaration of Independence was signed. But something else of importance happened that year, and in a way it was of even greater importance. True, it attracted almost no attention at the time. All the notice it got was one paragraph on an inside page of one small-town British weekly. Yet in effect the incident was the

X marking the spot where mankind turned a corner. Right about there mankind veered straight into the road to nowadays.

The scene of the incident was a grimy little colliery not far from Birmingham, in England. The date was the eighth of March, 1776. There on that day, in the midst of a small crowd of gaping onlookers, a pale, sober-eyed inventor started up a new machine to pump water out of the mine. He was a certain James Watt, age 40, tall, stoop-shouldered, hair prematurely gray; and his contraption was an iron monster that ate fire, belched smoke, and pumped like hell. Those who stood by and watched it were amazed.

Not that they had never seen a steam-pump before. Such devices had already existed in England for fully seventy years. (For that matter, the basic principle underlying them had been knocking about in books for almost seventeen hundred years!) Those earlier models, however, were crude, leaky, feeble affairs. To keep them going was almost more troublesome than pumping by hand.

But this machine of Watt's was in another class entirely. It did not merely boil and hiss and cough and rattle. It actually worked. The piston hammered up and down as though driven by a dozen devils, and gallons of water came sluicing out at every stroke. Up and down went that piston, up and down, up and down; and with each stroke, *whoosh* came the black mine-water.

The crowd broke into cheers, and one man, an ironmaster named Matthew Boulton, seemed hard put to keep from dancing. There was a special reason in his case: he owned a half-share in the invention. "Mr. Watt," he is known to have confided, "I hope and flatter myself that we are at the eve of a fortune!"

As it turned out, Mr. Boulton hoped and flattered himself

aright. But, had he realized what the world was at the eve of, one wonders whether the good man would not also have shuddered a little. For the monster which he had helped to let loose on earth did more than bring him and his partner a fortune; a great deal more.

It helped to bring the world a revolution.

To most people the word "revolution" suggests something sudden, convulsive, spectacular. They picture mobs brandishing scythes in flame-lit boulevards, bloody flags, bloodier gutters, and high-born ladies going to their death uncowed. But those are merely the superficial revolutions, the fleeting storms on the sea of history, the momentary crinklings and quakings in the external crust of the social earth. The really serious revolutions work slowly, and for the most part deep down. They work deep down and in stealth, gnawing the ground out from under age-old traditions, and wrecking the innermost order of life. They do not begin with chaos and slaughter. They usually end with them.

And to that far graver kind belongs the revolution of which I have just spoken. There was no building of barricades to signal its outbreak, no looting of mansions, no murder of gentry. For this revolution, being a serious one, did not break out at all. Instead it crept in . . . and went to work.

It quite literally went to work, for it was a revolution in man's way of working. Until the coming of the steam-engine, we humans were forced to rely primarily on brawn to make life comfortable. We used the delicate muscles in our fingers, the grosser muscles in our arms and legs, the still grosser muscles in the hocks and hams of tamed beasts. As a result we never did make life comfortable, not even approximately. We were too muscle-bound. Strain and sweat as we might, we could never produce even a steady supply of food for ourselves, let alone enough fair clothing or sound shelter. All through the ages we strained, we sweated, yet these things we never achieved. And life was therefore lean, mean, and sour with rancor. Men had to fight for the barest necessities; they had to fall out over the smallest crumbs. All society was shabby, and all existence was harsh, because there were not enough goods to go around.

True, we managed to survive, we got along—but always in considerable misery. And this left us chronically dissatisfied. After all, we were human beings, not dumb brutes. *They* might be content merely to get along; but not we. No, *we* had to get ahead.

That was why we kept seeking easier ways of doing things. We did not seek them methodically, of course. Before modern times we did not really hunt for improvements; we merely pottered around till we somehow stumbled on them. Fortuity was the mother of invention—then.

Nevertheless we did make progress. First we hit on simple tools like the hammer and the ax. Then came simple machines like the fire-drill and the pottery-wheel. The plow, the wagon, the lens, the compass, the printing-press: all these were devices which we invented to save ourselves labor. (And also the battering-ram, the cannon, the thumbscrew, the rack.) By the beginning of the Eighteenth Century we had stumbled on so many shortcuts to production—and destruction, too—that we might almost have been satisfied.

But we were not. On the contrary, it was just then that the urge to invent became at last conscious and resolute. Europe, which had first stirred from its sleep in the Eleventh Century, now finally stopped yawning and really went to work. And that led to a revolution more infernal and also more sublime than any other in human history. Thanks to it, man was able at last to acquire material abundance, and thus equip himself to seek a *sound* spiritual life.

Ever and again there comes a time when a strange yeastiness invades the race, and there is a stir somewhere on earth. Why that happens, no one knows; it just happens. It is like spring: secret forces become brazen, buried seeds begin suddenly to bear. The Eighteenth Century was such a time. It brought advance in almost every branch of human activity: in politics, science, morals, religion, even irreligion. But most of all it brought advance in technology—and in doing that it accomplished what was mundanely most imperative of all. Methods of manufacture which had been followed for ages became almost abruptly no longer tolerable. Tools which had been in constant use since the time of Tubal Cain were almost all at once discovered to be decrepit. Now a real hunt started for technological improvements.

History records the names of more than five hundred individuals who developed inventions during that Eighteenth Century. Some of these men were trained engineers, some were actually scientists. Most, however, were mere amateurs: tinkers, locksmiths, clockmakers, and hobby-riding curates. For these, as for the professionals, it was in part a treasure hunt, since an apt invention could be made to yield untold wealth. But that was not the only lure, nor even the most compelling one. The majority seem to have invented for the sheer fun of it—which was a lucky thing, seeing that fun was about all that most of them ever got out of it. The wealth, it appears, usually went to fellows who had a genius not so much for mechanical invention as financial circumvention.

That, however, is another story. No matter who got the money, the world got the inventions—and they were great ones. For example, there was the flying-shuttle, the spinning-jenny, and the coke-burning blast furnace. The first two ripped the swaddling clothes off the textile industry, and the third shattered the crib in which the metal industry had long been confined. There was also the primitive sewing machine, the primeval typewriter, the original mercury thermometer, the first practical water-closet. . . .

Yet these remained minor achievements. We were still hampered, for no matter how cunningly we contrived our machines, we still had to rely largely on muscle to move them. Even now most goods had to be literally *manu*-factured—"made by hand"—and all technology continued to be muscle-bound. True, we had long since learnt to harness the streams and the winds; but not very satisfactorily. Water-mills could never be more than creaking, poky establishments. As for windmills, they were too undependable for almost anything save grinding corn. So, despite all our inventiveness, we were only a little better off in A.D. 1775 than in 1775 B.C. Now as then our main source of motive-power was still brawn.

Finally, however, Watt produced his steam-engine, and then we were free at last. Or rather, *we had the means to become free.*

And the story of how we labored to make use of those means is in large part the story of our age.

The story opens on a small, fog-swathed, grassy island located in the North Atlantic: *lat.* 49° 57′ N. to 58° 40′ N., *long.* 6° 14′ W. to 1° 46′ E. This is in a way surprising, for in the past the natives of that particular island had always been markedly backward in industry. They had made good in a small way in mining and agriculture, and in a large way in piracy and other forms of commerce. But when it came to manufacture, they had never been anything but yokels.

Almost their only exports had been iron, wool, tin, and colonists—all raw materials.

The national symbol of those islanders was a bluff, gamey, heavy-jowled rustic squire named "John Bull"; and this was appropriate. Men after his image had dominated the tiny realm for ages. As a result, relatively little attention had been paid to so urban a pursuit as large-scale industry. That had been left almost entirely to people living on the mainland: Frenchmen, Flemings, Italians, and the like.

But then, belatedly, the islanders began to wake up. The change set in around the middle of the Eighteenth Century, and led swiftly to startling consequences. The very backwardness of those people gave them an advantage. Being innocent of experience in large-scale industry, they dared to experiment. Instead of copying the traditional methods used on the mainland, they contrived new ones of their own. Year after year they kept searching for ways whereby more goods could be produced with less effort. And finally—it was in a sense their crowning achievement—one of them perfected the steam-engine.

After that there was no stopping them. With a mighty clatter and snort the iron monster heaved John Bull out of the mud—and he was ready to outrace all his competitors.

For the latter continued to use their slow-poking watermills. In part this was out of necessity. A paranoiac named Napoleon happened to break loose just then on the Continent, and the people there became too busy shooting each other to have time to build steam-engines. In addition, those people were retarded by misguided thrift. They had considerable capital tied up in their old-fashioned industrial plants, so they hated to scrap them and start afresh. Besides, being human, they were inclined to be stubborn. If watermills were good enough for our fathers, they said, they're good enough for us. So they held out against the steam-engine.

And, because they held out, they lost out.

It was one more instance of a familiar paradox in history: when the time is ripe for a new advance in civilization, as often as not it will be a people from the rear that will come out in the lead. The Arabs proved that when they forged ahead of the Europeans in the Eighth Century; and the Europeans proved it again when they turned the tables in the Thirteenth. There are those who say the Asiatics are likely to repeat that story in the present century.

The explanation of this paradox is simple: he who builds last is free to build best. That is, if he has the means. And the British a hundred and fifty years ago had means galore. To begin with, their coffers were bursting with money gained during centuries of trafficking on the seas. To boot, they had a lively middle class with audacious ideas as to how money should be employed. Most important, their tiny island contained the iron out of which to forge the new engines, and the coal with which to stoke them. It was, therefore, as though God Himself had planned that the British should triumph at this juncture.

Being a very God-fearing folk, the British readily fell in with the plan. Before long they did triumph.

II. FROM WATT TO WHAT?

HAT came of Britain's triumph is a matter of record. That nation grew to be the richest and most powerful on earth. Of course, it had to pay a price for the victory, and so high a price that some insist the victory was really a defeat. They publish books to prove it, impassioned books full of glowing accounts of what Britain was like in the "good old days." Such authors, however, are usually better versed in rhetoric than in history.

They can be clever, those authors; they can write with verve and wit and caustic irony. Nevertheless, they are not to be trusted. Enjoyed, yes; but not trusted. For they gloss over the brute bleakness of existence in earlier times, the grim want that stalked the land, and the frustration and pain bred by that want. When they speak of "Merry Old England," their language is truer than they realize. The word "merry" is collaterally derived from the ancient Teutonic *murj*, meaning "short"—and that is precisely what life was in old England. It was recurrently short of food and chronically short of comfort. It was short of opportunity for the poor, and enterprise among the rich. It was short of roads to free the body, and schools to free the mind. In short, it was short of ten thousand boons which later became common property.

Life in those "good old days" was—by later standards—hardly life at all. For the bulk of the populace it was a process more like vegetation. Most people were like sessile plants, bound fast to the clefts where they were born, and knowing almost nothing of the great world all around them. Want and ignorance bound them close to the soil, so close that they were all but buried in it.

Yet it is difficult to deny one thing. Sorry as life may have been in England before the coming of the Machine, immediately thereafter it probably grew, for the bulk of the populace, even sorrier.

There were reasons for this, but they can wait. First let us look at the record. England got hold of mechanical power, and overnight—as time is reckoned in the history of a nation—she learnt to outreach and outsell all her industrial rivals. Overnight—that is, in about fifty years—she made herself the "workshop of the world."

But what a night it was! Looking back on it one gets the

impression that a pestilence befell the land. Just as Britain had once been ravaged by the Black Death, so did it now fall prey to the Black Life. Coal became king, Iron became his consort, and between them they brought on an indescribable Reign of Squalor.

It was not *all* bad. Behind and beneath the squalor there was grandeur of a sort: titanic heaving and straining and upthrust. At bottom the development was inestimably good. On the surface, however, the effect was awful. Whole counties became scabby with slums, with hideous mounds of huts encrusted at the base of chimney-stacks. They were called towns, but they were not really that. They were man-heaps.

At the top of these heaps stood a new class of masters: tough-gutted fellows many of whom had come up from the bottom, and all of whom seemed determined to stay up at any cost. By and large they were raw as coal and hard as iron. They were "masters" true enough—but not in the earlier sense of that term: because they had mastered a trade. Instead it was because they had made themselves masters of men.

And those at the bottom were a new class of slaves: mere "hands" hired by the week to tend machines. They were grimy, runty, cave-chested creatures, surly when sober, savage when drunk, and sick almost all the time. They were sick not alone in body but even more in spirit. And for good reason. Their kind had always worked hard and endured want, but formerly both work and want had followed a familiar pattern. Usage had inured the common folk to ancient wrongs; tradition had softened their deprivements. Life in the past, no matter how wearisome, had at least possessed a lulling rhythm. Now it became just hell on wheels.

But that had to happen. It was one of the unavoidable consequences of the advent of the Machine. Not that the Machine itself was to blame. It did bring the Black Life to England—and eventually to almost all the rest of the world—but it was no more culpable than is the shell for the death it spreads on the battlefield. Nor, in a final sense, were the owners of the Machine to blame. These were on a par with conscript soldiers who do the firing in time of battle. Many people will dispute that, but it seems true none the less. Those owners—the "capitalists" as they came to be called—were hardly free agents in what they did. They were hounded by the world in which they had their being, that world which kept bellowing to them: "Be a capitalist, or else—!"

Therefore, if we must have a villain, we might pick on that world. We might—and should—blame the prevailing state of mind for all the evils that ensued.

To understand that state of mind we must go back and see just what happened. The piddling industry existing in Great Britain in earlier days had been carried on chiefly by independent craftsmen. In most instances, of course, these were independent in name alone. In reality they were prisoners, for the wolf was always at their door. However, they did enjoy at least one glory: the door was their very own. They worked at home, using their own tools, and setting the hours to suit their own convenience.

This was particularly true in the textile industry. Villagers would receive the raw wool or cotton from traveling contractors, and work it up into finished goods on their own little wheels and looms during the winter months. Then the contractors would return, pay for the labor, and cart the merchandise to market. This was called the "putting-out" or "domestic" system, and it functioned quite passably in a clumsy, sluggish way.

But then the new inventions started to crowd in. One man discovered a way to speed up the process of combing the raw cotton. Another hit on a device which enabled a single pair of hands to spin several threads at one time. A third developed a contraption for weaving the threads almost automatically. Year in and year out more and more of such improvements appeared, and they wrecked the "domestic" system. The new machines were too large to be installed in village huts. Also they were too costly.

So another system arose. The pursuit called industry acquired money-glands, and became Industrialism—with the "I" capitalized in more senses than one. Thus far those glands had functioned almost solely in connection with commerce. Capitalists—in other words, men who used money to make money—had confined their activities largely to buying raw products in one place and selling them in another. Their plants had consisted mainly of ships and warehouses, for most of them had been pirates, brokers, or merchants.

Now they became manufacturers. An increasing number of enterprising fellows got hold of capital in one way or another, and started small factories. They built them preferably in rocky gorges, because water-power was needed to drive the huge new appliances. Then they went foraging for workers. They didn't forage for them among the village craftsmen. That would have been a waste of time. Those cottagers were proud fellows, poor but proud and stubborn. We're independent! they cried. We'll sell what we make, but we won't sell ourselves!

So the upstart manufacturers passed them by. They could afford to do that because they did not need craftsmen anyway. With their new appliances all they needed was a corps of dumb attendants. There had to be a certain number of eyes to watch the whirling spindles, and as many hands to mend any threads that broke. Nothing more. Even children could perform tasks as simple as these.

Wherefore the millowners went after children. Why not? Children were cheaper to employ than adults, and also easier to manage.

There was, however, one difficulty. Children were hard to find in the remote gullies where the water-powered mills had to be located. But that problem was soon solved. Just who showed the way is not recorded. All we know is that the way began to be followed almost universally. The millowners hied themselves to the nearest large cities—to London, Liverpool, Edinburgh and the like—and charitably contracted to empty the orphanages.

The victims of these raids were not necessarily orphans. The majority were just hapless waifs left on the hands of the parish authorities by parents reduced to pauperdom. (Merry Old England may have been short of many other things, but never of paupers.) These "infants" as they were called—and often they were literally that, for they ranged in age down to seven or even less—were handed over to the millowner ostensibly to be apprenticed to a trade. Actually they became his chattels. If he was indulgent, he might see to it that they washed on Sundays, so as to be fit to be marched off to church. He might even teach them to spell out the Ten Commandments, the Apostles' Creed, and other texts calculated to improve their souls. But if he was like most, he concerned himself only with their hands.

The millowner, after all, was not supposed to be a philanthropist. He was a businessman, and his first duty was to keep his charges busy. So he did his duty. He kept the mites at work twelve to fifteen hours each day. In return he fed them with scraps and watery porridge, and gave them shelter in sheds where they slept three and four in one bunk. Moreover, he was legally free to hold them on such terms until they died or grew to be twenty-one.

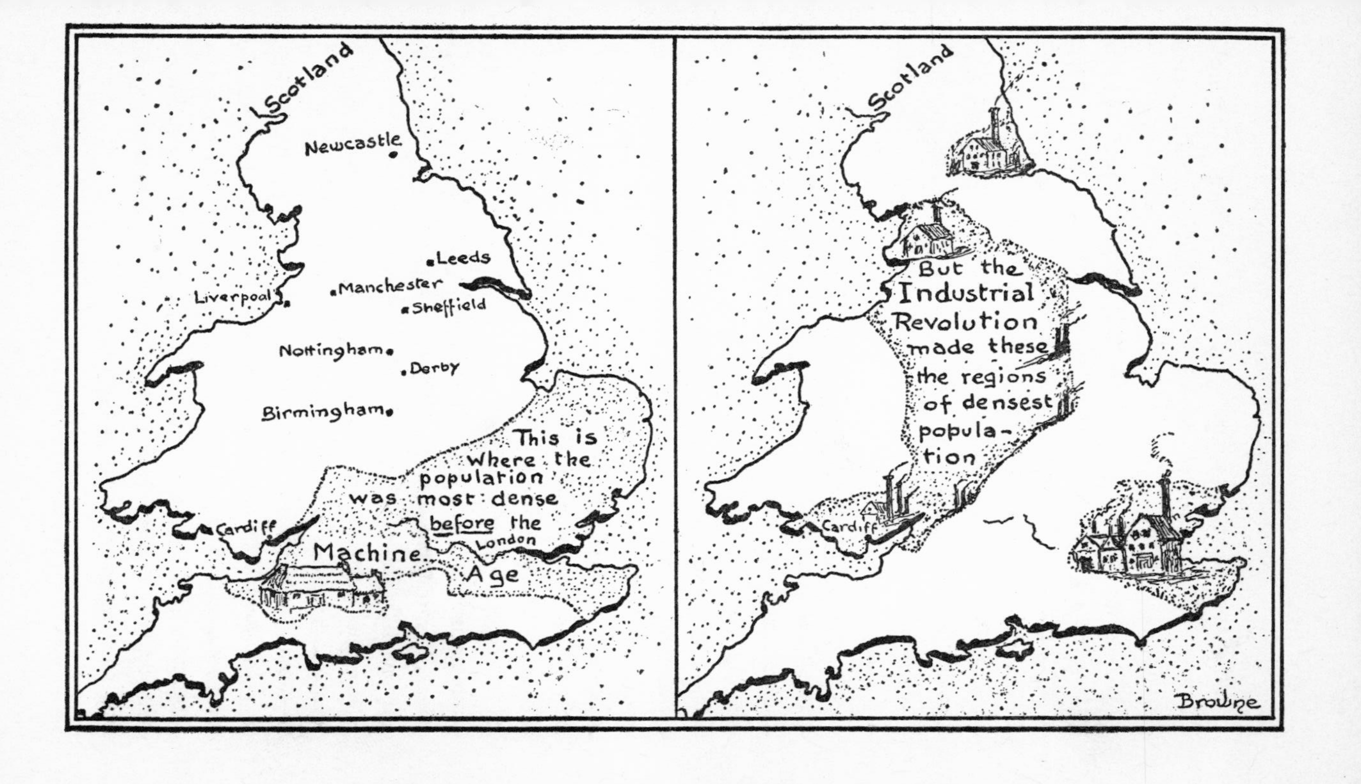
Scotland
Newcastle
Leeds
Liverpool
Manchester
Sheffield
Nottingham
Derby
Birmingham
This is where the population was most dense before the Machine Age
London
Cardiff
Scotland
But the Industrial Revolution made these the regions of densest population
Cardiff
Browne

Of course, if trade fell off and he had to close his mill, he often considered himself also free to cart them off in the dark of the night and dump them somewhere by the roadside.

Such were the circumstances in which the "factory system" got started, and none save an occasional crank seemed to see anything wrong with them. Sane and respectable people took child-labor as much for granted as they did wife-beating or smallpox. The children of poor folk had always been made to earn their own keep. True, in the past such children had usually earned it at home. They had worked for their own parents, doing chores in the fields, or helping out at the household looms. That, of course, was worlds removed from the slavery to which the waifs were subjected in the factories; but the difference went almost unnoticed. Most people in those days were inclined to take slavery, too, for granted.

Even the good church-going folk were prone to take slavery for granted. They had done so at least since 1565, when good Queen Bess put England into the slave-trade with a vessel named—sweet irony!—the *Jesus.* To be sure, the right to keep a fellow-human in bondage had in the meantime been abolished throughout Great Britain. As the saying went, "England's air is too pure to be breathed by a slave." Apparently, however, it was not too pure to be breathed by slave-traders. The Eighteenth Century saw Liverpool become the world's center for that trade, and all classes in the community yearned to invest money in it. "Many of the smaller vessels that carry about 100 slaves," reports a contemporary historian, "are fitted out by attorneys, drapers, ropers, grocers, tallow chandlers, barbers, and tailors." Such ships were constantly setting sail from Liverpool with calico and guns to be bartered in Africa for human flesh, which in turn was bartered in the New World for agricultural produce, which in further turn was carried to England to feed the machines and workers who produced the calico and guns. Thus all Englishmen, the most benevolent no less than the most villainous, were caught up in a vicious cycle of slavery. The sugar they consumed was produced by slaves. So was the tobacco they smoked, the rum, tea, and coffee they drank, and most of the spices they relished. Above all, the raw cotton on which the Lancashire mills were battening, that too was produced by slaves.

Slavery was woven right into the warp and woof of British life in that day. How then could reasonable folk be expected to protest when it showed up in the factories?

III. SUFFER LITTLE CHILDREN

O ONE thing went wrong right from the start. The Machine should have brought release to mankind but instead it brought greater servitude. Mankind, it appears, was not yet ready for release. Too much had come too soon, so the immediate result was too bad. Industrialism was like a fresh wine poured into an old bottle. It had to take on the taste of that which had been in the bottle before. Also the smell.

The evil of slavery crept into the new factories, and it stayed in them. True, the millowners did eventually abandon their raids on the orphanages, but hardly because of any change of heart. No, the cause was a change in technology. By that time the steam-engine had begun to come into common use, and factories were no longer dependent on running streams for power. That meant industry could leave the rocky gorges. Industry could move down into the valleys where there were towns, and where children were commoner than alley-cats.

Once that happened, the masters were able to become more masterful than ever. Formerly they had had lumbering water-wheels to reckon with, so they had been able to crowd at most a few score "hands" into each mill. But with the new motive-power they could make room for hundreds. Moreover, it was clearly profitable to use hundreds, since a single engine could turn appliances on three or four floors as cheaply as on one. The advent of steam proved therefore doubly advantageous. On the one hand it created a need for more workers in the factories. On the other it enabled the factories to spring up where more workers were to be found.

In general, the most favored towns were those with easiest access to coal mines. That was unfortunate from the human angle. Such sites lay necessarily along the canals, or down on the river-flats, where there was little wind to clear away the factory smoke. Consequently the factory populace was condemned to live in abiding reek and gloom. But those who selected the sites gave no thought to that. After all, they were not out to build health-resorts.

The average industrialist gave thought to one thing alone: maximum production at minimum cost. And now he was in a position to achieve that end as never before. Having built his new plant, he needed only to cry, "Suffer little children to come unto me!" and straightway hundreds, thousands, came—and suffered. Grown men, too, joined in the rush; but these the master was prone to turn away. Grown men demanded a grown man's wages. Women he liked better, for they asked less. But the master's real welcome went out to the children. They asked least of all.

So now the "apprentices" faded out of the industrial picture. Their place was taken by these other children who were known technically—but without conscious irony—as "free." The change delighted the average master. With "free" children in his employ, it was really he who became free. He did have to pay them wages; but on the other hand he was spared the expense of providing board and care. His whole relationship to them could be strictly impersonal and businesslike. "Apprentices" were legally wards of the government, and this had sometimes led to nasty complications. But "free" children belonged exclusively to their parents, and these were usually in too desperate a plight to complain. Consequently the masters were able to work the mites pretty much as they pleased.

They did. Not that they were ogres. On the contrary, most of those masters had right fine hearts; but, unfortunately, they were hearts of gold. Their one aim was to make money, and apparently the one way to make money was to keep paring the costs. Those who could manufacture most cheaply could endure and prosper; the rest had to go under. Therefore generosity had to be forgotten. The world of industry had become a jungle in which only the fiercest could survive.

Thus it came about that the "free" children were exploited as nakedly as ever the "apprentices" had been. Before dawn each day the factory whistles tore them from their slumber, and set them scurrying in their wooden clogs to reach the prisonhouse on time. Then for fourteen or fifteen hours they had to breathe dust and cough flue in the dank, close, overheated sheds where the cotton-spindles whirred. Sweat trickled into their red-lidded eyes as they trotted back and forth in front of those spindles; their legs swelled, their backs ached, their heads throbbed harder than the engines. Yet they had to keep going.

Listen to the testimony of Tommy Clarke, aged eleven, as reported to a Parliamentary Committee in 1833:

> "I go to the factory a little before six in the morning, sometimes at five, and work till nine at night. . . . I can earn four shillings [$1.00] a week, but my brother helps me. He is just seven. I don't give him anything. If it was not my brother, I'd have to pay him a shilling a week."

That was what went on in the cotton-mills. It was even worse down in the mines. Babes of four or five were set to guarding trap-doors in the damp, drafty, rat-infested blackness. Older children were put to more strenuous tasks. They had to lead the pit-donkeys that dragged the loaded trucks through the tunnels; or, if the borings were too small, they themselves had to drag the trucks on all fours with the aid of chains girdled around their naked loins. For this toil the pay was sometimes as high as six shillings ($1.50) a week.

Unnatural? Of course it was unnatural. Every instinct in the unhappy little tykes rebelled against such enslavement. But what could they do? Between hunger and terror they were helpless. The first drove them to work, and the second kept them at it. For, once the children entered the factories or the mines, terror dogged them unceasingly.

Overseers whipped them if they came late in the morning, and cursed and cuffed them if they dawdled during the day. Listen again to Tommy Clarke:

"They always beat us if we lark, or go for water, or fall asleep . . . Castles [the overseer] uses a rope thick as my thumb, doubles it, and puts knots in it. . . ."

Who was to blame? The overseers? Hardly. Those poor devils hounded the children because they themselves were hounded by the masters—who in turn were hounded by one another. It was "dog eat dog" all down the line.

But such things could not go on for ever. Eventually even a few of the millowners—and they among the richest ones—became revolted. All they could do, however, was plead with the government to intervene. They argued that so long as there were no legal curbs on the employment of children, so long were some employers bound to practice abuses. And so long as some did that, the rest had to follow suit. They were forced to it by the pressure of competition.

That was sound logic; nevertheless the government hung back. Upright gentlemen arose to point out that *free* children were involved, and the government therefore had no right to interfere. That privilege belonged solely to the individual parents. If the latter were too meek, or too depraved, to exercise the privilege, it was indeed very, very sad. But better that some children should be denied sun and air and health and life itself, than that all parents should be robbed of their constitutional prerogatives. To counsel anything else would be to Undermine the Family, and Destroy the Sanctity of the Home!

The debate dragged on for years and years. Even after the authorities were driven to the point of conceding the need for reforms, they still balked at enforcing them by law. As the Right Honorable Lord Lauderdale put it: "If the legislature attempts to enforce a moral code for the people, there is always the danger that every feeling of benevolence will be extirpated!" That, of course, was unthinkable.

Finally, however, Parliament was simply compelled to take effective action. After almost a generation of agitation, a child-labor bill with real teeth in it was at last made law in 1819. But even then the victory was less than complete, for the teeth were too few and too short. Nothing was said about work in the mines, for almost all of these were owned by noblemen. The new enactment applied solely to the cotton-mills, and there its most drastic provision prohibited the employment of children under the age of—*nine*.

But by the time that law was passed, it was the parents, not the children, who stood most in need of protection. The fate that had trapped the young had at last overtaken the grown folk too.

It was largely because too many peasants had come crowding into the factory towns. Year after year more and more of them had come crowding in, careless of the misery awaiting them because worse lay behind. For they were fugitives. Something had come over the British countryside which had not happened there in centuries. It was Change. For a thousand years, even longer, life had gone on almost unaltered in the rural regions. Generation after generation the fields had been plowed with the same plows, the grain had been threshed with the same flails, the sheep had been let out to graze behind the same old hedgerows. But now, seemingly of a sudden, everything had begun to change.

The reason is plain—to us. What had occurred in industry had begun to occur also in agriculture. The new technology had penetrated to the farms, and it was revolutionizing farm-life. New agricultural machinery had been developed, and new schemes for fertilizing the soil and improving the live-stock. Tilling and husbandry had begun to be "modernized," and that took the ground out from under the poor peasants. Most of them were mere tenants on great estates, and they had neither the wit nor the means to adopt the new agronomy. Only the landlords were in a position to do that.

Now, as a class these landlords were little inclined to try anything new. Throughout the past they had been content to hunt, drink, play politics, go to church—and collect the rents. They had been in a literal sense the *lords:* that is, the "loaf-wards," the bread-keepers. The hard chore of bread-winning they had left to their tenants.

Of late, however, some had begun to bestir themselves. Not all of them, of course. No, most of the landowners continued to act like typical sons of riches, sitting on their backgrounds and twiddling their titles. But a number did get busy. They saw what was going on in the towns: how the upstart industrialists were amassing fortunes, and putting on airs. That irked those rural gentlemen. They decided that they too would do a bit of amassing, for it looked easy. They already owned potential capital in the form of land. All they had to do was take full advantage of their ownership—in other words, become active capitalists.

They did do that. They ordered their tenants to clear off, tore down the ancient hedges, purchased improved equipment, and engaged managers to farm the estates on efficient, large-scale, capitalistic lines.

That is why there was so much migration toward the industrial centers. A certain number of the peasants were able to remain on the soil as cotters or hired laborers; but the rest had to move on. Some moved right out of the country.

They sold their belongings and bought passage to America, Australia, South Africa—any place where they could get back to the soil.

Most commonly they emigrated to the United States, where they took up homesteads on the frontier. If they were lucky or lazy, they lived out their lives on those homesteads, and so did their children and their children's children. More usually they continued to move. By ox-cart they moved, by paddle-boat, or on foot: first to Ohio or Tennessee, then to Wisconsin or Kansas, then to Dakota or Oklahoma. They kept moving westward, always believing—

> "When we've wood and prairie land
> Won by our toil,
> We'll reign like kings in fairy-land,
> Lords of the soil."

But the Machine kept catching up with them. The Machine kept pushing them out. Even four generations later many of their descendants were still being routed by that nemesis. Having been "tractored out" of their forty acres in Dakota or Oklahoma, they moved on then to Oregon or California. But by that time the futility of their flight was plain, for the only way they could try to escape from the Machine then was *in* it. They made that final trek in old automobiles!

That, however, is a story for later. Right now our concern is with what happened in Great Britain when so many peasants began to be driven from the manors. Only the more fortunate were able to go to America. The rest, lacking the means or the will, simply wandered to the nearest town. They put their belongings on their backs, took their young 'uns by the hand, and tramped off to find jobs in the factories. Thousands did that, tens and hundreds of thousands: bewildered clods, ragged and hungry, who came begging for jobs at any wage.

And the factory-owners were happy. They no longer cared much—at least, not *very* much—if Parliament passed laws against child-labor. They could get more than enough adult-labor now at minimum pay.

Even the cottage craftsmen began to beg for jobs in the factories. They had put up a stiff fight until now. In many localities they had actually banded together and tried to destroy the mills. Even now tens of thousands of them were still struggling to hold out. It meant they had to go hungry and bury themselves in debt, for they could not possibly compete with the power-plants. The most diligent artisan working at home could not produce nearly so much as any child in a factory. True, the artisan's product was finer in quality; but that did not help. The great demand now was for cheapness, not quality.

Nevertheless many artisans continued to cling to their spinning-wheels and hand-looms. In most instances their earnings were actually less than they could have received in the mills, but they felt they were compensated in other ways. A man who worked in his own home could sing at his work if he felt like singing, or knock off in the middle of the day and hoe turnips or go fishing. A man who worked in his own home was his own master—more or less. He was free—in a way.

So there were many in the land who stubbornly struggled to carry on under the old "domestic" system. But they became fewer year by year. Labor without joy was bad; but labor without bread was worse. In at least the textile industry it was already plain that the independent artisan was doomed.

IV. THE POOR SHALL NEVER CEASE

HE independent artisan was doomed. He went down first in the textile industry, and then in every other that lent itself to large-scale mechanization. If he could not get hold of capital and make himself a master, he had in most instances only one alternative: let himself be made a slave.

But not a docile slave. He drew the line there. He and his kind were not savages who had been trapped in African jungles and dragged in chains to another world. They were Christian Britishers living in their own homeland. From childhood they had been taught to sing, "Britons never, never, never shall be slaves!" And, foolish as it may have been of them, they took that boast literally. Therefore, no sooner did they begin to feel the yoke around their necks than some of them started to balk.

At first they had a very effective way of balking, for though driven like slaves, they were not actually chattel. They still had the right to quit their jobs. True, this was not much of a right, since if they quit they starved. But—and herein they had seen their one salvation—if enough of them in any factory got together and quit at the same time, their employer faced ruin. If they went on strike—indeed, if they merely combined and threatened to do so—they still had some chance of redeeming themselves.

So they did combine and threaten to strike. The movement started even before the close of the Eighteenth Century, and at first the masters paid it little heed. Some even relished the unrest—so long as it broke out in the mills of their competitors. Eventually, however, they learnt better. It became clear to them that their hirelings had laid hold of an exceedingly lethal weapon. Whereupon they ran to Parliament for help.

They got it. Parliament was controlled then by the landed aristocrats, and these as a class had little love for the upstart industrialists. Nevertheless, as between the latter and the common workers, they knew well how to side. (The French Revolution had just shown them what could happen when the rabble got out of hand.) The lawmakers hastily decreed (1799) that henceforth any workman who conspired with any other workman to extort an increase of wages, or a decrease in hours, was liable to three months in jail! Further, if any workman so much as attended a meeting called for the purpose of plotting such extortion, or if he urged any other workman to attend such a meeting, or if he gave aid to the family of any worker convicted for attending such a meeting, or if . . . or if . . . then he was likewise liable to three months in jail!

That attended to, Parliament heaved a sigh and laid down its pen. It felt that it had done its duty. The workers had been deprived of the one weapon still in their hands, and now all seemed safe.

But all was not safe, for all was not well. The strikes might cease, but the grievances remained. Want and squalor and disease and resentment were still unmitigated in the nether-world of the poor. Indeed, with each year, almost with each day, these evils increased. Conditions had been bad enough formerly. Wages had been so low that in some places—James Watt tells us this—the workers had actually stolen the grease out of the engines and used it for food. Yet now the lot of the toilers was more grievous than ever.

There were some even in the upper-world of the rich who saw this. One was a poet by the name of Shelley, who wrote brave verses counseling the poor to—

> "Shake your chains to earth like dew . . .
> Ye are many—they are few."

Several other poets of the day—most notably Byron and Keats—wrote verses in somewhat the same vein. But since most of the poor were illiterate, and the rest were unliterary, only fine ladies read those poems. That did not help much.

Similarly there were certain radical journalists and eccentric philosophers who espoused the cause of the lowly.

But their words, too, were largely wasted on the drawing-room air.

For the rest, a small number of intensely religious folk became wrought up over the situation. They realized only part of what was happening, but that part was enough. They saw that the masses were becoming debauched. The favorite potion down in the nether-world had ceased to be good, full-bodied ale. It was not even beer. What the poor craved most now was gin. The stuff was sheer poison to mind and body alike, yet they gulped down all they could get of it.

The masses were becoming debauched and depraved. No longer did they seek relaxation in dancing on the green. Now they spent their every idle moment in reeking public-houses. No longer could they be entertained by innocent Punch-and-Judy shows, or tumbling bears, or wandering jugglers. They preferred to watch what were called "up-and-down fights." Two champions would square off on a cindery lot, or right in the middle of the street, and maul, gouge, kick, and throttle each other until one lay numb on the ground. This was no new sport; but in former times it had been indulged in only at the annual fairs. Now such combats were everyday occurrences. So also were vicious wife-beatings, child-floggings, and sudden, inexplicable mob riots. It was as though some evil spell were creeping over the laboring-class, a dark rage that had to vent itself in savagery and murder.

All this was very appalling to the more righteous folk up above, and eventually it stirred some of them to action. Curiously, however, these saw no link between depravity and deprivation. For example, there was a great and good man named William Wilberforce, who devoted most of his adult life to grieving over the lot of the down-trodden. Yet when he was a member of Parliament in 1799 he was among the most eloquent supporters of the bill which made it a crime for workers to strike.

Mr. Wilberforce was typical of those pious uplifters. On the one hand, they did very fervently want to help the poor. On the other, they just as fervently did not want the poor to help themselves. Possibly that was because these uplifters were holy folk. Believing that the Lord would provide, and knowing that they themselves were peculiarly close to the Lord, they felt it should be left to them to hand out the provisions.

They did hand them out. They distributed bread on occasion, and also fuel and warm clothing. These, however, were in their own eyes the least of their benevolences. Far more precious, they believed, were the spiritual bounties which they were in a position to give away. Their real mission, they felt, was to restore the lowly to the light. Not to the sunlight, of course; no, to the Light of God. Bring the poor back to religion, they cried, and all would be well. The poor would then turn to prayer for solace, and to virtuous deeds for refreshment. They would become friendly, sober, and docile. In a word, they would be saved—and made safe.

Thus argued those holy uplifters. And they did more than argue; they went to work. Mr. Wilberforce set up headquarters at his fine home in Clapham, and began to gather funds with which to purchase Bibles, tracts, and hymn books. Then, arming his cohorts with these weapons, he sent them forth to do battle.

Most of the warriors were high-minded spinsters, and it must be recorded that they did do battle most valiantly. With hearts full of love—but jaws set a little grimly—they dared to venture into the toughest slums. They organized Sunday schools, prayer circles, sewing guilds, and refined entertainments. It took courage to attempt such tasks, and angelic patience to persist in them. The good ladies met with surliness from the workers and rage on the part of the masters. Often even the local curates were hostile. But, despite all rebuffs, they persevered. They scolded gamblers, pleaded with drunkards, wrestled with atheists, and drove harlots out of town. They were like so many godly gadflies in the dark stables where the poor were penned.

Nevertheless they did accomplish some good. The milk of human kindness may have been a little sour in many of those spinsters, but in the circumstances even sour milk was a boon. For one thing, they did dispense a certain amount of charity. For another, they taught a number of their charges how to read. For a third, they helped to keep at least a few of the rich from completely forgetting that the poor were still human beings. These may have been sadly inadequate benevolences; yet they were better than none. In the light of subsequent history they might even be ranked as important. They were the seeds which eventually flowered into three remarkable institutions: Organized Philanthropy, Mass Education, and the Social Conscience.

Yes, those missionaries did do some good.

However, many years had to pass before the seeds they planted could begin to burgeon. In part that was because the seeds were never deliberately planted; they were dropped by accident. To make matters worse, for a long time the seeds were poorly watered. The vast majority of the rich refused to interest themselves in the nether-world of the poor. They were hardly aware of its very existence. This was not true, of course, of the actual industrialists. Most of these were still small fellows who lived right next door to their factories, and they could hardly help knowing the conditions in the slums. Nevertheless, except in rare instances, they made no effort to relieve those conditions. They had more urgent things on their minds.

As for the rest of the rich, these seldom came within miles of the slums. Even many who drew their main revenues from those areas, the lordly owners of the coal-measures and the knighted shareholders in the mills, even they—and especially their wives—stayed away from them. They preferred to live in the fashionable districts of London, or on fine estates in the counties as yet unspoilt. If, on occasion, some business necessity did drag them to the factory sites, they drew the carriage curtains while traversing the alleyways, and held handkerchiefs to their nostrils.

Even so, they could not help hearing rumor of what life was like among the poor. The reports, however, were usually of so offensive a nature that they simply refused to believe them. Or else they shrugged their shoulders. They told themselves it was plainly God's will that the poor should be poor. What was more, such was His will, they told themselves, only because He loved the poor. Contemporary professors of moral philosophy had proved that quite conclusively.

For example, there was the Reverend Dr. William Paley, of the University of Cambridge: he had written what amounted to a treatise to show that poverty was really a privilege. The rich, he had argued, could afford to indulge their every whim; therefore their appetites were prone to be jaded. But the poor were always in need; therefore they were able to get a thrill out of the least little windfall. Again, the rich did not have to labor; therefore they could never know the full joy of rest. The poor, on the other hand, had to work hard all day long; therefore when night came they could fall on their beds and really relax. Still again, the rich had to worry about keeping up appearances. They had to dress in the fashion, run big establishments, send their sons to select schools, provide their daughters with seductive dowries. Also they had to contribute to charity. The poor, however, were burdened with no such responsibilities. All they had to do was stay alive. Everything considered, therefore, the rich were positively to be pitied. It was the poor who were the lucky ones.

That was one type of argument. In a sense it served the gentry as their first line of defense against any pricks of conscience. To be safe, they had a second line. This consisted of the blunt assertion that poverty, whether good or bad, was unavoidable. Had not God Himself declared through Moses that "the poor shall never cease out of the land"? Moreover, had not recent scientific research furnished statistical evidence to much the same effect? The Reverend Mr. Malthus in his erudite *Essay on the Principle of Population* had just proved—at least, so it was generally believed—that the very Laws of Nature ordained that part of the population must be eternally in a state of want.

Actually Malthus had proved nothing of the sort; nor had he tried to do so. He was a kindly man with a fine scientific bent and a stout moral purpose. But shallow readers, misconstruing his thesis, insisted that it added up to something like this: The earth could produce just so much food and no more; therefore there could never be enough to eat save for just so many people. But since far more than that number kept getting born, therefore the excess simply had to starve. Poverty was "Nature's medicine." It prevented the masses from growing ever more excessive, and thus enabled the classes to go well fed. Q.E.D.!

So the rich could feel secure from any qualms. Either poverty was a blessing, in which case nothing need be done to relieve it; or else it was a curse, in which case nothing *could* be done.

V. THE RICH SHALL NEVER REST

NEVERTHELESS the rich did have their worries, plenty of them. Roughly, the rich were of two kinds, the old and the new; and both worried themselves, if not thin, at least gray. The chief bane of the old rich was that they were being crowded by the new. Formerly the prime source of wealth had been land. Even the merchant-pirates, once they had grown to be merchant-princes, had invariably plowed their gains into land. But since there was a limit to the amount of land in the realm, there had always been a limit to the number who could be wealthy. That neat arrangement, however, was crumbling now, for wealth had acquired a third dimension. Industrialism had created a rival source of riches in machinery, and opportunity was therefore no longer bounded by the horizon. The sky had become the limit, and that meant more room on top.

So now there was a rush to get on top. Thousands of creatures from the lower ranks were heaving, shoving, clawing their way upward. The best of them were no doubt honest enough, but only according to their lights—and their lights, being those of smoky milltowns, were not very bright. As for the rest, they were just ruffians. Most of them were hard-bitten fellows with foxy wits and tigerish wills who wasted no time on gentlemanly scruples. They knew what they wanted and went after it. Ruthlessly, remorselessly, they went after what they wanted. If anyone dared to stand in their way, they knocked him down and walked on his face.

Not all of the poor were crushed by industrialism. A number managed to clamber up the sides of the smoke-belching juggernaut, and these rode high, wide, and handsome. They grew rich and began to act like rajahs. They did not need to be told that the words "rich" and "rajah"—and even "regal"—came from the same root; they seemed to smell it out. The moment they got hold of what they called "t' brass," that moment they started to act brazen. They learnt to strut, look down their noses, and clear their throats with a sound like thunder—for they had made themselves high and mighty folk.

All of which was very trying to those who had been *born* high and mighty.

But the new rich too had their worries. The proof is this: no matter how rich the newly rich grew, they kept struggling to get richer. Relatively few in those early days thought to build themselves palaces in which to make merry. Instead they built more factories in order to make more money. They kept saving and investing so as to get more savings to invest. They had their cake but refused to eat it because they felt they must acquire more cake not to eat.

Foolish? Not at all. There was sound reason for such conduct. These new-rich people could never feel completely secure. Their wealth was invested in business, and business, they had discovered, had its chronic ups and downs. Today they might be rolling in wealth, and tomorrow be floundering in debt. Therefore they had to keep worrying about the future. They had to keep saving for a rainy day—even if that meant living in a constant drizzle.

Now, in one way this persistent thrift was highly beneficent. *Because the capitalists were literally a "saving" remnant, all mankind was to some extent redeemed.* Those capitalists were driven to build more and more factories, and thus they enriched the world with more and more goods. And the world needed goods. There had never been enough simple necessities to go around, let alone pleasant comforts. At last, however, that lack was on its way to being filled. A well had been discovered which could provide waters of plenty for the entire land, the entire earth. So it was good that those who rushed to take possession of the well were impelled to pump with all their might. Without plenty there could never be health or joy or even common decency for the bulk of humankind.

But though good, the arrangement was not perfect. Unfortunately, the pumpers pumped with more vigor than wisdom. This was only natural, since each man felt constrained to get all the water he could out of his own spout. However, the combined flood coming from so many spouts could not always run off smoothly. The result? Every once in a while the waters backed up—and most of the pumpers got soaked.

No, the arrangement was very far from perfect. Thanks to the new machinery, it was possible now to produce lots of goods very cheaply. Once produced, however, the goods had to be sold. But to whom? Certainly not to the rich. Flimsy calico and coarse shoddy were no fit merchandise for such folk; nor were tin forks and spoons, or inch-thick mugs and platters. The rich might buy a little of such stuff for their servants, but for themselves they preferred hand-made goods. These were more painstakingly contrived, more durable, and usually more beautiful. In any case, they were less common, and therefore more impressive.

Obviously, therefore, most of the factory-products had to be sold to the poor. But just as obviously they could not be sold to the poor at home. In the first place, these lacked the price. The bulk of their wretched wages had to go for food and lodging. In the second place, even had they had the price, they would not have cared to buy all that was being turned out. The new industrialism was too specialized and unbalanced. For the most part its output was confined to textiles and ironware. Therefore there simply had to be a surplus of certain goods, and that surplus simply had to be sold abroad.

It was. Agents were sent out to forage for markets, and before long England's foreign trade began to boom. Here, for example, are the round figures for her annual export of cotton goods:

1780	$ 2,000,000
1790	8,000,000
1800	27,000,000
1830	86,000,000

Within little more than a generation the word "Manchester" became the hall-mark of cheap merchandise all around the globe.

But there was one bedeviling element in this foreign trade: it was chronically unstable. One year the demand for goods seemed insatiable, and the next it was gone. Here a war would suddenly destroy a market, there a famine, in a third place a plague. Therefore there could be no steady prosperity at the source of supply. Now the British mills were running day and night, and now they stood idle. That was very disturbing.

The situation had been different in former times, because making and selling had then been confined largely to local markets. Merchandising had been carried on from hand to mouth, so there had been relatively few hazards. But now that the hand was at such a distance from the mouth, anything could happen—and usually did.

There was another factor. In earlier days most of those who did the making and selling belonged to guilds. Each tradesman submitted to restrictions, and this insured a certain amount of common security. The guilds may have stultified progress, but they did at least prevent anarchy. All that, however, was changed now. In this new age the merchants and manufacturers were completely on their own. The one law to which they subscribed was "Each for himself and the devil take the hindmost." This was called the Competitive System, but in effect it was not a system at all. It was a chaos which showed promise—or threat—of some day becoming congealed. In the meantime, though savagely stimulating, it was almost as savagely confusing.

Here is an example of what could and did happen. In 1808 the British, having invaded Spain to drive out Napoleon, took occasion incidentally to extort a treaty which opened up Spanish America to their trade. This was practically a virgin market, and when the British go-getters learnt it was theirs for the raping, they fairly whooped for joy. Had they taken time to make inquiries, they might have been less jubilant. They would have discovered that South America was still largely a jungle, and therefore hardly nubile as a market. But those go-getters did not dare take time. Each of them feared that his rivals would go and get ahead of him. So all of them pounced together. A horde of traders loaded ships to the gunwales and set off at once for Rio.

It was farcical. Within the space of a few weeks more cotton goods were dumped in that port than the entire region had consumed in the preceding twenty years. Huge bales of fancy glassware arrived, giant crates of knickknacks and toys. Even ice-skates were shipped out in the excitement!

The final outcome, of course, was ruin. The adventure ruined the merchants who had chartered the vessels, ruined the manufacturers who had produced the wares, and ruined the bankers who had advanced the funds. There was a small panic when word of the fiasco got back to England. Banks in London slammed their doors, and mills in Manchester padlocked their gates. Only the churches—and the grog-shops—found much need to stay open.

That sort of thing happened over and over again. Now there would be a crazy boom, and now a sickening collapse.

First the go-getters would lose their heads, then they would lose their shirts. And nothing, it seemed, could be done about it. The situation might have been less hopeless had these ups and downs been due entirely to stupid blundering on the part of individuals. But they were not. Almost from the start the severest fluctuations were caused by a factor for which not individuals but all society was to blame.

That factor was war. For more than twenty years, from 1792 to 1815, there was virtually incessant fighting in Europe; and during all those years the British mills reacted like so many sweat glands to a fever. When the fighting was intense, the mills worked day and night; when it slackened, they fell idle. Boom and slump, boom and slump: so it went for two mad decades. Until at last there came the mightiest boom of all, and then—prostration.

It was late in the year 1812 that this climacteric boom began. Napoleon had finally taken one gamble too many: he had dared to invade Russia. That gave his enemies their chance. They waited until hunger, cold, and typhus wrecked his army, and then they closed in for the kill. Russia, Prussia, Sweden, and Austria rushed troops into the field. So did England, Bavaria, Holland, and Denmark. And the wheels of British industry began to whirl as never before. It was their task to produce equipment for all those armies. (And also—this must be whispered—for Napoleon's!) They had to pour out shot and cannon, and muskets, sabers, flints, and medals. They had to weave bunting for flags, shoddy for uniforms, and cotton for shrouds.

That meant profits for the owners of those wheels. War was a bonanza for them. All they could produce they could sell, and all they sold brought them profit. So they herded more and more infants into more and more factories to turn out more and more goods to be shot away in more and more battles. None stopped to ask what might happen when the shooting ceased. None dared. It would have been foolish—why look a war horse in the mouth? Besides, it would have been unpatriotic.

So all who could crowd their way to the well of plenty proceeded to pump and pump and pump. And they made money. An inquisitive London magistrate named Patrick Colquhoun tried to find out just how much money some people were making in that day, and this is what he discovered. In 1814 the average cash income of a worker's family was $55 *for the entire year!* But the income of those who worked the workers—he counted 400,000 such, including the landlords—was from $1,000 to $20,000!

That estimate, to be sure, was merely a wild guess, but since we lack a tamer one, we can ill afford to reject it. Even if we do, we must still concede that the warring must have brought profit to some people in England. For thirty months it certainly kept enriching the businessmen. And then—

Crash!

VI. A MAN WITH A PLAN

THE war ended in 1815. Napoleon was felled never to rise again, and there was peace at last. But not joy. Not for the British business-men, at least. No, to them peace brought only gloom. Even the most powerful among them were plunged into gloom. The weaker ones writhed in terror. They had borrowed right and left to build mills and install machinery, and now they were caught. Poor small fry, they had been fried good.

Yet theirs was not the harshest agony. That was reserved for the laborers. When peace pricked the industrial boom, the capitalists were merely out of luck. But the laborers suffered more, for they were out of work.

This was something new. Wars had always brought hard times in their wake; so had droughts, floods, pestilences, and other "acts of God." In the past, however, the poor had been able somehow to take care of themselves during such crises. They had had their own cottages to give them shelter, and their tiny fields and the surrounding forests to yield them food. But it was different in 1816. By that time hundreds of thousands of the poor were housed in towns where they subsisted entirely off industry. Once industry foundered, they were left stranded. Lacking money to pay the rent, they were put out on the streets. Being far from woods in which to pick berries or poach, they could do nothing but starve.

That spelled trouble, especially after the demobilized soldiers were added to the down-and-out mob. "Hard times brought hard crimes." The more the skies of England emptied of smoke, the blacker they grew with hate. The tougher fellows started to riot in the slums and loot in the countryside. Even the timid took to throwing rocks at passing carriages. The unrest grew so widespread that the rich began to take fright. It might have been better had they taken thought, but that apparently was beyond them. Instead of taking thought they reached for a club. (Did not Holy Writ declare: "A whip for the horse, a bridle for the ass, and a rod for the backs of fools"?) The Government suppressed the right of free speech, suspended the law of Habeas Corpus, organized a force of police spies, and called out the militia.

It worked. Cowed by the show of force, the poor slunk back into their kennels. What else could they do? They had been reared to believe that only their betters were privileged to revolt. Besides, they were unarmed and unorganized.

That, however, did not end the unrest. Afraid to bite, forbidden even to bark, the masses took to whimpering. They whimpered so agonizingly that at last the rulers were driven to relent a little. In 1817 Parliament appointed a "select committee" to inquire into ways and means of throwing the poor a bone.

And thereupon something very strange occurred. A certain industrialist by the name of Robert Owen arose and bluntly declared that a bone would not be enough. This Mr. Owen, a homely young Welshman with a large nose and gentle eyes, was already somewhat of a character in Great Britain. Though himself a most prosperous employer, his sympathies had always been with the workers. In this, it must be said, he was not unique. Nevertheless he was certainly peculiar.

Owen's whole career had been peculiar. He had left home at the age of ten to make his way in the world, and before he was twenty he had already established himself as a "cotton lord" in Manchester. By the time he was twenty-six, he and a group of partners were able to raise $300,000 to buy one of the largest mills in Great Britain. It was situated at New Lanark, near Glasgow, and employed some 2,000 workers, of whom 500 were apprenticed waifs. Conditions in the settlement were what one might expect. The millhands were the terror of the countryside, always stealing, getting drunk, and starting bloody brawls. Their bodies were filthy, their minds were dull, and their spirits were morose and debauched. Typical millfolk.

But Robert Owen was not a typical millowner. True, he was monstrously energetic, always hustling, bustling, and pushing ahead. At the same time, however, he was a man of some enlightenment. He had received very little education as a child—and that, characteristically, in a religious school conducted by pious spinsters—but he had since done a good deal of reading and thinking. Among other things, he had come to the conclusion that human beings behaved as they did not because of their nature but their nurture. If, for example, millfolk were prevailingly vicious, it was not at all because they were born vicious. No, said this Mr. Owen, it was because they lived in a vicious environment.

No sooner, therefore, did he take over the control of New Lanark than he set out to create a better environment for his workers. He could do only little to increase wages or reduce hours—his partners drew the line at that—but he was able to accomplish much in other directions. He renovated the mills, improved the housing, cleaned up the village streets, and opened a store where sound merchandise was sold practically at cost. Most important of all, he established a school. It was an extraordinary school because, though intended for the children of workers, it lacked all taint of snivelling piety. The one aim of the instruction was to develop keen and happy minds in clean and healthy bodies. The pupils were taught not alone how to read and write, but also how to play and dance and get on together. And, in part through the pupils, Owen tried to influence the parents. He sought to make the latter take an interest in their work and develop a pride in themselves.

On the face of it, the whole scheme was preposterous. Nevertheless it worked. Little by little Owen got his millhands to slough off their brutish ways and behave like decent citizens. What was even more amazing, his efforts paid. The more he spent on what his partners considered mad extravagances, the handsomer were the dividends he produced.

Within ten years Owen was able to pay back the entire original cost of the mills, plus interest at five per cent.

Rumor of the marvel spread far and wide, and many important people journeyed to New Lanark to see the place for themselves. One was no less a personage than the Grand Duke Nicholas, later Tsar of Russia; and he, like the rest, went away greatly bewildered. When Owen published a book on his educational theories in 1813, Napoleon himself found time to read it and scribble favorable comments in the margins. John Quincy Adams, then the American ambassador in London, sent copies of that book to the governors of all the states in the Union. "Mr. Owen the Philanthropist" grew to be a world figure. Despite his humble origin and peculiar ideas, even dukes and cabinet ministers, even the Archbishop of Canterbury, deigned to acknowledge his acquaintance. Consequently, when he raised his voice during the crisis of 1817, all Britain stopped to listen.

And this is what the country heard. Throwing the poor a bone, said Owen, would never do. At best it might provide momentary relief; but this crisis called for a permanent cure. Otherwise pauperism would grow worse and worse. It would spread until the whole land became one vast poorhouse. Why? Because more goods could now be produced with less human labor. This development, though calculated to be a boon, was proving to be a calamity. Thousands upon thousands of willing workers were losing their jobs. What was to become of them? They could hardly be asked to crawl off into a corner and die. Nor could they very well be kept alive by the rest of the population. Plainly there was only one solution: those multitudes would have to be restored to gainful labor.

That was Owen's basic contention. Something very grave

had gone wrong, and it would take more than mere wishing to set it right again. Machinery had thrown part of the economic system out of kilter, and unless society immediately adjusted that part, the whole system would surely go to pieces.

But how was this adjustment to be made? Obviously not by abolishing machinery. The only way out was to go forward. And Owen thought he knew how. He had a Plan. Said he: Collect all the unemployed in small colonies, give them sufficient land and mechanical equipment, and then leave them to provide for their own needs. Such a scheme might sound fantastic; but, Owen insisted, he had thought it all out, and he was sure it would work. (He was a very self-confident man.) The essential thing, said he, was to let the colonies be run as collective enterprises. The members must work side by side in the fields and shops, live together in one group of buildings, eat at a common table, and share as equals in all privileges as well as duties. This would insure a minimum of waste, a maximum of cooperation, and an optimum of happiness. True, no member would be able to wax rich; but neither would any be reduced to beggary. Indeed, life would become so idyllic in those settlements for the unemployed, that before long even the employed would want to join them. And not merely in Great Britain, but all over the earth. Whereupon such colonies would spring up everywhere, and the whole earth would be turned into one vast cooperative paradise!

That, in brief, was Robert Owen's Plan. He presented it first to the "select committee" appointed by Parliament. Then he hired a hall in London and announced it to the world. The result was sensational. Owen's picture of the Future, a smile on its dimpled cheeks and a ribbon in its golden hair, was enough to soften even the toughest-headed folk. The leading newspapers editorialized on his idea, high clerics preached on it, and fine gentlemen argued about it over their port. The economic depression had already lasted many months, and even the very rich were getting a bit white around the gills. They were in a mood to listen to almost any man with a plan for recovery—and Robert Owen was not just any man. Had he not amassed a fortune? Therefore, despite their prejudices, even the roundest-bellied people were tempted to take him seriously. For a while there were many who considered him almost a Messiah.

But only for a while. Then, almost overnight, he was metamorphosed into a fiend. The fault was in part his own. He allowed himself to be dragged into a squabble with the people who until then had been the chief pleaders for the poor. These were the pietists, and they wanted to know where God came into Owen's utopia. The man had given elaborate specifications for the building of model tenements in his colonies and for the building of nurseries, schools, libraries, recreation halls; but he had not even mentioned churches. What did he mean by that?

Owen was only too eager to tell them. He actually hired a hall again, so as to be able to tell them out loud. Religion, he roared, did not figure *at all* in his "villages of cooperation." Moreover, he'd be damned before he'd ever let it be smuggled into them. Said he:

> "My friends, I tell you that the fundamental notions of every religion have made man . . . a weak, imbecile animal, a furious bigot, a fanatic, a miserable hypocrite. And should these qualities be carried into Paradise itself, a Paradise would no longer be found!"

That finished him with the pietists. It helped to finish him with all other respectable people. These discovered that he was a heretic not alone about God, but also about marriage and even money. He seemed bent on standing the world on its head and shaking out all its dearest traditions. They decided he must be mad.

Nevertheless Owen carried on. Failing to win the support of the rich, he sought it from the poor—and got it, after a fashion. Eventually his movement acquired a name, and it was a very good one. What made it good was the directness with which it pointed to the crucial belief underlying all of his utopian fantasies. According to that belief, the sole way to end the woes of the world was through *social* rather than individual action. Therefore his movement came to be called "Socialism."

To most people in Owen's day, whether rich or poor, the entire scheme seemed not merely absurd but even wicked. They were sure, however, that it would never be taken seriously, so they let him go on preaching it.

He did. For more than forty years he continued to buttonhole statesmen and lecture to workmen in behalf of his idyllic "Socialism."

Toward the last, however, even he seems to have despaired of it a little. At the age of eighty-two he took up spiritualism.

VII. THE RELIGION OF MANCHESTERISM

OBERT OWEN failed—and that was only natural. Even had he been less indiscreet, or even had his plan been less unworkable, he would still have had to fail. The world was not prepared for a man of his sort, nor for a plan of any sort at all.

By the world I mean, of course, those people who had already begun to take possession of it: the up-and-coming fellows, the go-getters, the businessmen. In their judgment—and it was not altogether wrong—Owen was daft. True, there had been a moment when they had thought otherwise. The prolonged slump after 1815 had so shaken their nerves that they had almost accepted Owen's prophecy that business never would recover. But then they had got hold of themselves. Clenching their fists and gritting their jaws, they had growled: Times *must* get better!

And, lo, times did get better! No one knew why; it just happened. Gradually the old markets reopened on the Continent, and new ones were pried open in China and the Americas. The demand for manufactured goods reasserted itself, and the wheels of British industry began to turn again. They turned slowly at first, then faster, faster. By 1822 they were whirring at top speed once more. New factories had to be erected then, and deeper shafts sunk into the mines. More ships had to be built to fetch and carry across the seas. It was almost another boom.

Owen had absolutely no chance after that. All his theorizing had been based on the premise that the system of "dog eat dog" was done for. Machinery, he believed, had made the fangs of the top dogs too sharp. But, once the post-war crisis wore itself out, that system began to function better than ever. At least, so it seemed to those who remained the top dogs.

So they laughed at Owen and his socialism. Now they were surer than ever that individualism was the one way of salvation. Why draw up artificial plans for economic life? Wasn't a natural plan already in existence? Of course! It had been established by the very Architect of the Universe, and was operating in ways as sure as they were beneficent. Anyone could see that—if only he cared to look.

Those businessmen really believed that. Faith in the divine rightness of individualism became a deep religion with them.

Several scholarly books had already appeared which seemed to validate such a religion, and more were being written day by day. By curious coincidence, the first of those books appeared in 1776, the very year James Watt installed his first steam-engine. It was the handiwork of another Scotsman, a sweet, high-minded professor of moral philosophy named Adam Smith, and it bore the title, *The Wealth of Nations*. A distinguished company of economists had since arisen to amplify Adam Smith's ideas, and between them they had created a complete apology for capitalism. True, that had not been their intention. They had set out to develop a science of economics, and in a tentative way they had succeeded. But, as in the case of Malthus—himself one of that company—their purpose was misunderstood, and most of their findings were misapplied. Instead of functioning as a science, their whole enterprise was made to serve as a theology. It came to be called "Manchesterism," a very apt name, for in the popular understanding it was a doctrine which justified in principle what the Manchester millowners were doing in practice.

To be sure, the majority of those millowners did not give a tuppenny-damn whether their behavior was justifiable or no. All they cared was that it paid. But their behavior met with considerable opposition, not merely from sundry cranks who yearned for socialism, but far more redoubtably from the landed aristocrats, most of whom had a nostalgia for feudalism. It was therefore very necessary for the businessmen to show that capitalism was right as a matter of principle. They had to prove that in cleaving to it they were doing not alone well for themselves, but also good for all mankind. They were very glad, therefore, that scholars of unimpeachable integrity provided arguments which could be made to seem to offer such proof.

It was unfair, of course, and certain of the scholars, most notably the great John Stuart Mill, made loud protest. But the businessmen refused to listen. The latter insisted that though thinkers had evolved the theory of Manchesterism, only doers could properly appreciate it. These might miss some of its fine points, but not the really telling ones. And, in their own estimate, the most telling of all was this: that Manchesterism was not just a theory, but a gospel.

The crux of the gospel was the comforting doctrine that capitalism was *right*. Why? Because it conformed to the "Laws of Nature." The proof was simple. The mainspring of capitalism was "enlightened self-interest"—in plain talk, greed. And was not greed altogether instinctive in human nature? Again, the balance-wheel of the system was competition. And was not competition inherent in all animal nature? Therefore there was nothing to worry about. The Cosmic Clockmaker had apparently set everything in order, and it was left for man merely to let the wheels grind. If each individual would act "naturally"—in other words, be as greedy and competitive as possible—then all humanity would be better off. For, as the learned economists had shown, there were "iron laws" functioning in economics no less than in physics and chemistry. There was, for example, a law equalizing supply and demand, another regulating rents, a third controlling wages. And any attempt on the part of mortals to interfere with these "iron laws" was fated inexorably to cause mischief, and end in failure. Therefore, hands off! Let Nature take its course!

An old French phrase became the popular slogan: *Laissez-faire*, which might be vulgarly translated, "Let 'er go!" There was no chance, it was said, that anything might go too far. Not in the long run, at any rate. The relentless pressure of competition would see to that. The employer who was *too* greedy, and tried to underpay his workers, would soon find them drifting off to his rivals. The result? Either he mended his ways, or he lost his business. Ditto for the merchant who sought to overcharge his customers, and for the landlord who attempted to mulct his tenants. Competition was like gravitation: a Force of Nature. You just couldn't beat it.

True, competition was not yet working with perfect smoothness. But this, it was argued, was because it had never yet been given a proper chance. Competition was like the mills of the gods: it ground slowly, and one had to be patient with it. People should not complain because it caused incidental hardships. That was what it was supposed to do, and the more the better—in the long run. The Profit System was all the sounder because it was a Profit-and-Loss System. Bankruptcies, foreclosures, panics, and the like, were a healing medicine. They kept purging the business world of the reckless and the unfit, and thus served to make such catastrophes less and less possible. Eventually only the most competent would be left in control, and then all would be lovely. There would be steady profits for all the employers, steady work for all the employees, and a steady flow of goods for all mankind.

So let 'er go!

Such, in the common view, was the gospel of Manchesterism, and in time it won the British middle class almost to a man. Even the pious became its devotees. These were aware that the creed reeked of paganism, but they refused to let that repel them. They told themselves that "Nature" was but another name for Providence, and the "Cosmic Clockmaker" was obviously God. Thus they were able to make a vulgarized Manchesterism part and parcel of their own dear Christian faith.

Here, for example, is a quotation from a contemporary tract published by the pious Society for the Promotion of Christian Knowledge:

"It is curious to observe how, through the wise and beneficent arrangements of Providence, men do the greatest service to the public when they are thinking of nothing but their own gain."

Curious, they called it; but they might also have said wonderful. For the spreading belief in the righteousness of capitalism was undoubtedly accomplishing wonderful results. First of all, it was helping to clear the way so that the capitalists might be free to pump with all their might—and thus it was enabling them to flood the world with merchandise. By 1830 the noble historian, Lord Macaulay, could arise in Parliament and boast with complete truth: "Our houses are filled with conveniences which the kings of former times might have envied." To be sure, that gentleman was referring solely to the houses of the rich. (It is not recorded that he ever frequented any others.) But even the poor came in for some share of the stream of goods. To quote a less renowned writer of the period: "Two centuries ago, not one person in a thousand wore stockings; one century ago not one person in five hundred wore them; now not one person in a thousand is without them!" And what was true of stockings was true also of shirts and shoes, of knives and forks, even of books and pens. Capitalism was functioning like an over-active gland within the body of industrialism, speeding up all the vital processes and causing a veritable explosion of progress.

The effect was revolutionary—*really.* For generations there had been brave talk about Liberty, Equality, Fraternity, and the Right to Happiness; but only now was there much chance that those spiritual luxuries might be attained. Why? Because only now was mankind beginning to be supplied with enough material necessities. So long as wealth remained scarce, power was easy to monopolize, and tyranny was therefore hard to overthrow. So long as there were too few goods to go around, some people were certain to grab more than their just share of them, and privilege was therefore bound to prevail. So long as means of communication were slight, provincialism had to survive, and that spelled unending strife. And, naturally, so long as tyranny, privilege, and strife endured, the only right that mankind could conceivably enjoy was one to misery.

But now it looked as though those hoary evils would have to go. The gospel of Manchesterism was against them, and no sooner did it take hold than it refused to give them any rest. See what happened in Britain. In the past all good people there had been expected to "know their place." And keep it. They had been classified according to birth, the definitely "well-born" being on top, the definitely "ill-born" at the bottom, and the rest milling around in between. But the new creed thumbed its nose at all that. It insisted that what counted was not birth but worth—and what a man was worth could best be measured by how much money he had managed to save. Anything else was palpably "unnatural," and therefore immoral. If a man had made good, he *was* good, no matter what his origin. He belonged wherever he could push himself. Manchesterism was absolutely adamant on that point, and the result was a surge of social liberation in Great Britain.

There was a surge also of religious liberation. After all,

if a man had the right to profit as he pleased, logically he had also the right to profess as he pleased. He could be a Jew, or a Catholic, or even an atheist, and still be a good citizen—so long as he paid his bills. Before long Parliament began to erase every last mark of religious discrimination from the law-books.

But above all there was a surge of political liberation. Thus far Britain's government had been largely authoritarian, at least in principle. It had claimed the right to direct the entire life of its subjects, regulating not alone their comings and goings, but also their takings. In a word, it had been essentially feudal. And Manchesterism could not stand for that. So its devotees began to clamor that the sole duty of the government was to maintain public order, not to meddle in private enterprise. It should be a policeman, not a nursemaid. The pushing capitalists demanded "liberalism" in government—by which they meant liberation from governmental apron-strings.

And they got it.

They did not get it without a struggle, of course. For a while it looked as though there might even be bloodshed. The believers in authoritarian government, the so-called "Tories," started out with one advantage: they *were* the government. That left their opponents, the liberal "Whigs," legally helpless. Many a rural borough which had long since been depopulated was still sending two members to the House of Commons, whereas most of the new industrial towns—among them Manchester, Birmingham, and Leeds—were unable to send any members at all. Consequently most of the seats in the Lower House, like all in the Upper, remained in the possession of the landed gentlefolk.

And those gentlefolk refused to give them up. Not for nothing had they been dubbed Tories, which was an old Irish term for bandits. Under provocation they could act quite like bandits. Instead of surrendering their seats, they used them as battlements from which to snipe at the Whigs. Whereupon the latter became equally tough. They too deserved their nickname, which was originally a Scottish term for horse-thieves. Seeing no other way to get what they wanted, those Whigs turned around and aroused the masses. They started to shout that the Tories were to blame for the high price of bread—which was true. The Tories were maintaining a monstrous tariff on wheat in order to protect their interests as agriculturists. Since the Whigs were opposed to that tariff, it was easy for them to win the sympathy of the common folk.

Bread riots broke out in one town after another. Castles were attacked, jails were demolished, and monuments were burnt to the ground. Mobs in the capital went so far as to throw rocks at the great Duke of Wellington, then the Prime Minister.

The Tories grew panicky. For more than a generation, ever since the great revolution in France, they had lived in terror of a mass uprising. They decided it might be wise to compromise. One thing was plain: if they, the old rich, joined forces with the new, the poor could still be kept where they belonged. And that, after all, seemed to be the vital need.

So at length the landed gentlemen were forced to yield. They permitted the passage of a Reform Bill in 1832 which gave the urban upstarts a chance to have their full say in Parliament.

That meant the beginning of the end of Tory power. The Reform Bill did not establish political democracy in England, for even now only moneyed men were allowed to vote. But it did at least enfranchise the new industrial plutocracy. Once the urban upstarts got the upper hand in the House of

Commons, they proceeded to break up the old feudal game, scatter the stacked cards, and start a new deal. Socially the well-born might continue to look down on the self-made. Politically too they might try to hold themselves aloof. But economically they were forced to strike up a partnership.

Eventually the aristocrats and plutocrats became almost equally devoted to laissez-faire. Though their accents continued to differ, their voices became one in shouting to the very heavens, "Let 'er go!"

VIII. THE BLACK LIFE SPREADS

O THEY let 'er go in Great Britain, and she went. What had been a hard push before 1832, became a wild rush after that date. Free at last from governmental restraint, the capitalists began to drive the industrial juggernaut with all the brakes disconnected.

The pall of grime thickened over the blighted valleys of Lancashire. It streaked out in the wake of railroads until it enveloped half the other shires.

Thousands of factories reared their tall, black, ugly throats to belch sooty smoke against the sun. Tens of thousands of trains uncoiled like long, black ugly snakes, and spat cinders all over the landscape. Smoke and cinders spread everywhere. They filled the sky, they covered the earth, they fouled the streams, they buried the towns. Glasgow began to rival Manchester for noise and squalor. Liverpool, Birmingham, Newcastle, Nottingham, Sheffield, Bradford, Leeds, above all London, grew bigger and blacker day by day. Slums were exuded like pus from running boils. The Black Life ravaged mightily.

Nevertheless the net result was a gain. Machines multiplied, goods multiplied, and Britain "prospered."

Whereupon other lands grew envious. They too had their go-getters, and these were not content to let the British control the supply of plenty. They hungered to create wells of their own, and pump at them to their own profit. So a cry went up on the other side of the Channel, and even across the Atlantic, for machines, machines, machines!

The British capitalists, hearing that cry, were much moved. In the past all export of machinery had been forbidden by law; but now that ban was swept aside. There was profit in selling machinery to foreigners, better profit by far than could ever be derived from peddling machine-products. Why then forbid it?

True, such commerce did smack of selling the goose that laid the golden eggs. In the long run it held out the threat of ruining Britain's industry. But that consideration was ignored, and for very cogent reasons. In the first place, it was part of good capitalist theology that the long run would take care of itself. In the second place, it was part of good capitalist ethics always to sell whatever a customer would buy. In the third place, it was obvious that if the precious goose was not sold, it would be stolen. The foreigners would simply build their own machines.

So there was a rush to claw fresh iron out of the bowels of Britain's earth, and a rush to forge the ore into equipment. If the foreigners could not pay for this equipment, the Britishers were all the more pleased. They themselves advanced the money and thus made a double profit: an immediate one on the sale, and a protracted one on the mortgage. They went even further, and started industries overseas entirely on their own hook. Then, sending out their own managers to look after the enterprises, they sat at home and raked in the revenues. This was the most profitable procedure of all. It gave foreigners the privilege of feeding the goose while the British collected the eggs.

The Black Life began to spread. At first, however, it spread very slowly, for the rest of the world seemed not quite ready yet for industrialism. Belgium alone succumbed without much of a struggle, because there alone was the basic situation somewhat akin to Great Britain's. Belgium's soil contained plenty of coal and iron, the national spirit was markedly middle-class, the peasantry was largely landless, and access to foreign markets was easy and secure. The little country was palpably ripe for the Black Life.

English millwrights started to move in even before 1800, and several of them prospered fabulously. One by the name of Cockerill started an iron foundry at Liége which eventually, thanks to royal patronage, became almost the largest in the world. Native go-getters were quick to emulate such immigrants. They scrabbled for capital, bought machinery, and set up "modern" lace factories, carpet works, and paper mills. By 1830 Belgium was able to boast industrial centers which were nearly as busy and fully as squalid as those of England.

Elsewhere, however, there was no such rapid development. France, for example, continued to resist the Black Life even after 1830. One reason was the stodginess of the rich there. They were like tortoises who sullenly, stubbornly hug the ground for fear they may be thrown on their backs. They preferred to invest their wealth in land, not machinery. Another reason was the independence of the poor. Thanks to the French Revolution, the bulk of the peasants owned their own farms, and therefore had no need to beg for work in factory towns. Finally, France was lacking in mineral resources. Her coal-measures were broken and shallow, and they lay too far from the deposits of iron. Twenty years after James Watt could exclaim that England had gone "steam-engine mad," there were just fifteen of his contraptions in the entire realm of France. By 1830 there were barely six hundred, and as late as 1840 there were fewer than twenty-five hundred.

It was much the same in the United States. Before 1830 there was no large-scale industry over here at all, and even after that date it was slow to develop. Large-scale industry required money and machinery, and both these items had to be imported from England. Few native enterprisers cared to stoop to manufacturing, and those who did—for instance, the Lowells, Cabots, and Lawrences in Massachusetts—were for the most part people of small means and modest station. The established American capitalists saw more prestige and safer profit in growing and shipping raw-stuffs: cotton, tobacco, sugar, and wheat.

Besides, there was a lack of cheap labor. In England a millowner could get all the workers he needed at starvation wages; but not here. This was literally a free land—because it *contained* free land. The penniless immigrants who kept arriving had a way of demanding what they considered a living wage. If it was refused them in the towns on the seaboard, they pushed off to the clearings on the frontier.

So here, as in France, industrialism merely took root. It was unable to flourish—yet.

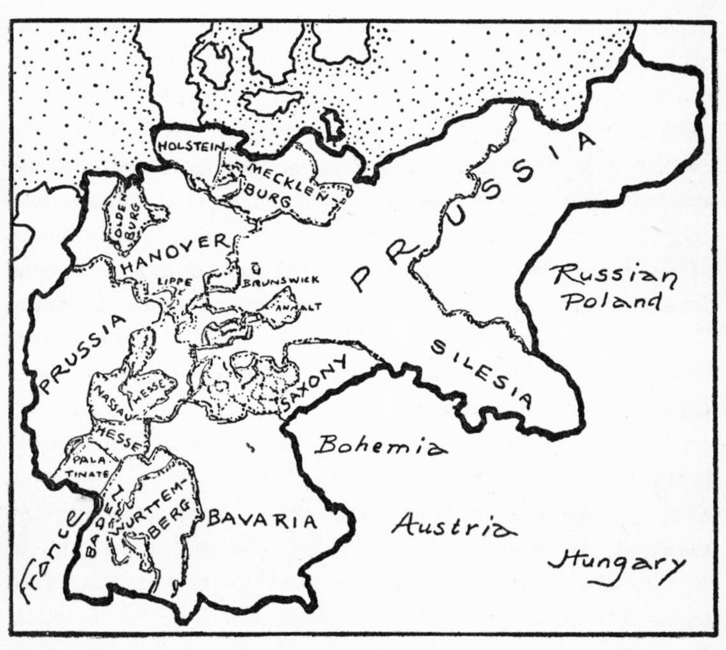

GERMANY *circa* 1830
Not so much a nation as an area.

And elsewhere industrialism fared even worse. In Germany, for example, it could hardly get even a start during that generation. The political situation was primarily to blame. The land was divided into some thirty-nine separate realms, many no larger than a handkerchief—lady's size. Each was a power unto itself, boasting its own ruler, its own troops, its own tariffs, often even its own coinage. Germany in the early Nineteenth Century was a little like the Balkans in the early Twentieth. It was not so much a nation as an area.

Consequently an ambitious businessman had almost no chance there. He needed elbow-room, gangway, space in which to let 'er go. Instead he was hemmed in by all those frontiers. Worse still, behind each frontier there was usually some flatulent potentate with his bottom glued to a throne and his feet planted square in the path of progress.

And there seemed to be no way to mend this situation. A businessman still ranked as a *Bürger*, and that term told the whole story of his plight. Centuries earlier, when gangsterism had been universal in Europe, the least unsafe place for an enterprising commoner had been the *Burg*, the "fortress," of the nearest gang-lord. That was where the merchants set up their booths, the craftsmen their shops, and the trollops their cribs. In time permanent markets developed around these strongholds, and later on walled towns. Finally the walls were torn down, and modern cities emerged. By 1830 this process was nearly complete in Germany—but only in a physical sense. Spiritually the walls endured, though they were built of tradition now instead of stone. Those who had once huddled behind them for protection were still there—as prisoners.

If a burgher wanted to start a new business, he couldn't simply go ahead and start it. First he had to fawn and bribe and pull wires until the local officialdom deigned to grant him permission. And thenceforth he had to let that officialdom pry and poke into every detail of his business, for such was still the law throughout most of Germany. The clay-cold hand of feudalism had as yet been barely budged there, and for that reason if no other—actually there was many another—industrial expansion was all but impossible. Here and there individual hustlers did manage to start modern plants—for example, Krupp in Essen and Borsig in Berlin—but these were usually very small, and they were operated under the most maddening handicaps.

The lordly rulers abhorred industrialism. In the first place, it was something new, and that made it abhorrent to them on principle. They liked to quote their idol, Prince Metternich, who used to say: "I detest even every New Year's Day because it is new!" In the second place, they had a very practical objection: industrialism menaced their interests. True, it did promise to open up new sources of taxation, and thus yield them larger revenues. (And that was a telling point, since most of those rulers were continually rolling in debt.) But it also threatened to yield even larger revenues to those from whom the taxes were to be extorted. Scurvy upstarts would quickly get rich, and begin to think themselves as good as their betters. The land would be overrun by a lot of burghers on horseback. That would never do. Better to have little and maintain the fear of the lords, than acquire great treasure and turmoil therewith.

Such was the attitude of most of the German rulers. Moreover, since they *were* the rulers, they were able to make their attitude prevail.

Much the same was true in Italy. That land, too, was carved up into many sovereign provinces—Sardinia, Tuscany, Piedmont, Sicily, the Papal States, et cetera, et cetera—so there, too, industrial development had almost no chance. There were other hindrances, most notably a lack of coal and iron. But the worst hindrance seemed to be this political fragmentation. It left the governing power in the hands of petty autocrats whose minds were as closed as fists. In Piedmont, for example, a royal edict actually commanded the preservation of illiteracy. Only those subjects who could

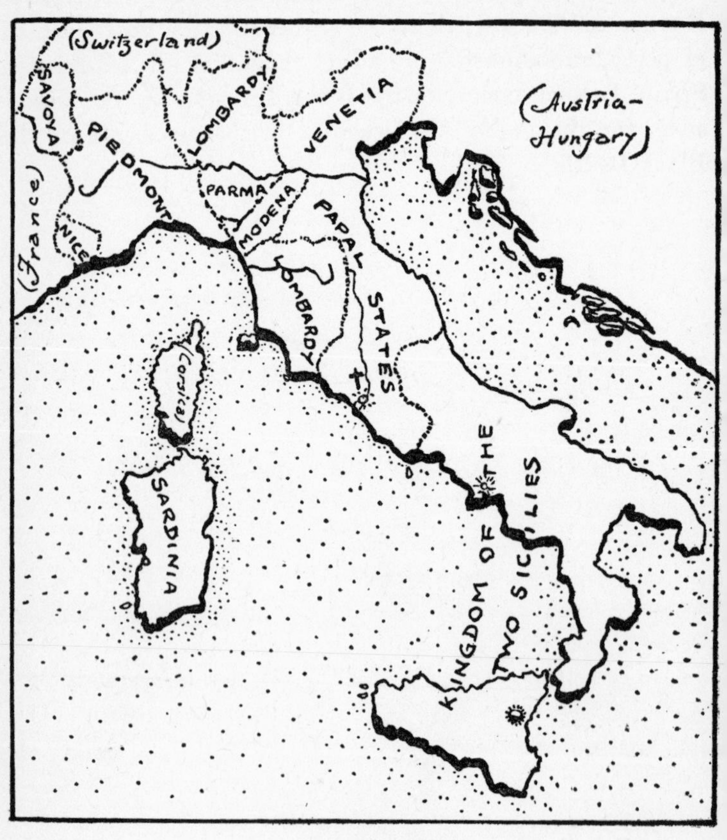

ITALY *circa* 1830

The rulers had minds as closed as fists.

boast an income of over 1500 lire were permitted to learn how to read and write! In much the same spirit, the Papal States as late as 1851 prohibited the building of a railway across the Romagna. The stated reason was that "railways breed commerce, and commerce breeds sin"!

As for the regions farther to the east, Austria-Hungary, Russia, and Turkey, there the autocrats were gross instead of petty, so industrialism had no chance at all. Likewise in Spain. In such countries the Black Life was as yet impossible, for they were still swaddled in the cerements of the Black Death.

IX. JOHN BULL TAKES A RIDE

O ENGLAND was able to retain her lead. Indeed, she extended it now. With the rest of the world mulishly lagging behind, England forged farther and farther ahead. There seemed to be magic in machinery, for the more it grew, the more it had to continue to grow. The 1830's saw British industry break all records for expansion. Several factors were responsible, but the chief was the critical need for better transportation. Wagons and barges were no longer adequate to fetch and carry between the mines and mills and markets. The country had to have railways.

It began to get them now. Attempts had been made to start railways in the early 1820's, but these had failed. Horses had been used to move the trucks, or stationary engines, or even sails. Not until a mechanic named George Stephenson developed a sound locomotive did such transport become really practical; and from then on progress was swift and wonderful. In 1830 a line was inaugurated from Liverpool to Manchester with a fanfare worthy of a coronation. The very Duke of Wellington attended the ceremony, and with him a whole host of lesser notables. Speeches were made, whistles were tooted, and flag-waving mobs shouted hip-hip-hooray. To cap it all, a former cabinet minister crossed the tracks at the wrong moment and was run over and killed. After that no one in England doubted that railways had a great future.

Tracks began to be laid all over the land. There was no plan in their laying, no attempt at a unified system. Rails were simply flung down and nailed fast wherever the builders could buy or filch a right-of-way. They were crude iron rails that buckled and sagged, and the clumsy high-wheeled trains swayed terrifyingly. But who cared? At least the trains did run.

It was marvelous! Never in the history of man had the rate of land-travel averaged more than five miles an hour. Even Napoleon in flight by coach from Russia had been unable to exceed that speed. But now any ordinary man going about his quite ordinary business could go four, five, even six times as fast! Was that not marvelous?

News of the wonder spread throughout the civilized world and at once there was wide effort at imitation. Several short lines were started in the United States, in Belgium, in France. Germany caught the fever, and Holland, Austria, Italy. Even Russia succumbed to what was called there the "iron samovar."

RAILROADS *circa* 1848
The Russians called it the "iron samovar."

Naturally, there was some opposition. Every new invention aroused the hostility of one or another element in the population. When the first railway line was projected in Bavaria, the medical faculty of the University of Erlangen declared that any vehicle moving faster than fifteen miles per hour must surely make the passengers bleed at the nose. Elsewhere on the Continent similar authorities gave warning that travel in tunnels might easily induce paralytic strokes. The Vatican, as we have seen, objected to the innovation on moral grounds, and innumerable Protestant divines quoted Scripture against it.

Nevertheless the railways continued to spread. At first they spread most thickly in England, for that was where they were most needed—and where they could be best afforded. Fifty years of profitable manufacturing had already begun to glut the country with capital. Fortunes were spent to wangle franchises and buy up rights-of-way. Great forests were leveled to furnish sleepers for the roadbeds; deep mines were scooped for iron to forge into rails. Tens of thousands of navvies were set to gashing the countryside, and soon all Britain was one mesh of metal tracks.

Railway building became a national mania. Crusty old squires might curse because train-sparks set fire to their haystacks. Doe-eyed poets might lament because cinders soiled the dew in their bosky dells. But they cursed and lamented in vain. The day of the haystack had passed; only smokestacks counted now. As for dew, what good was it? The real need now was sweat. What England needed was more men willing to sweat that there might be more engines to give off smoke.

And England got such men. For example, there was George Hudson: an immense sweaty blob of a man, round and solid, with a thick square head nailed to wide square shoulders, and a voice like a runaway train. He was just the type for that day. He believed in himself and he believed in railways. Also he was not squeamish. So he dug his stubby fingers into England's soil and clawed tracks for all he was worth.

And how people loved him for it! Thrice the city of York elected him Lord Mayor, and for long all England hailed him the "Railway King." When a grateful constituency elected him to Parliament, a special train raced to London to announce the glad tidings. The noblest lords fawned on the man; the stingiest bankers showered him with credit. Even the prim young Queen became a party to his schemes. On one occasion he presented Victoria with a royal train-carriage decorated with rare woods and shiny brass fittings, and when she beheld it, her tight stays almost burst. "Really," she gasped, "this *is* beautiful!"

It was beautiful, all right. Everything seemed beautiful just then. The boom was at its height, and railway shares were going up, up, up. The mines were busy, the mills were busy, and jobs were so plentiful that some of the poor even had sugar for their tea.

"God's in his heaven—
All's right with the world!"

Thus sang a fellow who was making quite a success of poetry at the time. Possibly he was indulging in sarcasm, but if he was, few of his readers suspected it. The rest took Robert Browning most solemnly, and from the depths of their bosoms breathed "Amen!"

For to those people all *was* right with the world. They were getting richer all the time, and with an ease undreamt of even yesterday. Then one had needed cunning and diligence to make money, an ability to think fast and a willingness to work hard. A man had had to go out and start his own little factory, work in it all day, worry about it all night, and live and die cherishing little else. What pleasure there had been in that had been the toilsome pleasure a beaver knows, the grim, harsh, exacting fun enjoyed by an ant. That was one reason why most of the real gentlefolk had kept aloof from industry. They had preferred to hoard their wealth, or sink it in land, or squander it on conspicuous luxuries. Had they put it into industry, they would have had to put in their energies, too. They would have had to become partners with raffish millwrights and traders. Their stomachs could not stand that—nor perhaps their brains.

But the situation had changed during the past decade or two. Railways and other such giant undertakings required investors rather than partners. They invited people to share in the ownership of industry without bothering at all about its operation. That seemed ideal. All one had to do, it appeared, was buy certain pieces of paper, large ones handsomely engraved, and then sit back and wait for quarterly dividends. Or, if one was impatient, one could sell those pieces of paper at a higher price the next day or the next month, and then go out and buy others.

For soon there was a wide variety of such certificates. Some were called "bonds" or "debentures," and represented straight loans on which interest was promised at a fixed rate each year. Others were called "shares" or "equities," because these were supposed to entitle their owners to an equitable share of the net profits. Bonds and shares alike were called "securities," a very comforting term. One could purchase securities in all sorts of enterprises located all over the earth. A man living in England might make himself part-owner of a railway in Germany, a tea-plantation in Ceylon, a textile-plant in Poland, or a deposit of guano—bird-droppings!—in Peru. All he needed was the money to buy the appropriate piece of paper.

The transaction was effected through an institution called a stock exchange. There had been stock exchanges in London and Amsterdam ever since the early 1600's, but formerly such institutions had been patronized almost entirely by professional speculators. Now, however, quite genteel people started to crowd around. The exchanging could no longer be done on street-corners, or in the back-rooms of smoky coffee-houses. The brokers began to set up shop in granite edifices built like Roman temples.

This happened most of all, of course, in England. Loose capital was most abundant in that country; therefore its owners were most tempted to play fast and loose. But much the same thing occurred, in varying degree, wherever else people felt money burning in their pockets. The boom swept most of Europe, and shares rocketed to the sky. Higher and higher they went, higher and higher.

And then—

s

m

a

sh!

The collapse came in 1847. Just what started it is still uncertain, but we know well what brought it to a head. Rumors leaked out in London of fraud in connection with some of the new railway companies. It was whispered that even George Hudson was involved. That was bad. Suddenly the stock market began to sag. It sagged, recovered, and then sagged lower than before. That was very bad. The Queen's ministers rushed to the rescue. They wrote her a speech and read it for her to Parliament—a splendid speech full of warm assurances that there was no cause for alarm. Too late. Those who owned shares wanted more than assurances. They wanted cash.

And then the awful truth became known: *there was no cash!* Where it had gone, no one seemed to know. (Actually, most of it had never existed, except on paper.) The luckless shareholders began to storm and rage. They collared George Hudson, and bellowed, Where's our money? He had no answer. The little eyes in his chunky head blinked and blinked.

He just did not know. He could not tell them where even his own money was gone.

Had they given him a chance, he might—perhaps—have recollected. Like an alchemist in reverse he had turned gold into iron, joining York to Darlington, Darlington to Newcastle, Newcastle to Manchester, and Manchester back to York. In his own brash, reckless, rip-snorting way he had done a fine job. But he was so shaken at the moment that he forgot all about that. Everybody else forgot about that. All they could remember was that once they had apparently had money, and now it was gone.

And then what had happened so often before happened again. With capital suddenly dried up, the machines began to slow down. It was as though they had run out of oil. The engines coughed, the wheels jammed, and the smoke paled over the factory towns. Railway construction halted, forcing scores of mines and foundries to close down. This threw thousands of toilers out of work, leaving them unable to buy goods. This in turn forced the mills which produced those goods to close down, throwing more thousands out of work, and rendering these likewise unable to buy goods. That was how it went, down and down and out and out, till at last the whole economy lay prostrate.

Nor did this happen merely in Great Britain. Capital had spread far and wide, and once the supply of it thinned at the center, it became thin everywhere else. As swiftly as the new telegraph wires could stutter report of the collapse in London, so swiftly did banks begin to close their doors in Paris, Amsterdam, Berlin, even St. Petersburg. Frock-coated brokers clawed at their side-whiskers; titled speculators blew out their brains. They felt the world had come to an end.

A fierce young German philosopher watched the crash

from Belgium, where he was living just then as a political refugee. His name was Karl Marx, and he was greatly stirred by what he saw. With a pen that jabbed the paper he wrote:

> "Commerce is at a standstill, the markets are glutted, products keep piling up, hard cash and credit are gone, factories are closed . . . liquidation follows upon liquidation, bankruptcy upon bankruptcy. . . . The industrial gallop . . . after breakneck leaps, ends where it began—in the ditch."

X. ARISE YE WORKERS!

O THEN there was revolution. Even in England there was an attempt at revolution in 1848. It was made, naturally, by the workers, for though the owners too were in a plight now, they could hardly blame the government for it. The owners *were* the government. But the workers were not, and that gave them good reason to want a revolution.

For those British workers were no longer what they had

been in earlier times. In the first place, they were more numerous. Their ranks had been swelled by both addition and multiplication. addition from the countryside, and multiplication in the towns. The entire population of Great Britain had been increasing at a phenomenal rate since the coming of the Machine, and the bulk of this increase had naturally occurred among the town laborers. That was one reason why they deserved to be called the "proletariat." No other element could keep up with them when it came to proliferating *proles*, "offspring."

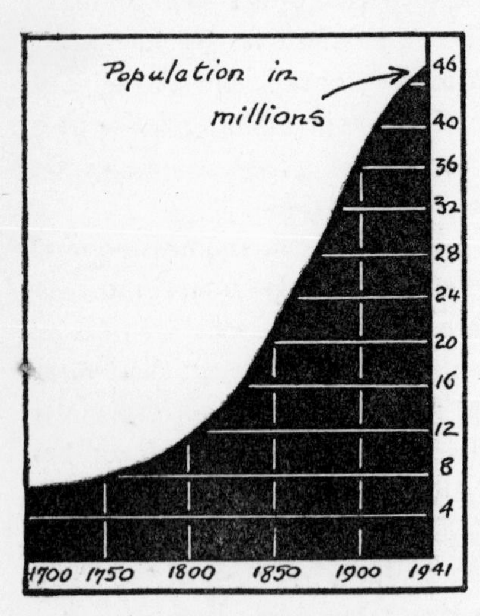

BRITAIN'S POPULATION

Laborers as a class had always been heavy breeders, but formerly most of their offspring had died at birth or soon thereafter. Industrialism, however, had changed all that. It had created great wealth, and a little of that wealth had gone to advance medicine. Doctors had become less crude, midwives less filthy, and hospitals less rare and appalling. Though morbidity had increased, mortality had fallen. More people might be sickly now, but fewer sicknesses were fatal. Certain plagues—cholera, smallpox, and scurvy—had been all but wiped out. And famines had been robbed of their terror. Most of the ships that sailed forth with factory goods, came back laden with agricultural produce. That meant more food for the British masses, more wheat and meat and sugar and tea—not to mention gin and bitters.

As a result, those masses were able to multiply as never before.

This, to be sure, was not altogether a blessing for them. As individuals, most of the laborers were glad enough to have large families. It gratified their carnal instincts, satisfied their religious beliefs, and offered them a mite of financial security. Children were an economic asset now. They could go into the factories and help support their parents.

But collectively the effect was calamitous. By increasing so rapidly the poor made themselves cheap, and at the same time made merchandise dear. They kept glutting the supply of labor and draining the supply of goods. Consequently their standard of living remained miserable.

True, it was not quite so miserable as in the first days of industrialism. Wages had gone up slightly, hours had been reduced to twelve or even ten a day, and the masters were no longer uncontrollable slave-drivers. Parliament had been forced to enact considerable factory legislation, especially during the early 1840's. But this mean improvement did not satisfy the workers. If anything, it made them the more mutinous. A little leniency is a dangerous thing. So long as the wage-earners had had their faces ground in the dust, so long had they been blind and hopeless. But now they could look up. Now they could raise their heads just a little and see what was around them—and above them. And a glare of rancor came into their eyes.

For these creatures were no longer tame villagers. They had become townsfolk—and that made a difference. A villager had to be respectful to his betters: to the squire and his fine lady, to the parson, to the bailiff. Whenever one of these shouted, "Come here, my man!"—instantly he came running, hat in hand. That was the tradition, and no proper villager dared break it. Also he had to behave respectably among his neighbors, for they knew who he was, and they had ways to make him feel it. Paul Pry lived next door, Mrs. Grundy across the green, and with such folk looking on, a body was too afraid even to think unconventionally, let alone act that way.

But a townsman was free of such restraints. His betters, usually, were a crowd of upstarts, and he was more prone to cock a snoot at them than tip his hat. As for his neighbors, most of them were total strangers. If they didn't like how he behaved, he told them to go *x* themselves.

Centuries earlier, when cities had first begun to arise in medieval Europe, there had been a proverb that "town air makes one free." That proverb still held good. Many of the factory workers in Great Britain had become free in at least this: they were no longer so easy to overawe. Where once they had been mice, now they were more like rats.

No wonder. Merely to live in those sooty, smoke-choked, stinking slums, was enough to make men as mean as rats. Sooty little houses like the droppings of some monstrous goat stood back to back along sooty little alleyways. Row on row they stood there, row on row, with privies in the basements and drains outside the doors. No trees, no grass, no touch of paint or sight of bloom; nothing but sooty brick and sooty slate and sooty iron and stone. And there in those warrens the poor were crammed a family to a room or two. There they had to cook and eat and sleep and multiply. Home, sweet home!

In Manchester, it is recorded, a district housing seven thousand souls was supplied at this time with but thirty-three water-closets. In all of Lancashire only one town could boast a public park. Many a slum lacked even wells, let alone piped water. The poor had to trudge to the "better" sections to fill their pails each day. Refuse was left in the gutters for the pigs to eat, or for the rains to wash away. Street-lighting was all but unknown—there where it was most needed—and almost the only time the police showed up was when a strike was brewing.

Schools were few, supported by charity, and run not unlike reformatories. Most of the teachers were starveling monitors who knew little save that one should not spare the rod. They would have made better animal-trainers. Hardly one child out of thirty in all the land ever learned so much as to read or write. In some counties the ratio was more nearly one in three hundred.

Churches were less uncommon, but even they were not much help. Here and there a devoted curate did manage to spread a little cheer. An occasional churchman of the "broad" variety dared go so far as to call himself a "Christian Socialist." These, however, were the rare, rare exception. The typical Man of God down in the slums was a surpliced prig who merely went through motions; or else he was a jumping, thumping, foaming exhorter who roared of the Wrath to Come.

That was why many of the slum-dwellers steered clear of the churches. They preferred to hang around the corner pub. The place might stink of beer and vomit, but at least it was friendly. A worker could get drunk there, and that was fine. When a worker got drunk he could feel like a lord. The ache went out of his back, and also out of his soul. He could forget the world he lived in, and be almost happy. "The quickest way out of Manchester," ran the saying, "is through the door of the nearest pub." Most of the workers went through that door as often as they had the price. Or oftener.

But not all of them. Some had stronger wills—or queasier stomachs—and these sought another way of escape. Usually they were workmen who had learned to read, and who through reading had learned to think. Not all the products of the charity schools grew up to spell out nothing but religious tracts. Some discovered the pamphlets published by Robert Owen and his kind. Furtive little printing-shops in a dozen different towns were putting out a flood of literature about the "rights of labor," the "crimes of capital," and the virtue of that thing called "Socialism." Such pamphlets were not always easy to understand. Many of the words were strange, the sentences were involved, and the print was usually close and smeary. But those who read them, men with moving lips, could get at least the gist of the pamphlets—and that was enough. They learned from them that it was foolish, nay wicked, to try to deaden themselves to the world. A man's duty, they learned, was not to forget the world, but fight it.

Whereupon they cloaked themselves in a mantle of wrath, took up the sword of hate, and fought.

First they agitated against the law of 1799 which forbade them to combine and strike. And when they got it rescinded —in 1825—they set out to organize militant unions throughout the country. There had been unions all along in several industrial sections, but these had usually masqueraded as "burial societies" or "choral clubs." Now they came out into the open, and began to flourish like morning-glories under a hot sun. Robert Owen, who had become labor's tribune, was talked into leading the movement, and by 1833 he had more than a million members enrolled in one Grand National Consolidated Trades Union.

At the same time—again under Owen's influence—small cooperative stores were started in the factory slums. The members pooled their pennies, bought flour and tea and candles wholesale, and thus struggled to reduce the cost of living. By 1835 there were already some five hundred of these stores in Great Britain.

Such things helped. The unions enabled the workers to stand up to the millowners, and the cooperatives gave them a way to hold down the shopkeepers. Because some of the poor ceased to be meek, it began to look as though all might cease to be poor—some day.

Labor was on the march.

But then came 1847, and an abrupt halt. Worse: there was actual rout. Jobs became so scarce that the workers were glad to take them for any pay. The unions crumbled and the cooperatives collapsed. Almost overnight everything that labor had won seemed lost.

It was not the first time. Much the same thing had happened a decade earlier, then too as a direct result of a financial panic. Dreadful convulsions had ensued then, prolonged strikes and bloody brawls. Birmingham was all but laid waste in 1839. Mobs set fire to many factories there, and plundered countless fine homes. The Duke of Wellington, who suppressed the outbreak, later testified that in all his experience he had never seen a city worse sacked.

But now the labor leaders knew better than to try blind violence. Their first need, they realized, was a hold on Parliament; otherwise the government would again be free to call out the troops to shoot them down. In other words, the workers had to wrest the right to vote. At present, only the rich had that privilege, the male householders whose dwellings had a rental value of at least ten pounds ($50.00) a year. That, incredibly, was so steep a qualification that it disfranchised nearly ninety-five percent of the population! So a call went out to the workers to rise up and yell. They were told to yell for a "People's Charter" which would make manhood suffrage universal in the land. Then the government, which had once been aristocratic, and was now plutocratic, would at last become actually democratic. At long last it would be run by and for The People.

A queer character named Feargus O'Connor became the leader of the agitation. He was a hulking, wild-eyed, fire-breathing Irishman who had long been struggling to win the masses to "Chartism." Now, in the hard winter of 1847–8, he saw his chance. First he got millions of workers to sign a monster petition demanding immediate enactment of the "Charter." Then he called for a horde to march on London and ram the petition down Parliament's throat. He set a date for the event—the tenth of April—and picked a place on the outskirts of the capital for the host to assemble.

The authorities did not like the sound of that. They rapped out an order forbidding the march. But O'Connor had the pluck of a madman—he actually did end up in a mad-house—and he roared that the government could not frighten *him*. Come the tenth of April, said he, and the workers themselves would be the government!

The gentry in London began to shiver. Word reached them that mobs were gathering in Manchester, Bristol, York, even Edinburgh and Glasgow: ragged folk with hunger in their bowels and fury in their eyes. The aged Duke of Wellington was once more pressed into service. Troops were stationed at the bridge-heads across the Thames, and guns were mounted around the Houses of Parliament and the Bank. One hundred and seventy thousand patriotic clerks and lackeys were enrolled as special constables.

At length the dread day dawned. The whole town waited, taut with apprehension. Finally O'Connor appeared. But he was not leading an army. He was riding in a hired cab, the monster petition in his lap. Six million workers—more or less—had been willing to sign that petition; but not even fifty thousand had dared come along to present it. So he was bringing it alone.

That was his finish. When O'Connor reached the House of Commons, the honorable members waved him away with a snort. They knew they had nothing more to fear from him or his rabble.

They, the owners, were still the rulers in Great Britain.

XI. 1848—THE FIGHT THAT FAILED

BUT the story was different on the Continent. There 1848 became known as the "Mad Year," for not one class but two dared to rebel. In France, Germany, and a dozen other lands the financial collapse left the burghers as sore as the workers, so they combined and began to topple thrones all over the place. Within six months there was hardly one old régime left intact between the Atlantic and the Russian border.

Suddenly, however, the storm gave out. Swift as had been the revolution, even swifter came the reaction. Within another six months most of the old régimes were back in power again.

Two factors were largely responsible for that reversal. First, the revolution had lacked general support. It had been engineered entirely by city folk, and industrialism had as yet taken too little hold on the Continent for city folk to carry decisive weight. The bulk of the people were peasants: slow, dumb, torpid creatures afraid of change. They were the "masses" in the original sense of that term: just dough to be kneaded. (The Greek verb *massein* actually meant "to knead.") They may not have been satisfied with the mean life they led, but they had lived it so long that they could not conceive of a better. So they refused to join the insurgents. Instead, they actually rallied to the other side.

Even at that the revolution might have prevailed, for what its supporters lacked in numbers they more than made up in brashness—and brains. But hardly had they stormed the first battlements before they fell to quarreling among themselves. The burghers discovered that the workers at their side were out for more than had been bargained for. The burghers wanted merely to abolish feudalism; but this, it seemed, was not going to satisfy their allies. The workers talked of abolishing capitalism as well!

Not all the workers talked that way, but those who did were fearfully loud. Just what they wanted in the place of capitalism was not quite clear even to themselves. Some spoke of establishing "socialism," others "communism," still others "anarchism." The good burghers recoiled in terror. Most of them had never even heard those terms before. They had been so busy struggling to get ahead that they had had no time to watch what was stirring among those they were leaving behind.

But now they knew, and it made their flesh crawl.

INDUSTRIAL CENTERS *circa* 1847
The Black Life had taken hold.

Hostility to capitalism had been brewing on the Continent for fully a generation already. As early as 1817, the year Robert Owen sounded off in England, a treatise appeared in France which attacked the system with a cleaver. Its author was an ambitious, impoverished, half-cracked nobleman named Claude Henri Saint-Simon, whose imagination was exceeded only by his naïveté. According to him, capitalism was the Anti-Christ in the new world which was being created by the Machine. Properly, said he, all the means of production should be owned by the state, and their management left solely to artists, scientists, and technicians. These should form a new aristocracy—more accurately, a technocracy—bound by vows to run the entire economy for the benefit of the entire populace. This would ensure such a vastness of wealth, and so little chance to hoard it, that all the present ills would vanish at once. It would bring on practically the Kingdom of Heaven.

Saint-Simon was naturally a laughing-stock in his day, and when he died in 1825—after at least one attempt at suicide—his queer gospel seemed fated to die with him. But it did not. Ten years later, by which time the Black Life had finally begun to take hold in France, Saint-Simonism became all the vogue in certain circles. Bright young engineers became fascinated by the vision of a world reordered—and run—by their kind. Bright young ladies, too, found the cult alluring, if only because it advocated complete equality—and intimacy—of the sexes.

Soon, however, a number of rival cults appeared, for newer prophets kept arising who sought to improve on Saint-Simon. In France there were Blanqui, Fourier, Cabet, and Proudhon; in Germany there were Franz von Baader, Adam Müller, Rodbertus, and Hess. Each of these managed to attract apostles who proceeded to evangelize with the most formidable zeal. They organized meetings in cafés and beer-halls, and they argued endlessly in fashionable salons. They published books, pamphlets, journals, broadsides, and occasionally chalked slogans on palace walls.

Nevertheless the total effect was slight. Radicalism seemed to appeal almost entirely to eccentrics: seedy noblemen, frustrated ladies, hot-tempered poets, and sore-headed clerks.

Good, honest toilers would give it hardly a sniff. That is, so long as those toilers had jobs. But once their jobs were gone, they began to take in radicalism by the lungful. They were ready for it then, ready and savagely eager. The financial panic of 1847 had thrown more than a hundred thousand workers on the street in Paris alone. Lyons, too, swarmed with jobless folk, and so did Cologne, Milan, Berlin, Vienna, and every other newly blackened town.

We have already seen what ensued. The burghers, having their own cause for rancor, urged the workers to turn on the princes. But no sooner were the latter momentarily dislodged than those same workers turned on the burghers. Armed mobs came pouring out of the slums like lava out of the bowels of the earth. In bands they came, in gangs, in droves, bawling:

"Blood must flow now,
Blood must flow now,
Blood, blood, blood!"

In hordes they came, bearing red flags and howling: "Long live the Revolution! . . . Down with ALL Masters!"

No wonder the burghers quailed. They saw that they had thrown off a yoke only to put their necks in a noose. So they began to back away—and that gave the reactionaries their chance. For a while the proletariat struggled to resist the counter-attack. In Paris they barricaded the streets, and fought pitched battles against the "loyalist" troops. They fought from house to house, even from room to room. When they ran out of gunpowder, they tried to stand their ground with knives and sledge-hammers. They hurled rocks and paving-stones, they poured hot lead from the roof tops. Not until ten thousand of them lay dead or wounded were the rest ready to give in.

Then the revolution was over.

XII. THE BRAND OF GAIN

BUT the upheaval of 1848 had not been entirely in vain. Though it may not have cured anything, it had at least lanced a few boils. True, the hereditary princes did manage to crawl back into the saddle, but their seat was shaky, and they knew it. The less imprudent took heed and tried to ride with new care thenceforth. They gave over using whip and spur, and began to hold out the oat-bag. The Austrian Emperor agreed to abolish serfdom, and Napoleon III of France consented to legalize labor unions. The rulers of Sardinia, Holland, Denmark, and Prussia promised to abide by written constitutions.

The dead hand of feudalism continued to rest on most of Europe, but less oppressively now. And one eventual result was a new surge of prosperity. The burghers were somewhat freer now politically. Moreover—and this was supremely telling—gold had of a sudden come pouring out of a fabled place called California. Thanks to the flood of new bullion those burghers were able to make a fresh start economically.

The wheels of industry, which had been creaking since 1847, picked up speed again and began to hum. It was absurd, in a way. Those wheels were made of iron and driven by steam. Rationally their motion should have been no more dependent on the supply of gold than is the sun's on the noisiness of roosters. That, however, is beside the point. Industrialism may not have needed the shiny metal, but capitalism did. And capitalism, it must never be forgotten, was the vital gland that governed industrialism's growth. Consequently a lucky strike by a hobo working on a cattle ranch somewhere in the Wild West was able to start a boom throughout the world.

The effect, naturally, was felt first and most sharply in the United States. California had begun to yield more than $50,000,000 worth of gold each year, so the nation was free to run amuck with enterprise. Gone now was the old dependence on England. Having money of their own at last, the Americans grew more venturesome. Here, they saw, lay a whole continent aching to disgorge its wealth. Red men had roamed it for millennia, and white men for centuries, yet thus far barely a corner of it had been even scratched. What was needed was more machinery: more railroads, freighters, sawmills, foundries, cotton looms, tool shops, and whiskey stills.

They got busy. Instead of importing machinery, they learnt to make it for themselves. They built locomotives far larger than any used in Europe, and steamboats far more navigable and capacious. They developed totally new devices: a mechanical reaper, a handy sewing machine, a practical typewriter, a rotary printing press. In 1831 an official of the United States Patent Office had urged that it be abandoned on the ground that "small prospect remains of further inventions." Now patents began to be issued at the rate of more than forty a week!

American industry found its feet at last, and strode forth like a young and slightly drunken giant. More and more chimney stacks sprouted in New England, more and more mine-shafts pocked the Appalachian hills. A black maze of railways thickened around the Great Lakes, and steamboat lines began to snake down every broad stream. Commerce pushed farther and farther westward, traversing the plains, the mountains, at last even the yonder sea. By 1860 the Yankee traders were handling half the business of the port of Shanghai.

All that took money—and made money. The number of banks doubled within the space of four years; the number of corporations quadrupled. Forgotten was the day when the stockbrokers in New York had been satisfied to do their trading under an old buttonwood tree on Wall Street. Now they moved into grand offices equipped with plush chairs and gilded cuspidors. They could afford it. A boom was on, and whoever had cash or could raise credit rushed to speculate. English, French, and German capitalists reached out blindly across the ocean to snatch up options, concessions, and shares. A billion dollars were sunk into railroads alone, and no one knows how much more into mines, mills, farms, docks, stores, and fancy saloons. And profits went up, up, up.

People began to say the "Golden Age" had finally dawned.

The boom was not confined to America. The arteries of business encircled almost half the earth now, and a distention anywhere meant excitement everywhere. England reacted almost at once. Idle mills reopened in Manchester, and long-silent foundries started to clank again in Birmingham. The Americans needed supplies: pins, pans, engines, derricks, shirts, shovels, and shootin' irons. True, they had begun to produce such articles at home, but not in nearly sufficient quantities or low enough prices. Only the English were in a position to do that; so the English got busy. By 1855 their exports were almost double what they had been in 1850.

The French, too, got busy. They were not up to much as makers of humble wares, but when it came to fineries they were peerless. No other people could match their silks, jewels, scents, and ornaments. And now there was a new and voracious market for such elegancies. Miners on a spree in San Francisco liked to lavish fancy things on their fancy ladies; bankers in Philadelphia felt it their duty to swill champagne. The French found reason to get very busy.

So did the Belgians. They had carpets to sell, and laces, crystals, and fine linens; also coal and iron. The Dutch, too, got busy, for they had many ships to carry freight across the seas, and also well-grounded banks to handle exchange. Ultimately even the Germans, the Austrians, the Italians started to get busy.

It did indeed appear to be the dawn of the "Golden Age," and those who basked in the aureate glow felt wonderful. Their triumph was not complete yet, but it looked secure now, absolutely secure. The world, it seemed, lay all before the middle-class folk, for them to make it over as they alone thought best. The glories once mourned by Isaiah were to be restored at last: merchants were to be princes, and traffickers the lords of the earth.

Was that good? Yes—*on the whole.* Merchants and traffickers might have their grave limitations, yet as a class they were far above those whom they supplanted. Though they could see no farther than their noses, at least they were not always looking toward their behinds. What they lacked in tradition they more than made up in grit and enterprise. True, they were prevailingly crude, and their rise brought on a reign of ineffable vulgarity. They strutted, they splurged, they wallowed in immoderation. Whatever was bigger seemed to them better; the more showy a thing the more they thought it fine. They loved to clutter their dwellings with bric-a-brac and junk, loved to heap every inch of space with trophies of their money-chase. Floors sagged beneath the weight of monstrous statuary and crowded furniture; walls seemed ready to cave in beneath their burden of paintings and tapestries. Thick curtains of velours covered every window affording a vista; tasseled portières reeking of camphor barricaded every open door. Books too dull to read were armored in bindings too heavy to hold and displayed on tables too rickety to support even one elbow. Everything was overcarved, overpadded, overgilded, overdone. It was as though the highest ideal of this new ruling class was to domicile itself in warehouses.

The ostentation was worse than vulgar; fundamentally it was dishonest. These parvenus seemed bent on making everything look grander, solider, at least costlier than it really was. Plaster was fixed up to pass for marble, glass for onyx, papier-mâché for precious wood. The rubber plant in the bay window was actually made of hemp and canvas; the fruit on the mantelpiece was really painted soap. Even the proud posterior of the hostess was nothing but cotton-wadding. No object was too humble to escape romantic fakery. The butter-knife masqueraded as a Turkish dagger, the umbrella-stand as a knight in armor, the boot-scraper as a sleeping cat.

The yearning for pretension was so intense that it invaded even the workshops. Boilers were ornamented with Doric columns, wheels with tin posies, treadles with cast-iron vines. All life seemed one frenzied hunger for make-believe.

But that was to be expected. The burghers as a class were as yet too unsure of themselves to dare be themselves. Try as they might, they could not shake off a sense of inferiority. The trouble was that they had barely arrived in their Zion; they were not yet at home in it. Their whole conduct was so lacking in grace because the world had not yet accorded them that which the word grace had meant originally—namely, "welcome."

It was merely a phase, however. There had been a time when the nobility too had been boorish. Indeed, for long centuries that class had been positively bestial. It is significant that our very earliest record of the word "gentleman" as a token of rank occurs in an indictment dated 1413 which reads:

> "Robert Erdeswyke of Stafford, gentilman, . . . charged with housebreaking, wounding with intent to kill, and procuring the murder of one Thomas Page, who was cut to pieces while on his knees begging for his life."

If the nobility could outgrow that sort of thing, surely there was hope for the bourgeoisie.

All that the upstarts needed was time. Endowed as they already were with money, brains, and enterprise, once granted time, they were bound to improve. Moreover—and this was the important point—the bulk of mankind was bound to improve with them. Businessmen could hardly do what priests and soldiers had so often done: raise themselves to the status of an aloof and exclusive caste. The very nature of their economy dictated that they could thrive *off* society only in the measure that they strove *for* it. Consequently, they were —at least for the present—like a locomotive coupled to its tender, like an army bound to its supply-train. Businessmen could not really get ahead unless they dragged along all humanity.

Actually, they had already dragged it an enormous distance. Thanks to their insensate urge to multiply machines, they had provided the race with almost limitless means to health, wealth, and power. They had given man bowels of fire and sinews of steel, endowing him with potential might to make all Nature do his bidding.

Nor was that the whole of their achievement. More prowess called for more freedom, and this too the upstarts had wrested for mankind. Consider these achievements—

Item, they had blasted the very foundations of feudal despotism, and set up a new order based on equal rights for all who could grab them. *Item*, they had completely overturned politics, converting the state from an effective agency of restraint into an ostensible guarantor of liberty. *Item*, they had uprooted millions of laborers from the swamps of rural doltishness, and turned them loose in towns to learn a more galvanic way of life. *Item*, they had provided women with means of support outside the home, and therewith cracked the main prop of the age-old tyranny of male over female. *Item*, they had created an imperative need for wider literacy —workers simply had to be able to read, even if it was only the signs which declared, "No loitering here!"—and thus they had assured the eventual establishment of universal education. *Item*, they had laced up whole continents with rails and wires, and bridged wide seas with cables and steamboat lines. *Item*, they had carried commerce to the remotest fastnesses, and rumor of civilization to the wildest tribes.

These were colossal, world-shaking achievements. They provided, as has already been said, the first real chance of attaining Liberty, Equality, Fraternity, and all the other ideals that noble philosophers had exalted, and brave revolutionists had espoused. In effect they pushed back the night and readied the earth for the dawn of a totally new era.

Of course, very few of the men who wrought those achievements had any idea of what they were really doing. All they knew, and indeed all they cared to know, was that they themselves were getting ahead. And this lack of vision, though natural enough, was a grievous defect. It explains why so much pain and confusion accompanied the achievements. It accounts for the thoughtless cruelties that so many capitalists visited on their hirelings, and for the needless distresses that all of them inflicted on themselves. The booms and slumps, the strikes and hunger marches, the filth, the ugliness, the insane spoliation—these and most of the other horrors of the period were directly due to that shortsightedness. The capitalists refused to look beyond their noses, and darted after gain as bees dart for nectar—blindly.

But, for all that, their rise was a blessing to mankind. Like the bees, they wrought better than they knew, scattering pollen wherever they moved, and robbing only to enrich the world they ransacked. Whether they would function thus throughout the future was still uncertain, but none could deny that they had functioned thus up to now.

No man living in that day loathed the capitalists more lushly than did that German philosopher whose name has already been mentioned, Karl Marx; yet even he had to give them their due. Said he:

> "The bourgeoisie, during its reign of scarce one hundred years, has brought forth more massive and more colossal creative forces than have all the preceding generations put together."

He was right.

But, as we shall see, Karl Marx had other things to say about the bourgeoisie, and in at least one of them he was equally right. It was that they were better able to bring forth forces than control them. That was why their whole career thus far had been marked by incessant mishaps. Each advance had ended in a crash, each spurt in a headlong sprawl. And this, said Marx, would continue. What had happened in 1816, and in 1825, 1837, and 1847, would happen again. It was inevitable.

The good capitalists ignored him. Perhaps it was just as well, for had they weighed his words they might have been tempted to silence him for good. They themselves had absolutely no misgivings as to what lay in store for the world. The drunken boast first uttered in America in 1849 had become a sober truth to them by now: this *was* the "Golden Age." And it was here to stay. California seemed full of gold, so there could never again be a scarcity of cash; and the world seemed to be filling up with freedom, so there could never again be political interference. Prosperity, therefore, seemed assured forever and aye. The capitalists were ready to bet on it.

They did bet on it.

And they lost.

Out of a clear sky in the summer of 1857 a rocketing trust company in Cincinnati blew up in debts. It was not much of a disaster, but coming so abruptly it created sharp alarm. The very next day many a depositor in New York ran to see if his own bank was safe. He saw and was satisfied, but nevertheless withdrew his money. It seemed prudent to do that—just in case. But when more depositors did the same on the second day, and still more on the third, things began to look bad. Those New York banks, like all the others in the land, had been over-optimistic. They had loaned out so much money that they were $12,000,000 short of cash. Within a week they had to close their doors.

Boston was next. Then Philadelphia, Pittsburgh, Chicago, Montreal. The clatter of closing doors became so loud that it was heard three thousand miles away in London. British capital was heavily invested in the United States, and the brokers on the Royal Exchange grew jumpy. They kept up a bold front before strangers, but to their intimate clients they whispered: "Sell!" Soon everybody was selling, and not alone American securities, but British ones too.

The *Times* lumbered into action, solemnly informing its readers that the financial situation had never been sounder than right now. At this, like a rude punctuation mark, a bank blew up in Glasgow. The next day banks started to blow up all over Great Britain. Within a month they were blowing up in Paris, Amsterdam, Hamburg, and Stockholm.

And Karl Marx, having prophesied it all, smacked his lips.

XIII. THE GOSPEL ACCORDING TO MARX

ARL MARX smacked his lips. He was ill at the time, his wife was ill, and he had no money to pay the rent. Nevertheless he was full of ghoulish glee. "I have not felt so cozy since 1849," he wrote to his closest friend.

That was just like the man: always perverse. Even in appearance he seemed perverse, especially in England, which was where he was living now. He was short, chunky, and very professorial-looking in a snuffy German way, with a huge head framed in a thick forest of beard, and small red-lidded eyes that flared defiantly. His clothes were always threadbare and stained, and he usually wore them as though he had flung them on in the dark. He could rarely converse without disagreeing, and rarely disagree without growing disagreeable. He could be tender when he forgot himself, but most of the time he snapped and barked. Perhaps that was because his spiritual underpinning was all askew. He had been born a Jew, baptized a Christian, and become an atheist. Or perhaps it was because he was sickly. His stomach was weak, his liver unmanageable, his nerves were jangled, and he suffered from boils.

But Karl Marx rates a chapter in our tale because, no matter what his defects, he had ideas. And what ideas! At a time when capitalism was just coming into its own, he kept insisting that it was already doomed.

Here was his argument. The sole aim of capitalism is to increase profits, and therefore its constant effort is to reduce costs. This leads to two stratagems, the first and most obvious of which is to force each laborer to do more work for less pay. That maneuver, however, can be carried just so far and no farther. Laborers are merely human, and if driven too hard will either die or rebel. Consequently the capitalists have to resort to a second stratagem: they must install more machinery. But even that has its drawbacks. New machines throw men out of work, and until those men can find other jobs, they are unable to do much spending. Moreover, even when they do find other jobs, they can still hardly do much spending, for they are in no position to haggle over the wages they are offered. Usually they are glad if they can get enough to keep themselves and their dependents alive. Therefore the installation of new machinery solves one problem only to create another. The capitalists equip themselves to produce more goods, but leave *proportionately* fewer people able to buy them.

And that, said Marx, was why capitalism had no future. There was a crucial flaw in the system: the farther it was pushed, the more it had to frustrate itself. True, it had managed to work thus far, but only because it had been enjoying its springtide. Even at that, it had already had its bad moments. Over and over again it had run into crises: financial panics, industrial breakdowns, social prostrations. And it was fated to continue to suffer such crises—progressively worse ones, too—for they were not just strokes of bad luck. They were part and parcel of the system itself. So long as production was made to gallop and consumption to crawl, so long were breakdowns absolutely unavoidable. Production simply had to stall periodically in order to let consumption catch up.

But that sort of thing could not continue indefinitely. Those periodic crises tended to make the structure more and more top-heavy, since they kept battering the smaller capitalists and fattening the big ones. The latter were able to buy up bankrupt plants at bargain prices when times were bad, and thus they put themselves in a position to corner more business when times got good again. It followed, therefore, that eventually the big capitalists would be doing almost all the business—and then their tactics would necessarily change. They would become monopolists. They would see that they had nothing more to gain by the disorder born of "free enterprise," so instead of continuing to compete, they would begin to combine. In other words, they would seek to end the economic chaos by congealing it. They would form super-trusts to regulate production and stabilize prices—and guarantee profits. And thus, having begun by looking no farther than their own noses, they would end by filling nothing but their own mouths. Ultimately the capitalists would start to imitate the feudal tyrants whom they had once hounded from power. They in turn would become in a literal sense the lords—the "bread keepers."

But, Marx hastened to add, that too would not last. "Accumulation of wealth at one pole," he explained, would be "matched by accumulation of hunger, hardship, slavery, ignorance, brutality, and mental degradation at the other." And such a situation could not possibly endure. True, there had always been gross inequality among men, and in the past it had been maintained without much difficulty. That, however, proved nothing. Conditions were different now, for the Machine had come into the world, and the Machine made a reign of oppression at once easier to start but harder to sustain. For the victims were less scattered than in former times. They were no longer poor peasants who lived lost in lonely villages; they were townsfolk. They lived in packs, were lashed in packs, got overworked and underpaid and kicked around in packs. That did something to them. It encouraged them to howl in packs. It taught them to band together in unions, brotherhoods, confederations—and fight.

This process had already started, and it was bound to continue. At present even the most militant workers were content to fight like guerillas, turning now on one employer, now on another. Or they came shuffling up to the governments, hat in hand, and meekly begged for drop-in-the-bucket reforms. This, however, would cease after a while. The nearer capitalism approached its logical conclusion in the triumph of a few monopolists, the more clearly would the oppressed see the need for tougher tactics. By that time their ranks would include not merely born workers, real proletarians, but also many people from the bourgeois class. There would be bankrupt shopkeepers among them, and ruined millwrights, jobless technicians, and land-robbed farmers. Above all many intellectuals would join them: men like Marx who had "raised themselves to the level of comprehending theoretically the historical movement as a whole." That would mean better leadership for the masses. The new recruits, though brought down to the level of the mere "hands," would have heads—and know how to use them.

Then the real fight would begin. No more pleading and nagging, no more furtive agitation and futile sabotage. This would be—*the works.*

War would break out along a front gashed clear across the face of society. On that side would stand the owners, on this the owned, and between the two a struggle would ensue which could have only one possible outcome. The owners would be swallowed up! The whole institution of private property would be liquidated, and with it would go all the economic anarchy, social tyranny, moral hypocrisy, and religious cant which that institution had so lavishly fostered.

And then? Then mankind would be free at last. With the bourgeoisie gone, no class would be left to usurp privilege and arouse resentment. Only the masses would remain, and they would proceed to establish their own institutions. Just as the aristocracy had brought forth feudalism, just as the plutocracy had brought forth capitalism, just so would this, the ultimate democracy, bring forth—Communism!

Such, in the crudest outline, was Karl Marx's gospel. Naturally, he himself did not call it that. He was ready to grant—indeed, he was scornfully insistent—that other critics of capitalism preached gospels. But not he. They were uplifters, but he was an upheaver. Proof? They kept talking about what *ought* to happen, whereas he showed what *must* happen.

They staked all their predictions on faith, hope, and charity, whereas he staked his solely on what he considered strict logic.

That was why he preferred to call himself a "communist" rather than a socialist. He did not want to be confused with men like Robert Owen and Saint-Simon, apostles guided more by their hearts than their heads. According to those men, the chief objection to the capitalist system was that it was cruel, and their dearest hope was that the capitalist class would itself some day be moved to adopt a kindlier one. "Utopians!" Marx called them with a curling lip. "They dream of establishing castles in the air . . . pocket editions of the New Jerusalem."

He himself claimed not to give a hang whether capitalism was morally defensible. All he asked was whether it was economically workable. And, since his calculations proved the answer to be emphatically *No*, that settled the matter. Why wish or weep for the bourgeoisie to relent? Better goad the proletariat to revolt.

And Marx set out to do just that. "Thus far," said he, "philosophers have been content merely to interpret the world. The task now is to change it." So he devoted himself to rhetoric as well as logic; he became an agitator as well as a theoretician. At the age of twenty-four, having written himself out of a job as a liberal journalist in Cologne, he moved to Paris, where he turned into an active radical. Deported a year later, he moved to Brussels, and there he and another brash young German, Friedrich Engels, proceeded to draw up a manifesto calling for world revolution. The Panic of 1847 was at its height just then, and they felt the time was ripe for such a call. They entitled the screed *The Communist Manifesto.*

It was a brilliant document, clear, compact, and blastingly vehement. It opened with a staggering boast: "*A specter is haunting Europe—the specter of Communism.*" And, ten thousand words later, it closed with a roaring challenge: "*The proletarians have nothing to lose but their chains. They have a world to win. Workers of all countries, unite!*"

Those words were written in December 1847, and—was it mere coincidence?—hardly had they reached the printer when some workers actually did begin to unite. They threw up barricades in the streets of Paris and roared, "*Vive la Révolution!*"

Marx was beside himself when he heard the news. Now it was coming, he thought. The French uprising was a confused affair; few of the workers seemed to know what they were fighting for. He felt he must tell them—at once. Not waiting even for his wife to pack, he rushed off to Paris.

Once there, however, he was swiftly disillusioned. Not even the leaders, let alone the rank and file, would listen to him. He decided to move on to Germany, where the insurrectionary movement was as yet less advanced. There, he felt, he would have better luck. Engels joined him, as did a number of other Germans who had become converted to the communist cause while in exile. Throughout the "Mad Year" of 1848 they went storming up and down their native land, shouting to the workers to make this *their* revolution. It would not be enough, they cried, to destroy feudalism. Capitalism too must go—even though it had barely come yet in that country.

But the German workers were relatively few, and almost as difficult to convince as those in France. Far from winning them over to the red revolution, Marx and his cohorts simply scared the burghers into black counter-revolution.

The next year Marx was once more in flight. Completely penniless now—his aristocratic wife had to pawn the last of her family plate to pay the fare—the fugitive was forced to take refuge in England. The bourgeoisie he so hated had made that country the world's stronghold of liberalism, so he knew he would be safe there. Settling his family in two dingy rooms in a London slum, he got himself a visitor's card to the British Museum. The Reading Room there was quiet and full of books, and these were his chief needs now. He was through with agitation—for the present. "A new revolution," he told his comrades, "can come only with a new crisis." Meantime there would have to be another boom, and while that lasted he intended to devote himself to research. He dreamed of writing a monumental treatise giving all the philosophical, historical, and economic reasons why capitalism could not possibly survive.

Day in and day out he repaired to the Museum, and from ten to seven remained buried, beard and all, in notes. Occasionally he took time off to write articles for liberal newspapers, especially the *New York Tribune*, which was then edited by Horace Greeley, an avowed socialist. At long intervals he delivered lectures before small crowds of radical workmen. For the rest, he subsisted off the charity of the ever faithful Engels, who had taken a post in one of his father's cotton-mills in Manchester.

It was a sad existence. More than once the family had nothing to eat for days save bread and potatoes. Periodically Marx had to pawn his overcoat to pay the rent. Yet he refused to abandon his research. He dearly loved his wife and children, but he insisted that the Cause came first. This may seem strange, seeing that the man claimed to be an out-and-out materialist, believing neither in God nor in the soul. Nevertheless, that was how he behaved.

During eight long years he continued patiently to pile up notes; then, in the summer of 1857, he began to write furiously. The crisis he had so long predicted had come at last, and he wanted to get at least one volume done before he was called back to the barricades. For he was utterly sure that this time *the* Revolution would come.

Engels was equally sure of it. Gleefully he reported from Manchester:

> "The general aspect of the Exchange here has been altogether delicious this past week. The [businessmen] grow black in the face. . . . I hear the Cookes, owners of the colossal factory on Oxford Road, have sold their foxhounds. . . . [Another] has discharged his servants and put a 'To Let' sign on his palace."

Engels himself had lost his money in the crash, but that made him feel all the better. "The bourgeois filth of the last seven years . . . is washed off, and I am another man again." As proof he confided that he was devoting all his time to the study of military tactics!

And Marx, hearing these tidings, felt the blood pound in his veins. It was coming now! At last, he gloated, at last it was coming!

But he was fooled.

XIV. YANKEE DOODLE GOES TO TOWN

MARX was fooled. What he had hoped would be the beginning of the end of capitalism, proved merely to be more of the end of its beginning. A revolution did come after 1857, but it was quite unlike the sort he had looked for. It was confined at first to the United States, and instead of toppling the "bourgeois tyrants," it actually set them more firmly on their thrones. Eventually he himself recognized it as a revolution; but at first, like everybody else, he called it merely the American Civil War.

Today we can see that it was much more than that. The ordeal which beset the United States in 1861 was related to the upheaval on the Continent in 1848, and to the spasm which shook England in 1832. In a veiled and confused yet crucial way it, too, was a test of strength between the industrial way of life and the agrarian.

When the Machine first reached this country it took root in the North, and there alone was it able to make even small headway. The ruling elements in the South were inclined to despise the innovation, for they had black slaves to do their hard labor. In this they were merely repeating history. The slave-owners in ancient Greece had had a similar attitude toward machinery; so had the slave-owners in ancient Rome and China and Mexico. These, it must be realized, had not lacked the cunning to invent mechanical devices. We know that because they did invent quite a number of them. To cite but one instance, a Greek mathematician named Hero, who lived in the First Century, actually built a working steam-engine complete with cylinder, piston, valves, and clacks. But did it occur to him to put the contraption to practical use? It did not. Instead he installed it in a temple to amaze the worshippers by the way it worked the doors.

That was typical. The clock and the compass, gunpowder and the printing press—these were all invented in relatively ancient times. Yet until relatively modern times they were kept mere playthings. Ingenious patricians with time on their hands were continually thinking up cunning devices; but never with the idea of applying them to save toil. They themselves did not toil, neither did any of their friends. They had slaves for that. So why bother?

And that was precisely the attitude of the white gentry

who ran the South. In their eyes an interest in machinery was vulgar.

In the North, however, the very opposite held true. Bondage had long since been outlawed in that section, in part because for climatic and other reasons it had too obviously failed to pay. Having no slave-labor, the Northerners had naturally been forced to try to save labor. Since this could be done more easily in industry than in agriculture, there had been an equally natural compulsion to favor the factory over the farm. The great boom of the 1850's was almost entirely confined to the North, and it equipped that region with so much new machinery that it was able to manufacture six times as much merchandise as the South. As a result the interests of the North, especially New England, became increasingly wrapped up in the fortunes of industrialism.

But, as the collapse of that boom had revealed, those fortunes were maddeningly insecure. When the Panic of 1857 finally waned, and the Yankee industrialists began to pick themselves up from the dust, there was blood in their eyes. They felt they had been betrayed. For years they had been complaining that their foreign rivals had them at too great a disadvantage—especially the British, who were better heeled financially, better equipped mechanically, better established in the world markets, and freer to pay low wages. For years, therefore, those Yankees had been pleading with Congress to come to their aid. Specifically, they had asked it to do these things: first, build high tariff walls to keep out cheap foreign merchandise; second, lower all immigration bars so as to allow the importation of the cheapest foreign labor; third, increase the subsidies to shippers who carried American merchandise overseas; fourth, advance more generous loans to men who offered to extend the railroads; fifth, create one stable national currency to replace the present seven thousand varieties of unstable state bank notes; and sixth, free all the blacks so that they, too, might have at least a little cash to spend.

But the Southerners had opposed that program to a (white) man. Moreover, being superior politicians, they had always been able to make Congress vote their way. Now, however, the Northerners had their dander up. Throwing caution to the winds, they forged a political alliance with the radical farmers in the West, and elected a cagy frontier lawyer named Abraham Lincoln to the Presidency. Whereupon, there was war.

The Southerners decided to secede from the Union. They felt they would rather have half a continent of their own than a whole one run by damn Yankees. For those Southerners had never become real nationalists. Like agrarians everywhere else, their outlook had remained essentially provincial. Their minds were a little like the trees amid which they dwelt—moss-hung—and as a result they could not see very far. They believed that a citizen's first loyalty belonged not so much to his country as to his immediate countryside.

The Northerners, however, had acquired a wider outlook. They realized that the United States could never become great unless it stayed big. The South with its capacity to produce raw materials and consume manufactured goods was absolutely essential to the nation's well-being. Therefore, rather than let that region secede, they were ready to lay it waste.

They did—and grew rich in the process. No sooner was the first gun fired at Fort Sumter than the entire North re-echoed with a thunderous "Boom!" The war started a frantic rise in production, for never before had there been such ferocious consumption. And that gave the Northern industrialists their chance. With the Government furnishing the capital, and patriotism the incentive, they rushed to lay hold of more and more machinery. Had the Southern planters lain awake nights worrying how best to help their worst enemies, they could not possibly have improved on what they did when they invited that war.

At the time it was called the "Civil War," and later this somewhat sinister name was softened to the "War between the States." In effect, however, it was the "Second American Revolution." The first had secured the triumph of republicanism on these shores; this insured the triumph of industrialism.

For the boom did not end with the carnage. The Yankees had attended to politics as well as business during the war, and had succeeded in putting their entire economic program on the nation's law-books. An obliging Congress had built towering tariff walls, legalized coolie-labor, reformed the banking system, made the public treasury a trough, and turned the black men into cash customers. So there was every reason for the boom to continue.

Great years ensued for America, wondrous years full of furious toil and fabulous achievement. An iron track was laid clear to the Pacific, and hundreds of thousands of farmers, miners, trulls, and gamblers sallied forth to gouge the earth and one another. Silver and gold were discovered in Nevada, and copper in northern Michigan. So many new iron deposits were uncovered around Lake Superior that the total output of the metal more than doubled within ten years. The output of coal almost quadrupled within that same period, and the output of steel increased precisely a hundredfold. Petroleum was belatedly found to be good for illumination as well as snake-bites, and a thousand farms in western Pennsylvania suddenly bristled with derricks and pumps. Myriads of new factories raised fuming throats to the sky, and tens of myriads of new stores hung out "Open for Business" signs. In San Francisco a "Palace Hotel" was built containing eight hundred rooms, seven hundred and fifty-five toilets, and nine thousand cuspidors.

Yankee Doodle had gone to town.

XV. MADE IN GERMANY

OCTOR MARX had erred. What he had diagnosed as the death-pangs of capitalism proved to be merely more of its growing-pains. The system reacted to the shock of 1857 as it had to all the earlier ones, stumbling only to recover and go racing faster than before. This happened not alone in the United States. In Germany, too, the money-minded elements were now goaded to make a final bid for power. And there too they triumphed.

But not as completely. The German go-getters did get much of what they wanted, but hardly in the way they wanted it. Unhappily for them—and, as it turned out, even more unhappily for the whole world—the feudal spirit was peculiarly virile in Germany, and it was able to bring forth at this critical juncture a supremely virulent man. His name was Otto Eduard Leopold von Bismarck, and he was what was called a Junker—that is, a descendant of those medieval *junge Herren* ("young lords") who had hacked their way eastward and colonized the Slavic borderlands.

The typical Junker was a sinewy, bull-necked, bear-tempered gentleman who seemed to live only to fight, hunt, drink, and keep his estate intact. He was at once sentimental and insensitive, conventional and profligate, shrewd yet slow-witted. Bismarck shared all these traits except the last. Perhaps that was because he was only half a Junker. His mother was a city-bred woman, and came of a family of professors and civil servants. But unfortunately he grew up to hate her, and the intelligence she passed on to him served only to help him balk all that she represented.

He spent four years at a good university, where he devoted himself diligently to duelling, drinking, and the other studies deemed suited for a young Junker. In these he achieved a notable record, and was rewarded at the age of twenty-one with an appointment in the Prussian diplomatic service. Finding the work uncongenial, he soon resigned and went home to take over the management of the family estate. For eight years he lived the riotous life of a maverick country squire, only to be thrown at last by a pious young lady, harnessed in marriage, and converted into a model family man. Domesticity's gain was humanity's loss. Thenceforth Bismarck vented his wilfulness in politics.

His purpose was clear almost from the beginning. It was

to create a greater Germany for the greater glory of his own reactionary class. This was no light undertaking, for thus far the idea of political expansion had appealed only to progressives. Most of the landowners were lumpishly provincial in their outlook, and preferred to keep Germany a collection of petty states. It was the burghers who favored the cause of "nationalism," in part because they as a class had most to gain if that cause triumphed. They would be freer to manufacture what and how they pleased, since they would no longer be under the thumb of local princelings. Also they would be able to sell farther afield, since they would no longer be hampered by provincial frontiers. Again, they would be in a better position to resist competition from abroad, for they would cease to be so divided among themselves. Finally, they might even be able to cope with disaffection at home.

This last item was particularly important. Most of the German laborers had been serfs until yesterday, and the abrupt shift to free life in raw factory settlements seemed to be affecting them with peculiar intensity. They were growing insolent. What they needed, plainly enough, was some sort of pious distraction, some safe enthusiasm like that which Christianity had once been able to provide. For that religion, being a product of the past, had lost much of its influence in this new day. Laborers who worked amid modern machines were hard to awe with tales of ancient miracles. People who had to live in slums were hard to scare with threats of Hell. What was needed, therefore, was a new religion.

That was where nationalism came in. It seemed just what the situation called for, since it appealed to the most primitive emotions and yet was as up-to-date as a steam-train. Once a worker succumbed to it, he ceased to think of himself as anything but a citizen. He identified himself not with his class but with his nation, and docilely agreed that he and his employer, beings sons of one Fatherland, were brothers. That made him safe.

So the burghers had very practical reasons for favoring nationalism. In addition, however, they had even more compelling spiritual ones. They learnt these usually from their sons who attended the universities and heard erudite discourses on the "heroic German spirit," the "eternal German soul," and so forth. There had been a swelling flood of such talk in the country ever since the time Napoleon had temporarily reduced it to a parade ground for his troops. A very learned, very virtuous, and very wordy professor of philosophy named Johann Gottlieb Fichte had arisen then and delivered a series of addresses which were destined to become a new Holy Writ in certain intellectual circles. The essence of Fichte's preachment might be summed up in the statement that though he doubted the existence of God, he was sure that the Germans were His chosen people. They alone, he insisted, spoke a really "pure" language, had created a "genuine" art, and were capable of comprehending "true" philosophy. Whereas the spirit of other peoples was at best comparable to a bumbling bee,

"the German spirit is an eagle whose mighty body thrusts itself on high and soars on strong and well-practiced wing into the empyrean, that it may come ever nearer the sun whereon it delights to gaze."

Fichte was appallingly successful. Pouring a thimbleful of fact into a gallon of prejudice, adding a fistful of metaphysical terms and mixing in plenty of metaphors, he had stirred briskly and served piping-hot. And educated Germans learned to drink themselves berserk on the stuff.

The whole development, it should be realized, marked a sharp break with the past. As recently as the Eighteenth Century most German intellectuals had looked down on nationalism. Their ideal had been cosmopolitanism. One of the greatest of them, the poet Schiller, had cried: "Germans, don't try to be a nation! Be content to be human beings!" And his words were widely echoed—then.

But in the Eighteenth Century most intellectuals had been aristocrats, at least in spirit, whereas now most of them were brazenly bourgeois. Now they were usually the sons of prosperous burghers, and—like their fathers—they had sound practical reasons for favoring nationalism. The triumph of that cause promised to enrich them with the choice plums of officialdom which at present were still reserved for the sons of noblemen. The would-be bureaucrats therefore had a definite economic stake in nationalism. However, they rarely mentioned that.

Most of them, indeed, were not even conscious of it. They honestly believed that their patriotic fervor sprang pure and undefiled from the deepest depths of their ineffable German souls. And this, it must be said, was equally true of their fathers. Nationalism was no deliberately perpetrated fraud. Had it been, it could neither have spread nor have endured. Fundamentally it was as innocent as the measles.

Now Bismarck was obviously no proper Junker, or he would have opposed nationalism on principle. Being an improper one, however, he had intelligence enough to see that any such opposition was doomed. The whole trend of civilization was toward nationalism. Therefore he set out to do what seemed to him the next best thing: capture the trend and divert its course. Thus far nationalism had been a distinctly liberal influence. It had sought to widen men's horizons, lengthen their tethers, emancipate their minds. That was why its loudest advocates thus far had always been the progressives, the people who believed in Liberty, Equality, Fraternity, Democracy, Machinery, and every other portent of progress. Nationalism spelled freedom to such folk, for it opened a way of escape out of provincial confinement.

Bismarck made up his mind to change all that—and he succeeded. His opportunity came when, after fourteen years of patient political climbing, he was appointed Prime Minister of Prussia. At once he set about enlarging the army, for his whole scheme hinged on force. "Not by speeches or majority resolutions can the important questions of the day be decided, but by *blood and iron!*" Those were his words the very week he took office, and he lost no time in proving that he meant them. First (1864) he ganged up with Austria to pounce on Denmark and filch the duchies of Schleswig and Holstein. Then (1866) he turned on Austria, and throttled it into agreeing to Prussian suzerainty over most of northern Germany. Finally (1870) he welcomed a war with France, and in the heat of it welded Prussian rivets on all the rest of the land.

Thus Germany emerged a political unit at last. What countless burghers had failed to accomplish in sixty years, one Junker managed to do in six. The various kingdoms, duchies, and city-states had all been made part of one Empire, and there were no longer internal tariffs to impede the flow of commerce, or internal passports to restrict the drift of labor. There was a uniform currency now, a uniform system of weights and measures—and also a uniform conscript army. Germany was a real nation at last.

But not the sort of nation the burghers had dreamed of. Instead of its existing for them, they were told they existed for *it*. This Germany was not Liberal but Conservative, not humanitarian but militaristic, not an ostensible democracy but a gloved despotism. At bottom—and even more on top—it was one vast Junkerdom.

The burghers did not like that.

But most of them grew reconciled—in time. Though they continued to oppose Bismarck throughout his long term in office—twenty-eight years—their vehemence waned steadily. One can understand why. They began to see that, despite himself, Bismarck was really helping them.

His policy of blood and iron kept increasing the need for coal and iron. Moreover, it kept providing the means to fill that need. Bismarck had extorted a billion-dollar fine from the French, and that had meant so much fresh capital for German economic expansion. Also he had seized Alsace and Lorraine, one a store of machine equipment and the other a mine of metal resources. German industrialism could really begin to flourish after that.

Now the German industrialists had the advantage once enjoyed by the British: they were building last, and therefore could build best. They were free to adopt the most advanced techniques and install the very latest machinery. In addition they possessed a certain advantage all their own: they were forced to build as nationals rather than as individuals. Germany, thanks in part to Bismarck, had never been allowed to succumb to the doctrine of laissez-faire. Its government was still authoritarian, and private enterprise was still subject to public control. And this, though irksome to the enterprisers, proved in the long run distinctly helpful. It clamped brakes on murderous competition and suicidal speculation. If profits were less spectacular, they were also less unstable.

Nor was that all. Much as the German government might control capital, it controlled labor even more. To be sure, it also made an effort to care for labor, insuring all workers against sickness and unemployment, and paying them pensions in old age. Bismarck had discovered that such benevolences were highly prudent. They stole part of the thunder from the socialists, and thus short-circuited their lightning. The German workers were led to believe that they were true children of the Fatherland, not stepchildren. Thus they were encouraged to be loyal—and docile. The thought of rebellion grew so shocking to them that they became reluctant even to strike.

That was immensely pleasing to the German capitalists. It convinced some of them that Bismarck, though hardly their friend, was yet their ally. And this conviction was sound, for at the same time that he protected their rear he also cleared a path for their advance. He fostered scientific research at state expense, and thus assured them of a constant supply of new inventions. He forced through legislation to raise the tariff walls, and therewith "protected" the domestic markets. He encouraged every member of his diplomatic staff to be a tacit commercial agent, and by such means helped German goods invade the foreign field. Above all, he maintained a supremely powerful army, and with it made known both at home and abroad that what he had created was here to stay—and grow.

It did grow.

XVI. THE MACHINE GROWS UP

NOW industrialism was able to acquire a new character. It grew not merely bigger, but better. Germany and the United States were not content to copy British methods and mechanisms. They invented totally new ones. Technology experienced what amounted to another revolution, one even more profound and convulsive than the first. A hundred years earlier it had shot up from infancy to adolescence. Now it began to approach maturity.

Science deserves most of the credit for that. It had played only a minor rôle in the earlier revolution, for scientists had been relatively rare then, and usually too proud to apply themselves to "practical" things. Most of the major inventions of the late Eighteenth Century, like all of the minor ones, had been fathered by amateurs. But it was altogether different now. Technology had acquired the dignity of a profession, and even highly-trained physicists and chemists were willing to devote themselves to its problems. Invention ceased to be a casual, rule-of-thumb, hit-or-miss affair pursued by ardent hobbyists. The laboratory supplanted the attic; precise blueprints took the place of barn-made models.

Formerly science had looked down on industry as a haughty princess might look down on a low-born swain. Now, however, the swain had come up in the world, so milady swallowed her pride and let him make her his wife. It was a marriage of convenience, but its fruit was noble. Machines began to appear which were not simply larger than any that had come before, swifter, more efficient, less capricious. Many were completely novel.

The great triumph of the late Eighteenth Century had been the harnessing of steam-power. Now in the late Nineteenth Century came an even greater triumph: the harnessing of electricity. When an English chemist named Michael Faraday devised a primitive dynamo in 1831, a prominent politician is reported to have sneered, "What's it good for?" To which Faraday supposedly replied: "You might put a tax on it, sir!" And that is just what politicians were doing a few decades later. A German engineer named Werner Siemens developed a practical dynamo, and this coupled with the alternator contrived by a Jugoslav scientist, Nikola Tesla, eventually enabled an American inventor, Thomas A.

Edison, to produce light and power and even justice by electricity. The State of New York ceased to hang her capital offenders after 1888. Her solons decided it was more civilized to "electrocute" them.

Simultaneously a second source of energy was discovered in petroleum. In 1876 a German named N. Otto produced a practical gasoline-engine, and ten years later another German, Gottlieb Daimler, improved the device so that it could be hooked to a bicycle or a wagon. Thus was born the "horseless carriage." A French firm named Panhard and Levassor clamped pneumatic tires on the contraption in 1892, another named Renault Brothers added gears in 1897, and five years later an American named Henry Ford set up shop in a barn in Detroit. Dawned the "Flivver Age."

Ford started out as an unlettered mechanic, and so did most of the other men who succeeded in saddling the explosive power of petroleum. They received their training as wheelwrights, gas-fitters, or bicycle repairmen. Edison, who did most to buckle the harness on electricity, sprang from much the same class. But their practical achievements depended fundamentally on theoretical discoveries, and they knew it. That was why, once they went into production, they unfailingly hired consultants who were trained scientists. And they paid them well. Not extravagantly, of course, but well enough—especially when compared with what scientists had once been paid. The great Michael Faraday, head of the Royal Institution, had been content to work for $500 a year, coal and candles included!

Even Ford found himself forced to hire trained scientists. Edison, who had a far livelier intellect, recruited a staff of them as soon as he sold his first patent. He knew it would pay him. And it did.

The recruiting of scientists was found to pay in every industrial field. Geologists put new profit into mining, metallurgists into smelting, physicists into steel-construction, hydraulists into cement-mixing, geneticists into agriculture. Above all, chemists earned their salt. They found uncanny ways to refine petroleum, cure rubber, preserve food, tan leather, harden steel, synthesize dyestuffs, and conjure precious products out of sheer swill.

The earlier technology had been appallingly wasteful. Valuable commodities had been allowed to pour down drains, go up in smoke, fly away in the wind, pile up in refuse heaps. Now there was an end to such profligacy. In one industry, pork-packing, the "chemical engineers" wrought so wondrously that their employers could boast that nothing went to waste except the squeal!

All this meant more merchandise for the world, more to eat and wear and enjoy. The London markets began to display fish from Newfoundland, lamb from Australia, dates from Egypt, bananas from Honduras. Canned and bottled goods became common everywhere. Prospectors on the Klondike were able to feast on bully beef, and pauper children in Glasgow had orange marmalade with their tea—on Sundays. Textiles improved in quality and appearance. Leather shoes began to displace wooden clogs, and cheap handkerchiefs came to the relief of coat-sleeves.

Innumerable new conveniences and comforts crowded into everyday use: sewing machines, bicycles, fountain pens, tooth brushes, typewriters, rolled cigarettes, and rubber overshoes. All life was made at least potentially cleaner and more healthful. Sanitary devices multiplied, surgical appliances were improved, new and better medicines came on the market, and false teeth were made that really fitted. And a new brightness came into the world. The noxious, hissing gas-jet which had just begun to supplant the oil lamp was already beginning to give way to the electric globe.

Rail-transport picked up new speed. The chuffing "iron horse" became a sleek steel Pegasus capable of pulling a train at seventy, eighty, ninety miles an hour. The first white man to cross from Florida to California had spent eight hard years on the journey. Now the same distance could be traversed comfortably in half as many days.

Water-transport experienced an even profounder change. The paddle-wheel steamboat had proved a failure on the open sea, and as late as the 1870's almost all navigation had still been carried on in sailing vessels. But now the screw-propeller was introduced, new boilers were developed, welding replaced oakum and tar, and ocean voyages became as regular as ferry crossings. Ships appeared that were veritable floating hotels, their decks turned into tennis courts, their masts into derrick props. Seamen were still called "sailors," but they were really engine-tenders.

Yet these changes, on land and sea alike, were mere improvements. The real revolution came when the dynamo and the oil engine were perfected. These brought on the electric street-car, the automobile, and—eventually—the airplane. Thereafter man could really go places.

Even more wonderful: man could make places come to him. He had already learned to do that back in the 1830's, when the telegraph and the photograph first came into his ken. But after 1876 he had the telephone, after 1891 the motion picture, and after 1896 the wireless. Then his power over space and time became almost limitless.

So the marriage of science and industry proved a very princely event. It turned what had been a mere stream of plenty into a roaring flood. That was good.

But not perfect. The same thing happened now that had happened a century earlier: technology was revolutionized, but not psychology. Though the means were at hand to make life infinitely more bountiful and beautiful, not enough will emerged to take those means in hand. Man had, so to speak, educated himself beyond his intelligence. He had learned, but he had not understood. Therefore, despite all his newly-acquired power, he remained weak.

One trouble was that he kept trying to fit his new machines to old designs. Just as he had built the first railway cars to resemble stage-coaches, just so did he make the first automobiles look like buggies. Pushing is easier than pulling, and properly the motor should have been installed in the rear. Instead it was put in front, for that was where the horse had been. The most luxurious model was characteristically dubbed a "limousine"—because once upon a time royal coaches had been drawn by horses bred in the French province of Limousin. Even the humblest model usually sported a flower-vase on the dashboard—because people were used to seeing a whip-socket there.

These may seem trivial details, but they are revealing. Instead of erecting a brave new world, technology was employed to shore up the slavish old one. Consider, for example, what electricity might have accomplished now—had it only been given a chance. It might have dispelled the Black Life within a generation. No longer was there any need to concentrate industry in blighted, smoke-choked valleys. High-tension wires could deliver power to factories on mountain-crags, or far out on open moors. The same was largely true of commerce. The telephone was here, so why pile offices one on top of the other? The automobile was coming, so why continue to crowd the already overcrowded shopping-centers?

The herding of humans had been physically imperative in the steam-engine age. But not now.

Yet the herding actually increased. Though technologically wasteful, and socially disastrous, herding was financially profitable. Did it not improve real estate "values"? So the population of New York more than tripled between 1870 and 1910; that of Chicago multiplied sevenfold. Birmingham, Alabama, which had not even existed in 1870, contained over 130,000 inhabitants in 1910. Similar swarming occurred in every other industrial region. Tenement areas kept growing and growing. They suppurated in Osaka, in Johannesburg, in Calcutta, in Madrid. Factory slums ceased to be mere boils on the face of the earth; they became carbuncles.

Something that had gone wrong from the start kept going constantly wronger.

XVII. THE MIND STANDS STILL

REVOLUTION is another word for turn, and mankind had just made a good one. It had again ferreted out new and better means to exploit nature. But this good turn deserved another—and did not get it. Properly not alone the means should have been renovated, but also the ends. Just as science had been employed to direct the how of making goods, just so should it have been invoked to decide the when and where and for whom. More than horse-sense was needed to run an economy driven by horse-power. Unhappily, however, that need was not realized, and the second Industrial Revolution saw the fallacy of the first repeated and compounded. Once more a supply of new wine was spilled or spoiled because it was poured into cracked old bottles.

The economic system remained what it had been before. Commerce and industry continued to be carried on primarily by private individuals seeking immediate private gain. All the change that occurred was confined to method, not motive. Instead of growing essentially better, enterprises grew merely bigger.

This was especially true of the manufacturing enterprises. See, for example, what happened in the United States. In 1900 that country actually had fewer cotton mills than in 1850; but the average amount of capital invested in each had swelled from $68,100 to $442,882. There were only two hundred additional iron and steel mills; but the average annual output of each had jumped from $43,650 to $1,203,545. The number of factories making farm implements had been cut almost in half; but the survivors were producing forty-eight times as much merchandise.

The same thing happened in Great Britain, Germany, and all the other industrial nations. In each the manufacturing units waxed enormously in size and productivity. And this of course was only natural. Just as one revolution in technology had forced the domestic workshops to give way to small factories, just so did the next force the small factories to give way to giant plants. To be sure, this second change served to correct certain of the evils wrought by the first, for it took part of the crude muddling and caprice out of industry. Mammoth establishments could afford to hire scientists to develop new techniques. At the same time, they could not afford to foster all of the old abuses. It actually paid them to install safety devices in their workrooms, and to improve the lighting and sanitation. At times it even paid them to raise the wages or reduce the hours. A small manufacturer could get stubborn when threatened with a strike. He was free to close his shop and go off and sulk until his workers gave in, or his funds gave out. But the president of a great corporation had to reckon with his shareholders—and public opinion.

So far, so good. But so far was not far enough. This growth of giant plants tended to buckle the economy's balance-wheel. Business was no longer a free-for-all scramble. Any upstart could still start up; but if he wanted to forge ahead he had to form or join a gang. That boded no good for the economy. Formerly a man had needed merely a little money and a lot of enterprise to make good in the business world; but now the prerequisites seemed to be a lot of money and even more caution. A man who was at best a capable manufacturer could become at most a captain of industry. He had to be a shrewd financier to become a general. That boded no good at all. It put the fate of the economy into the hands of men who were more eager to conspire than compete.

For example, there was John D. Rockefeller. He was an extraordinary character who started out in a quite ordinary way. Born of poor parents on a mortgaged farm, he set himself to learn bookkeeping, and then went out into the world to make his fortune. With characteristic shrewdness he chose a field in which men of his pious kind—he was exceedingly pious—were as rare as they were needed. It was the petroleum industry, one of the newest in the world, and also about the rawest. As late as the 1840's, petroleum had been used solely as a quack medicine. Wandering mountebanks—among them John D.'s own father—had hawked it as Seneca Oil, "the one and only *genuwine* Indian remedy for snake-bites, cholera morbus, liver troubles, bronchitis, and fits." Late in the 1850's, however, people discovered that it could also be used for lighting and lubrication, and then there was a rush to drill wells and build refineries. Cleveland, the railroad-junction nearest the main oil-fields, became a boom town. Fortunes were made there in a day, and lost in a night. It was like San Francisco during the gold rush, only worse, for no one knew just how much oil was "worth." In 1859 a barrel of it fetched twenty dollars, and in 1861 fifty-two cents!

That was what appealed to young Mr. Rockefeller. He abhorred gambling, but loved a sure thing; and here he saw one going to waste. Oil, he believed, could be made as stable a commodity as coal or iron, and even more lucrative. All that was needed was a little organization. So he got busy. Finding himself two partners, he started a small oil refinery in 1862 with a capital of four thousand dollars. Eight years later he was the president of a million-dollar corporation called the Standard Oil Company.

That, however, was only the beginning. As yet he had resorted to none save quite conventional business methods, the ones he might have learned from his own father. The time came, however, when young John D. felt impelled to improve on what he had been taught. Instead of continuing to beat his competitors according to the rules, he set out to beat the rules.

His method was beautifully simple. First he quietly persuaded several of the largest refiners around Cleveland to form a syndicate, and then he gently bludgeoned the railroads into giving this syndicate special freight rates. That accomplished, he turned to the smaller refiners in his locality and blandly invited them to sell out or go broke. They sold out.

But then there was a howl. Rockefeller had wriggled himself into a position where he had the actual producers of petroleum by the throat, and the ultimate consumers by the tail. Both those groups began to howl, and with such violence that the railroads blanched—and welched. So Rockefeller tried another dodge. Hiring the lawyer who had led the crusade against him, he evolved a new type of combine which had no legal existence, and could do anything it wanted without ever baring its face. He called it a "trust," and began to recruit partners with the most elaborate stealth. He warned them not to disclose the scheme even to their wives, and begged them not to build large houses, or start driving fast horses, or reveal in any other way that big money had suddenly begun to come their way. He himself avoided extravagance as though it were rum or tobacco. Despite that he soon became one of the richest men in the land—eventually the very richest—he would not buy either a yacht, or a race horse, or a box at the opera, or a house on Fifth Avenue, or even a private art gallery. His only indulgence was philanthropy, and even that he kept—in those days—largely secret.

This stealth, however, did not imply a sense of guilt on his part. On the contrary, Mr. Rockefeller felt he was performing a righteous mission. Was he not exorcising the devil of competition? If he practiced guile, evasion, even deception at times, it was because he recalled the Gospel injunction to missionaries: "Be ye wise as serpents . . . lest they deliver you up to the councils and scourge you in the synagogues." Of course, he also remembered that the Bible said something about being "harmless as doves"; but he believed he was fulfilling that injunction, too. Did he not teach Sunday School regularly?

The public, however, put a different evaluation on his conduct, especially after other businessmen began to copy his monopolistic scheme. By 1887 a Senate Committee was moved to thunder that the formation of trusts had spread "like a disease through the entire commercial system of the country." All sorts of industries had begun to be monopolized: whiskey, sugar, glass, copper, farm tools, coffins, school slates, even castor-oil. A handful of timber barons had bought up so many of the nation's forests that they could have provided the logs for a bridge five miles wide clear across the Atlantic. Rockefeller himself had succeeded in getting control of nine-tenths of all the oil refineries in North America.

So a cry arose to "bust the trusts." It came first from the myriads of little businessmen who had already been, or were about to be, bust *by* the trusts. And the general public was not far behind. In 1888, an election year, both the Republican and the Democratic parties proclaimed their bottomless horror of all "combinations of capital." In 1889 half a dozen states passed laws against such combinations. In 1890 Congress itself joined the stampede, voting almost unanimously in favor of a sweeping "Anti-Trust Act." And in 1892, after fourteen months of stertorous litigation, the Standard Oil Company, archetype of all the trusts, was ordered dissolved.

Was Rockefeller daunted? Not in the least. Nor were any of the other panters after monopoly. Denied the right to combine in "trusts," they combined in "pools," "trade-associations," "joint-agreements," "communities of interest," and—last and best of all—"holding-companies."

This ultimate device was initiated in New Jersey, a small state where big businessmen were able to do almost as they pleased with the crumb-hungry legislature. By dint of various kinds of suasion they prevailed on it to enact a law permitting any corporation chartered in that state to buy an interest in any other corporation chartered anywhere in the country. That enabled monopoly to function behind a wall that was, as the saying went, "horse-high, hog-tight, and bull-strong." A similar law was soon enacted in Delaware, which was an even smaller state with an even crumb-hungrier legislature. By 1901 nearly two hundred giant holding-companies were pyramiding one enterprise on top of another. Between them they were already in control of capital to the extent of over four billion dollars—nearly twice the amount of money in general circulation throughout the land.

Monopoly had won out in the United States.

It won out in Germany too, and there even more sweepingly. Bismarck was in large part responsible for that. Being feudal to the marrow, he loved monopoly. Did it not foster authority and order? By the same token, Bismarck loathed competition, for that spelled freedom and chaos. Had he had the power, he would probably have consolidated all business in the hands of the state, and run it like the army or the school system. With some types of enterprise—for example, the railways and utilities—he actually succeeded in doing that. He made them government property.

Most enterprises, however, did not lend themselves to such tactics, so Bismarck compromised. Unable to take them over, he laid plans to keep them under, and therefore deliberately encouraged the businessmen to organize among themselves. He knew that the more they organized, the easier would they be to keep in line.

And most German businessmen fell in with his policy. They had never been able to work up a really deep devotion to individualism. They had not been given the chance. Only yesterday they had been the vassals of princelings, and the vassal spirit was still strong in them. They actually preferred to work in teams. They abhorred scrambling; they liked to march.

But even in Britain, where individualism was almost a national cult, even there more and more businessmen began to combine. The same was soon true in France and Belgium and every other land that developed extensive industries. In Japan fully 50% of all business fell into the hands of eight families. Throughout the world there was a swift growth of "trusts," "cartels," "syndicates," and similar monopolistic devices. Everywhere there was a steady drift toward setting production quotas, parceling out markets, and fixing prices. It seemed to make little difference whether the phenomenon was damned, blessed, or ignored; it came as irresistibly as caution to an aging hound.

There were two reasons for this. In the first place, the more that industrialism expanded, the more it had to be reduced to order—and order was impossible without some consolidation and centralized control. In the second place, the more that capitalism matured, the more it had to develop prudence, for without prudence it seemed bound to claw itself to shreds. It had been all very well for Adam Smith to advocate unbridled competition. In his day the field of business had been almost a wilderness, and there had been plenty of room for all who cared to rush in and grab. But the situation had changed since then. Competition had begun to prove itself inherently self-defeating, since the longer it was carried on, the fewer were the competitors who could survive. Smith had believed that the game would be umpired by an Unseen Hand. Instead it had begun to fall prey to an ungloved fist.

Here then was one more thing that went wrong. Monopoly did spell less chaos in industry, and thus definitely increased the potential capacity to produce. At the same time, however, it tended to rig prices, and thus it choked the relative capacity to consume. That meant trouble for the economy, even worse trouble than it had ever known before. Thus far it had been run by little businessmen, so the incidental ills had been likewise little. But now that big businessmen had begun to take over, correspondingly big ills had to follow. For those big businessmen, though superior in shrewdness, were equally lacking in vision. They too could look no farther than their noses. It never even occurred to them to ask what an economic system was really for. They, like the rest, took it for granted that the prime motive was merely the begetting of profit. Consequently, though they broke the old rules of business, they continued to play the same game. They too sought only to keep cutting costs and padding prices.

But costs included the wages paid to labor, and if these were held down, how was the bulk of the population to pay high prices? The whole arrangement was awry. Goods could be produced, but to whom were they to be sold?

XVIII. BUSINESS IS BUSINESS

ISTRIBUTION was the snag. The making of goods was easy now, but selling them still remained a problem. It would have been a problem even had the economic system not been so awry, for there was a technical hump to hurdle. Commerce had failed to become as efficient as industry, largely because it had been slower to succumb to the big businessmen.

Considerable capital was required to start a modern

manufacturing plant, but almost anyone could open a store—and almost anyone did. As a result, most trading continued to be carried on in ways as crude as they were hoary. Usually it was conducted in dark and cluttered little shops run by ferret-eyed vendors to whom each transaction was a battle of wits. Prices were rarely marked. The shopkeeper asked all he dared, the customer offered what he liked, and then they chaffered to and fro till they struck a bargain—or parted scowling. Save perhaps for the absence of oaths, and brandished fists, the whole procedure was precisely like that which had obtained in the bazaars of ancient Babylon. The first need, therefore, was improvement in the technique of merchandising.

This did come, of course; but all too slowly. One sign of advance was the emergence of a new kind of retail establishment called a "department store." Its inventor is said to have been a Parisian merchant who opened an emporium in 1852 which he named Le Bon Marché—"the good bargain." His success was modest at first, but he persevered, and in time other merchants copied his idea. Department stores began to appear in most of the larger cities throughout Europe, and eventually even in many small ones in the United States.

Another mark of progress was the rise of what came to be called the "chain store." This was an older type of institution, for there are records of its existence in ancient China and Rome. Not until late in the Nineteenth Century, however, did it begin to become somewhat common. Shortly before the Civil War it occurred to two Yankee merchants that if they bought tea right at the dock by the shipload and then sold it widespread by the pound, they could cut prices and still make a fine profit. So they started a concern which they bravely named "The Great Atlantic and Pacific Tea Company," and proceeded to open small stores in one town after another. Before long they too had imitators; indeed, so many of them, that eventually half the groceries consumed in the country were being bought from chain stores.

Still another advance was the invention of what came to be known as the "dime store." In 1879 a bright young man named F. W. Woolworth rented a small shop in Lebanon, Pennsylvania, stocked it with notions and gimcracks, and put a sign in the window reading, "No Article Over 5¢." That was a completely new wrinkle, and it caught on instantly. Before this Mr. Woolworth died he was opening similar shops even in Europe. Moreover, other merchants were emulating him in Australia, Africa, and Asia.

Then there was the "mail-order" house. The first of these to offer a general line of merchandise was founded in Chicago in 1872 by a man named Montgomery Ward. Later other such concerns arose in America, most notably Sears, Roebuck and Company and the T. Eaton Company of Canada. Eventually their like arose in most lands where there was free rural delivery.

All these developments were obviously steps in the right direction. True, they did crush the toes of the little shopkeepers; but see how they advanced the stride of the general public. They enabled the middleman to buy in large quantities, and thus tended to narrow the margin between what the producer charged and the consumer had to pay. They enforced plain marking of prices, and thus made the act of purchase a simple rite instead of a minor brawl. They encouraged standardization of brands, and thus helped take some of the gamble out of shopping. Above all, they fostered expansion, co-ordination, and efficient management, and thus began to shorten the lag between mass-production and mass-distribution.

The total effect, however, was far from adequate. These new institutions never conquered more than a corner of the entire retail field, and even within that corner the buying public was still at a disadvantage. Prices might be marked, and goods labelled, but the intrinsic quality of an article continued to be kept a secret. So far as that item was concerned, the rule was still *Caveat emptor*, "Let the buyer beware!"

This, to be sure, was not universally true, for there had been some growth of "co-operative stores" throughout this period. Robert Owen had plowed the ground for them back in the 1820's, but the seed had not taken firm root until after 1844. That year a group of laborers living in a Lancashire milltown named Rochdale started a "buying club" based on a new financial principle. They agreed to apportion the profits according to the amount of goods each member bought, and to disburse this profit not in cash but in capital shares earning 5% interest. Thus they assured their enterprise of a growing supply of capital, and at the same time gave themselves an unflagging stimulus to seek its success. The more they bought of its wares—and they were sound wares, fairly priced—the more they appeared to increase their personal savings.

The scheme proved so successful that it soon began to be copied in the neighboring towns, and then throughout the length and breadth of Europe. Even in the United States, where individualism was most stoutly intrenched, a society called the "Sovereigns of Industry" started to propagate co-operative stores. By the middle of the 1870's there was a chain of them extending from Maine to Maryland.

But again the total effect was slight. These cooperatives were able to form mere microscopic clearings in the jungle of commerce, for they labored under crippling handicaps.

The whole might of capitalism was pitted against them, and their own strength was chronically sapped by lack of initiative and excess of mismanagement. Therefore, despite their patent virtues, they failed to win wide patronage. Even where the cooperatives were least unsuccessful, in Great Britain and Ireland, they were able to boast fewer than 2,000,000 members by 1901—barely 4% of the entire population.

So the principle of *Caveat emptor* reigned unchecked, and this naturally encouraged all sorts of abuses. Some merchants did not hesitate to resort to outright villainy in their eagerness to earn an extra penny. They adulterated flour with plaster, whiskey with raw spirit, pepper with sawdust brown sugar with sand. They applied chemicals to tainted meat to make it look fresh and colorful, or added embalming fluid to milk to deter it from going sour. And though such practices may have been exceptional, others which were general were no less harmful in their ultimate effect. They put such suspicion into the hearts of the buying public that "sales resistance" became almost endemic.

This was no new affliction, but in the past it had not been important. Goods had been so difficult to produce that it had been almost an advantage if they were slow to sell. Now however, "sales resistance" threatened to throttle the entire economy.

Ways simply had to be found to break that bottleneck—and found they were, in the course of time. They were hardly the most intelligent ways, nor the most adequate; but they were at least adroit, and they did help a little. One stratagem was to make goods look better than they really were. Shoddy was fabricated to resemble pure wool, cotton was mercerized to shine like silk, tin was plated to look like sterling silver Anything that was costly was reproduced in cunning coun terfeit: jewelry, cut glass, leather, fur, and chinaware. Machinery which might have produced sound wares was deliberately employed to turn out trash. For trash had a twofold virtue: it was cheap and did not last, and could therefore be sold easily and often.

But there were some people who could afford to buy costly wares, and more who were slow to replace even cheap ones. This created a need for a further stratagem, one that would compel people to buy new merchandise before they could wear out the old. So the fashion-craze was popularized. Formerly fashions had changed only at long intervals, and they had interested solely the rich. Now such changes were deliberately stimulated each year, and even the poor were encouraged to pursue them. A new profession arose, that of the "fashion expert," and female apparel was re-designed relentlessly. There was no effort to make the new styles more sensible or more beautiful. The one ideal inspiring the entire fuss and flurry was simply change. The feather was put here instead of there, the bustle was raised, or lowered, or taken off, or put back again—that was all. The whole thing was worse than silly; it was cruel, for it caused immeasurable pain. Half the British navy could have been floated in the tears of poor womenfolk struggling to make one year's wardrobe do for the next. In addition it encouraged unconscionable waste. Essentially the whole artifice was nothing but a cancer.

That, however, was just what endeared it to the merchants. A cancer consumed, and consumption was their chief problem. They wanted to keep selling, and here was a means of inducing the public to buy. Before long they began to graft that cancer into other lines of merchandise: ornaments, draperies, furniture, automobiles. The time came when even the fashion in pet dogs was changed every year or two.

It was all done by means of propaganda. Every ruling class in history had had to resort to propaganda, and the stalwarts who were now struggling to become such a class resorted to it hard. They advertised. Back in the Eighteenth Century the current oracle, Dr. Johnson, had boasted that "the trade of advertising is now so near to perfection that it is not easy to propose any improvement." He spoke too soon. More than a hundred years later improvements began to come so fast that what had once been a mere trade suddenly blossomed into a mighty profession. All the Muses were seduced into its employ, and most of the Furies too. The greatest artists were hired to paint posters proclaiming the peculiar virtues of some particular brand of soap, soup, or sausages. Poets were paid to compose sonnets to that same end, and humorists were engaged to grind out limericks and slogans. Advertising multiplied and fructified till it threatened to smother the whole earth.

Wherever one turned one could not escape the adjurations to buy, buy, BUY! Glaring billboards were erected on the housetops in the cities, and on the hillsides along the roads and railways. Leaflets were scattered in the streets, free samples were stuffed in the mails, and arty calendars were hung in every kitchen and outhouse. The daily press began to carry almost more advertising than news, and even learned journals became freighted with commercial appeals.

In a sense it was a siege. Giant mortars of selling propaganda were set to pounding at the buying public day and night, Sundays included. And this seemed altogether necessary. In the language of an American writer of the time, the one sure prescription for business success had become:

> "Early to bed, early to rise,
> Work like hell, and advertise."

The whole system may have been foolish, and was certainly wasteful, but the businessmen were convinced that no better one could be devised. They badgered and wheedled and baited and begged because they believed that thus alone could the public be made to buy more goods. And it did buy more. The rate of consumption within the industrialized countries increased enormously as the years elapsed. But this, it must be recorded, was due only incidentally to high-pressure salesmanship. What helped far more was the increase in the public's buying-power. Wages had been steadily rising during all this period. No matter how the masters might struggle to hold them down, the workers always found ways to force them up. They joined unions and struck; or, better still, they merely threatened to strike and then agreed to negotiate. Where such methods were ineffective, the workers started riots and hurled bombs. The result was that in England, for example, the average wage nearly doubled between 1850 and 1900; in the United States it more than tripled.

That was good. The more the workers earned, the more they were able to spend. But there was a cloud behind that silver lining: by the time the workers had, say, twice as much to spend, the merchants had at least three times as much to sell. No matter how labor might advance, machinery advanced faster.

So in the end the situation was little better than it had been in the beginning. Despite all that the merchants thought up, and even all that the manufacturers gave up, consumption continued to lag behind production.

One more thing that had gone wrong from the start kept going wronger.

XIX. JOHN BULL'S DILEMMA

NOWHERE in the industrialized world was home consumption able to drain home production. Though the machines were allowed to stand idle all night, and periodically all day too, they still turned out far more than the domestic markets could absorb. The only solution, therefore, was to sell abroad. As the years elapsed the great producing countries found themselves forced to do more and more selling abroad.

Great Britain especially felt that need. The sudden spurt in the industrial race toward the close of the 1860's had goaded the British to install more machinery than ever. True, it was not the best machinery. Radical innovation was rather frowned on now by the typical British industrialist. He feared it would entail too much renovation. A novel device might require scrapping an old factory, and that would mean writing off considerable capital. He did not care to do that. For that matter, he did not see the need. Hadn't the old devices served him well enough in the past?

It was the German and American industrialists who showed the sharper enterprise now, for they were less encumbered by obsolete notions and obsolescent plants. As a result they began to gain on the British. Not alarmingly, of course. John Bull's juggernaut may have been less up-to-date, but it still retained the advantage of bulk. In addition it was more compact and better greased. It seemed able to keep ahead on sheer momentum.

It did keep ahead, but only by hitting up a madcap pace. Britain's annual output expanded stupendously between 1870 and 1900. Here are some figures of the increase:

Cotton goods	40%
Woolens	100%
Pig Iron	150%

And this increase meant so much more surplus to dispose of each year.

Now once upon a happy time a surplus of manufactured wares had presented no problem at all to the British. The whole world had been eager to take it off their hands. But conditions had changed since then. Other nations had got hold of machinery, and these were manufacturing for themselves. Not as cheaply perhaps, for their equipment was less extensive as yet. But they were making up for that handicap by walling in their home markets with "protective" tariffs. The United States had not been the only country to resort to that maneuver. Germany had adopted it too, and so had France, Italy, Austria, even Russia.

"Protection" was threatening to make the whole world a maze of walls, and to John Bull that seemed outrageous. He for his part believed in "Free Trade"—all markets open to all comers, everything fair and square, and may the best man win. John Bull had been pursuing that policy in his own realm ever since the 1840's, and he felt it ought to be pursued everywhere else. To be sure, he himself stood to gain most if that were done. His peerless industrial resources would then enable him to continue outselling and underselling all rivals. But this, he argued, was neither here nor there. It was the principle of the thing that counted. According to the teachings of "economic liberalism," the most profitable policy—in the long run—was to let competition go the limit. "Protection" was therefore inexcusable. Its whole aim was to put competition on a leash.

But John Bull argued in vain. His rivals refused to think about the long run; they were too intent on winning the short one. The latter agreed that "Economic Liberalism" was a very noble ideal, and they hoped Britain would never abandon it. For themselves, however, they preferred "Economic Nationalism." That gave them a better chance in the battle for business, since it enabled them to fight in packs against the British who fought as individuals.

John Bull did not like that. Where was he going to sell his goods if other nations continued to gang up against him? At home? Impossible. Most of his subjects were too poor, and most of his products were too specialized. Britain was producing more textiles than ever, yet even less food; it was turning out whole mountains of ironmongery, but only handfuls of fine wares. British industry could not conceivably serve the British market alone; it was geared to serve the whole wide world. So John Bull found himself with a growing surplus on his hands—and a growing ache in his head.

The problem was not confined to goods; there was also a growing surplus of capital to dispose of. John Bull had been enriching himself hand over fist ever since he took to the Machine. By 1870 his total capital amounted to nearly thirty billion dollars—fully twelve times what it had been in 1770. This was called Britain's "national wealth," but the term was inaccurate. Most of the treasure belonged to the very rich, and these were relatively very few. They could not possibly spend all they had; nor would they try. They believed with something akin to religious fervor that their first duty was not to spend but to invest. A thousand pounds to them was not a thousand pounds. It was sixty pounds per annum—or more, if they could get a higher rate of interest.

This, as we have seen, was a good thing in one way. Had the rich considered their increment a flower to be plucked, instead of a seed to be replanted, the age-old curse of scarcity might have endured forever and aye. Only because the profits of British industry were plowed right back into it was British industry able so swiftly to expand.

But the time came when that process seemed to reach a saturation point. Britain might be Great in name, but it was small in size. Once the basic mines and mills had been established, and all the essential railways had been nailed down, further industrial expansion necessarily yielded diminishing returns. Consequently the British capitalists found themselves forced more and more to look abroad for places to invest their wealth. Not that there was no room for it at home. The industrial plant may have been large enough, but it was not nearly good enough. Much of Britain's mechanical equipment had already become obsolete by 1870, and almost all of it could have stood improvement. As for what might be called the social plant, that was in unspeakable shape.

No effort had yet been made to raze the slums which had festered around the first factory sites. On the contrary, these had been allowed, even encouraged, to spread. Crowding, squalor, stink, and grime were actually commoner in 1870 than they had been even in 1830. There were industrial towns in England, containing tens of thousands of inhabitants, which still lacked a single public park or public bathhouse. Schooling had been made universal, but almost all the schoolhouses were as cramped as they were foul. What few free hospitals existed were so dreadful that even the deathly sick fought against being taken to them.

And conditions in the British countryside, though less sordid, were almost as squalid. There were, of course, many beautiful estates and unspoiled woodlands, but these were usually walled in and marked, "No Trespassing!" The common farmfolk had to subsist in the most abject surroundings, for they had been reduced to virtual pauperdom. Their houses might be picturesque to look at, but they were noisome to live in. What with their straw roofs and mud walls and earthen floors and steaming dunghills, they were not so much homes as lairs. In many respects life in the British countryside was as primitive as it had been in the Middle Ages.

To talk of an excess of capital in Britain was preposterous. Actually there was not even nearly enough for all that cried to be done in the land. The virus of the Black Life was still raging in the industrial regions, and the ghost of the Black Death continued to haunt the rural parts. To have stamped out both would have called for public works costing billions.

But those who owned the billions were not interested in public works. Public works did not yield dividends. Those owners were cool even toward private works unless they yielded high dividends. So they insisted on shipping more and more of their capital abroad.

This, however, like shipping more and more goods, was ceasing to be quite easy. Earlier in the century the British had been able to invest to their heart's content on the Continent and in the United States; but now the fairest opportunities in those regions were being snapped up by native capitalists. Worse still: the latter were beginning to compete with the British in every other part of the world. Germans were developing industries in Russia, Belgians were building railroads in China, Frenchmen were opening up mines in Mexico, Italians were starting plantations on the North African coast.

No wonder John Bull began to fear he was in for trouble. He had equipped himself to serve the world, and now he was being denied the run of it. That spelled serious trouble. It threatened to curtail his power not merely to sell and lend, but also to buy—and he had to do lots of buying.

He needed raw materials for his factories. The two basic ones, coal and iron, were abundant right at home; but there were others quite as essential, especially in the newer industrial processes, for which he had to forage overseas. He had always had to go abroad for raw cotton. Now he had to do likewise to get petroleum, rubber, manganese, brimstone, copper, lac, and scores of other such commodities.

And even more vital than raw materials for his factories was his need of food for the factory workers. John Bull still liked to picture himself a country squire, but it was completely a pose. Agriculture had become at most a sideline with him; yet he had more need now of agricultural products than ever before. By 1870 England and Wales alone contained more than twenty-two million mouths that had to be fed each day. By 1900 they numbered more than thirty-two million.

So John Bull had every reason to start worrying. He was at the mercy of the world—and the world's mercy, he had learned, was nothing to rely on. He got ample proof of that when the Civil War broke out in the United States. The Southern ports were blockaded by the North, and that cut off the supply of raw cotton to Lancashire. The result? Lancashire, which lay full three thousand miles beyond the range of the American guns, became as sore stricken as though it were right inside the war-zone. The mills had to close down, the millowners had to go bankrupt, and the mill-workers had to roam the streets. Britain's most important industry was all but paralyzed.

John Bull was never the same after that. He began to see that if he intended to survive economically, he would have to expand geographically. His empire of machines demanded an empire of land.

He set out to get one.

XX. GOADS TO EMPIRE

THE BRITISH developed a ravenous appetite for land. It was not the first time. Much the same thing had happened in the early Sixteenth Century, right after an Italian adventurer in the hire of Spain discovered a new world beyond the Atlantic. That discovery had been largely accidental. In the apt language of one historian, Christopher Columbus set forth without knowing where he was going, got there without knowing where he was, and returned without knowing where he had been. But this ignorance was soon dispelled, for half a dozen other European nations rushed to hire adventurers of their own to comb the seas.

Their incentive was not so much greed as need. During more than a thousand years hordes of dark-white tribesmen had been pressing in on them from the East. Century after century those tribesmen—Huns, Arabs, Tartars, and Turks—had come storming in across Russia and Anatolia. And now the nations at the western end of the European continent found themselves being pushed right into the sea. These nations had waxed in population, and needed more living-space than before. Instead they were being left with less and less. So they had to move out.

It was sheer need, therefore, that led to the great explorations of the Sixteenth Century. Those who took part in them may have thought themselves adventurers, but in reality they were more akin to refugees. Luckily, they found what they were after, and much more of it than any of them had dreamed. Land, they discovered, was everywhere. No matter in what direction they sailed, invariably they found land—if they sailed far enough. Whereupon what had started as a rout ended as a prowl. The Spaniards prowled, the Portuguese prowled, the French, the Dutch, and the Scandinavians prowled. And the English, they prowled too.

But after a while they all began to tire of prowling. Even the English tired of it—though not until they had bagged next to the largest collection of prizes. Thereafter they continued to pick up colonies only absent-mindedly, in a sort of kleptomania. And finally even that ceased. Halfway through the Eighteenth Century the English seemed actually to sicken of colonies.

Note what happened when thirteen of Britain's choicest

possessions dared to declare their independence in 1776. King George was forced to hire German mercenaries to go out and fight the rebels. His own subjects, it seems, had neither the time nor the will to bother about any revolution in America. No wonder. They had a more exciting one on their hands right at home.

The British nation had got itself embroiled in the Industrial Revolution, and this, as we have seen, raised a new class to power. Money-minded men, capitalists, got control of Parliament, and these had little use for the Empire. The pig-iron had entered their hearts, hardening them so that they could not respond to any appeal based on sentiment alone. Even when their country was locked in a death-grapple with France under Napoleon, they had insisted that French holders of British bonds should be paid interest at regular intervals. Right in the midst of their Crimean War with Russia they gladly floated a loan for Russia through the London banks. Such gestures were typical of those money-minded men. In their eyes business came before patriotism or any other pleasure.

It was natural, therefore, that they should be cool toward the Empire. They felt it was a source of waste and silly fol-de-rol. It necessitated maintaining a large army and navy, and thus tied up capital which could be put to use in industry. Besides, the Empire was a public institution run by public officials for public pride—and these capitalists believed solely in private enterprises run by private individuals for private profit. They recoiled from the very word "public," for it spelled government to them, and government spelled officiousness, extravagance, taxation. They were confirmed Liberals. "The less government the better!" they believed.

So they proceeded quite deliberately to neglect the Empire. Some even urged that it be scrapped forthwith, but these were branded Radicals and voted down. The majority of the Liberals felt that Britain ought to retain a certain number of colonies if only as dumping-grounds for convicts, missionaries, black sheep, retired army colonels, and other people who were in the way at home. Therefore instead of scuttling the Empire, they left it to rot away at anchor.

This remained the official policy for nearly two generations—from 1815 until about 1870. Britain might have seized all of South America during that period; but instead she urged the United States to proclaim the "Monroe Doctrine." Twice the chieftain of the Fiji Islands offered to deed her full sovereignty over his realm—he was trying to dodge a fine of $45,000 levied on him by the United States—but each time Britain resolutely refused. The only territories she seized in all those fifty-five years were three coaling stations needed to protect her shipping, and a bit of South African coastland where her colonists were being troubled by the Boers. At the same time, she turned around and granted complete autonomy to four of her largest dependencies: Canada, Newfoundland, Australia, and New Zealand.

But finally there was a revulsion. It was fomented by the Tories, who had never reconciled themselves to the new policy. They were opposed to it not alone because it was new, but also because it was bad—for them. They had heavy stakes in the Empire, spiritual as well as material ones. In the first place, it propagated all that was most dear to their souls: warfare, glory, tradition, authority. In the second place, it furnished many of them with that which they most needed: government jobs. Men of good family but poor means—and that type had grown all too common in Tory circles—could hardly be expected to seek employment in "trade." They might marry into "trade," but to stoop lower than that would have been too demeaning. If such personages were reduced to the necessity of actually working for a living, obviously their only fit employer was Her Majesty the Queen.

So the Tories never ceased to wail against the neglect of the Empire; and in the end their wailing took effect. In large part that was because they learnt to wail in the right quarters. For one thing, they carried their agitation into the so-called "public schools," which were actually private academies attended exclusively by the male children of the rich. They appealed there to the idealism of the youths, ardently warning them that as true sons of Britain they must grow up to think of more than mere money-making. Nature had appointed them to fulfill a high destiny, the highest ever assigned to any race. It was to tame the savage peoples of the earth, curb the foolish ones, spread light and civilization—in short, make "cricket" universal. Years later one of those youths, having grown up to become a poet, put the whole message into four words. He called it "The White Man's Burden."

That, however, was a distinctly secular notion, and could appeal only to more or less paganized minds. (Was there anything in the Bible distinguishing white men from black?) England still contained innumerable very pious folk, so for their benefit the same message was offered in another version. They were assured that not merely Nature, but Christ Himself expected every Englishman to do his duty; and this duty was to spread not just civilization, but religion. The White Man's Burden was really the Cross. Thus the imperialists were able to recruit a following in the churches as well as the schools. They readily granted that a missionary needed only the grace of God to do his holy work.

However, they argued, if in addition he had the support of the Queen's army, could he not do his work much faster?

But where the Tories won their readiest response was in the common public-houses. There they were able to reach the masses, and these proved peculiarly eager to shout hurrah for the Empire. The reasons were numerous, but they all came down to one: imperialism offered those wage-slaves a way of escape. To the more courageous among them it held out the promise of physical escape. They saw themselves riding pickaback on good old John Bull to lands where there was enough food to eat, sweet air to breathe, and perhaps ignorant natives whom they could make *their* wage-slaves. As for the timid, they were drawn to imperialism because it offered them a way of mental escape. Though they themselves might never venture out to the colonies, they wanted the satisfaction of at least knowing that the colonies were there. They wanted to be able to read about them in the penny press, and sing about them in the music-halls. They wanted to be able to point them out on the map, and gloat: "See 'em? They're all ours!"

Fools? Certainly they were fools. But to call them that is to say no more than that they were human beings. Like all human beings, they wanted to count for something, wanted to feel important—and imperialism gave them the means. It served them precisely as nationalism was serving their laggard contemporaries on the Continent, for imperialism was nothing but nationalism boiling over. Both alike enabled the timid to puff themselves up until their heads reeled and they could imagine themselves giants. Both alike brought comfort to the downtrodden by encouraging them to identify themselves with the treaders. And Britain, it must be realized, contained millions who were downtrodden.

It is true that the lot of the average toiler there had improved somewhat. He had more to eat than in former times, knew the taste of more comforts, and was less at the mercy of his masters. But these gains, far from making him content, had served only to leave him the more frustrate. He had managed to rise just high enough to see how low he stood. This filled all his being with gall.

Yet what could he do? How was he to allay his sense of frustration? He could no longer easily steep himself in religion: he had lost the necessary innocence. He did not dare shout for revolution: he did not have sufficient courage. He could hardly keep getting drunk: he had too much sense and not enough money. Apparently there was only one way for him to assuage the misery in his soul. He had to drug himself with patriotism.

And thus it came about that the Tories were able to whip up a popular clamor for reviving the Empire. Nevertheless the government refused to act. Parliament was still controlled by the Liberals, and these were still averse to coloneering. Being good businessmen, they believed in economic exploitation, not military exploits. Whereupon certain of the wilder Tories decided to "dish the Whigs" as they had once been dished by them. The latter, it will be recalled, had managed to attain power in the 1830's by enforcing a new deal in politics which gave the urban upstarts the right to vote. Now, thirty years later, the vanquished gentry set out to turn the tables by going their victors one better. They demanded votes for the urban downtrodden.

Here was irony with a vengeance. The highest in the land struck up a partnership with the rabble. (How the ghost of Feargus O'Connor, the old Chartist, must have roared!) Haughty British aristocrats, musty dukes and crusty squires, suddenly draped themselves in the mantle of righteousness and began to snort for more democracy.

The turnabout was engineered largely by one man, and he, significantly, was neither an aristocrat nor quite a Britisher. His name was Benjamin Disraeli, and his grandfather had been literally a merchant of Venice. Few characters in modern history present a more fascinating psychological study than does this "Dizzy." His whole career was like the costume he affected—dazzling, dashing, excessive. A Jew, it has well been said, is just like anybody else, only more so; and in at least that respect Disraeli was all too true to his stock. Whatever he set out to do he overdid.

That may help to explain why he joined the Tories in the first place. He wanted to prove himself thoroughly, utterly, supremely a Britisher. It may also help to explain why, once he joined them, he insisted on becoming their leader. He must have felt that he needed to confirm what he had already proved. He it was who led the aristocrats into that strange alliance with the mob. He was canny enough to see that if the workers were given the vote, they would inevitably use it to send gentlemen rather than businessmen to Parliament. And in this he was right—at least temporarily. When, in 1874, the enfranchised rabble got its first real chance to flock to the polls, the Tories carried the elections overwhelmingly.

Then the Empire was reborn.

XXI. PHILANTHROPY PLUS FIVE PER CENT

ITH the Tories in control of Parliament, and Disraeli in control of the Tories, the dawn came up like thunder on a new day in history. It was preceded by a stroke of lightning: Britain snapped up a block of shares in the vital Suez Canal Company. And then the thunder pealed forth: Britain's Queen was formally proclaimed Empress of India. After that, Disraeli retired to the House of Lords as the Earl of

Beaconsfield. His work was done. He had slipped the leash on the British lion, and now he could sit back and watch it prowl.

And how it did prowl! First it stalked westward out of India to devour Baluchistan, then eastward to swallow Burma and Malaya, then northward to claw at Thibet. It pounced on Wei-hai-wei on the coast of China, on Cyprus in the Mediterranean, on Fiji, New Guinea, and countless other islands in the South Seas. And then there was Africa. Starting from the north, it bolted Egypt, Somaliland, Kenya, Zanzibar, and most of the Sudan; stalking from the south, it seized Bechuanaland, Zululand, Matabeleland, Uganda, and the Boer Republics.

For thirty years the British lion kept prowling and preying thus, and not until a fourth of the entire planet lay between its paws did it think to rest. Then, sinking to its haunches, it seemed to glare at the sun and growl: Try and set on me now!

Never before in history had any nation acquired so enormous an empire, and the feat, needless to say, was not accomplished with ease. Luck certainly set the stage for it, but pluck was what kept the show going. Whole armies of hale young Englishmen—and also Scotsmen, Welshmen, Irishmen, and a hundred other breeds—gave their lives to wrest the new colonies. They were ambushed in mountain passes and drowned in steaming swamps. Thirst tortured them, fevers laid them low, boredom drove them mad. Those soldiers were real heroes, God rest their souls!

Yet it must be recorded that valor accounted for only part of the triumph. Cunning accomplished even more. The British employed every type of cunning from diplomatic artfulness to brazen treachery. To be sure, compared with

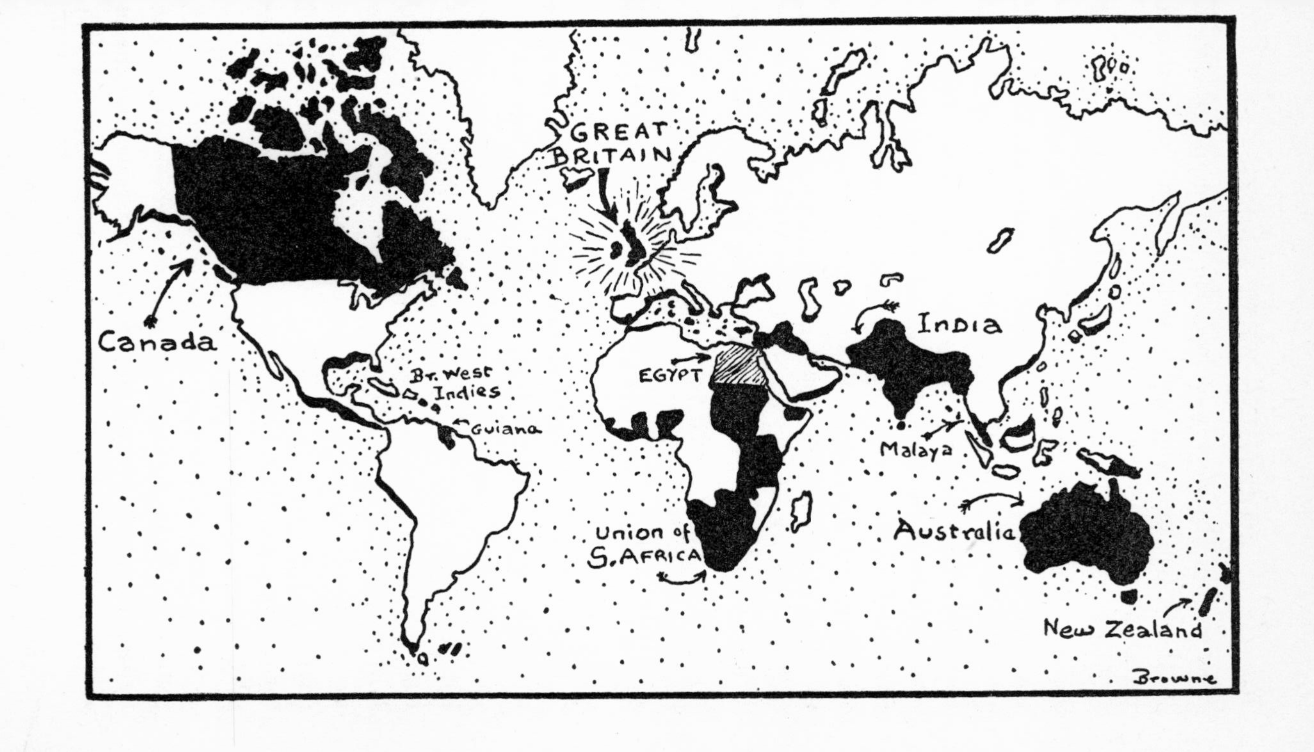
GREAT BRITAIN
Canada
Br. West Indies
Guiana
EGYPT
Union of S. AFRICA
India
Malaya
Australia
New Zealand
Browne

earlier empire-builders—and later ones—their conduct was almost saintly. But it could have been saintlier.

Consider, for example, how they helped themselves to what was called Matabeleland. The inhabitants of that region were a ferocious Negro shepherd-folk who asked nothing but to be left alone to roam and fight on the grassy plateau which they had made their home. But one day in 1888 three Englishmen—among them a fellow of All Souls College, Oxford—approached Lo Bengula, the Matabele chief, with a proposition. They would give him, they said, a thousand rifles, a hundred thousand cartridges, and also a monthly stipend, if he would give them merely the right to see if there was gold on the frontier of his realm. Lo Bengula shook his head. His people, he said, wanted white men to keep their distance. But when the delegation offered to throw in a second-hand steamboat, covetousness—and champagne—got the better of the chief. Trustingly, he put his mark on a piece of paper, and the strangers departed.

But soon other strangers came, whole swarms of strangers who proceeded to stake out claims as far as the horizon. Apparently Lo Bengula had signed away the rights to all the minerals in his entire domain. The white men had that piece of paper to prove it, and waved it in his face when he tried to order them away. Whereupon the chief dictated a letter of protest to the fabled Queen who ruled over those white men. Twice he wrote to her as one monarch to another, requesting that she denounce the shabby trick that had been played on him. But when a reply finally came, it curtly informed Lo Bengula that he must surely be mistaken, since the Britishers involved in the dispute were known to be most honorable gentlemen.

That was the last straw. Rallying his black braves, Lo Bengula prepared for battle. Three months he fought like a hero—and a savage—until at last his whole army was cut down. And then, having chased him into hiding, the white victors proclaimed all his lands forfeit to their Queen.

That was a typical incident—a bit flagrant perhaps, but none the less typical. The pukka British attitude seemed to be that a lie was not a lie unless it was told to someone important enough to deserve to be told the truth. That, obviously, ruled out mere "natives," and in consequence the path of British glory was paved thick with skulduggery. Not as thick, certainly, as the path of Mongol glory in the Thirteenth Century, or that of Nazi glory in the Twentieth. But thick enough.

There was of course some suspicion of this at home, and it aroused no little protest. The Socialists protested, the Anarchists protested, and the brotherly-loving Quakers shook their heads and deplored. But who cared to listen to such folk? The ordinary Britisher preferred to believe that the empire-builders were practically paragons of virtue. Were they not carrying Christian decency into the sinks of heathendom, and British civilization into the haunts of savagery? Were they not teaching head-hunters to see the naughtiness of their ways, and cannibals the indelicacy of their diet? Were they not suppressing banditry, daughter-slaughter, widow-killing, slave-snatching, and all the other wicked practices which heathen breeds seemed to adore? Of course they were!

So the cries of protest were drowned out in a chorus of cheers. Eventually nearly everybody at home learnt to cheer, including even the businessmen. For the latter tardily discovered that they had been wrong about imperialism. Apparently it was not at all an indulgence born of folly and breeding waste. On the contrary, it seemed to be a sound investment. It actually paid.

Imperialism paid, first of all, because it compelled savages to put on clothes, taught them to crave forks, umbrellas, and guns, and thus created new markets for British goods. Moreover, being controlled by Britain, these markets were safe from ever being "protected" against her.

Imperialism paid, secondly, because it opened up new sources of raw materials. No longer need Lancashire depend for its life on cotton imported from the United States. Egypt could supply a far better grade, and India as good a one far more reliably. Tin could be procured from Malaya, zinc from Burma, hardwood from Ceylon, copra from Fiji, bullion from South Africa, rubber from Central Africa, hemp from the West Indies. Moreover, such commodities could be procured cheaply, since the British could see to it that the natives did not learn about trade-unions.

And imperialism paid, finally, because it opened up new fields for capital investment. Money was needed to clear jungles, dig mines, dredge harbors, and lay out towns. It was needed to build smelters, railways, docks, and warehouses. And British money naturally got the best chance to finance such enterprises, since British officials ruled the lands where they were started.

So it was no wonder that businessmen learned to cheer. They came to see that the prowling lion bore a halo made of solid gold. Before long, indeed, many businessmen were not content merely to cheer. They personally took the lion by the mane and tugged to show it just where to prowl. There was Cecil Rhodes, for example: he tugged so hard that he enriched Britain with more than half-a-million square miles of African soil. At the same time he sieved enough diamonds and gold out of that soil to enrich himself with well over a hundred million dollars. But this, he believed, was as it should be. Imperialism, in his authoritative opinion, was nothing but "philanthropy plus five per cent."

And most of the people back home seemed to agree. Only the most skeptical Englishmen thought to analyze the nature of the philanthropy, and only the most jaundiced stopped to ask who got the five per cent. The rest were carried away by the idea that a way had at last been found whereby they could serve God and Mammon at one time. The joke, of course, was on them. Whether they were really serving God, only God knows; but most of them were certainly not serving Mammon. The average Englishman was not making a ha'penny out of the colonies. On the contrary, seeing that he had to foot the bill for the army and navy and Colonial Office, he was really out of pocket.

Imperialism was actually a sound investment only for those who actually did the investing. There was immense profit in it, but solely for a few soldiers of fortune and captains of industry and princes of finance. Certain shipping magnates made millions out of the colonies; so did certain promoters, importers, adventurers, and munitioneers. But the rest of the home population got nothing out of them at all—at least, financially. This, however, was not generally understood. It was imagined that what enriched *some* Englishmen, enriched *all* of them.

It did—on paper. The proof of it was that after 1870 the "national wealth" of Great Britain began to grow—on paper—at the rate of nearly a billion dollars a year.

XXII. THE GREAT WHITE LIE

UT Britain was not the only nation to wake up suddenly to the value of colonies. France discovered it even sooner, and had she not been halted by misadventure at home, she might have seized what became the lion's share. As early as 1852 the ruler of France, formerly a mere President, officially proclaimed himself an Emperor, for he had already laid plans to coloneer all around the globe. Nor did he lose any time in carrying out those plans. First he seized Algeria in North Africa, then New Caledonia in the South Seas, then Cochin-China in the Far East. He even made a clutch at Mexico. But in 1870 he committed the fatal blunder of tangling with Bismarck, and that finished him together with all his proud schemes.

France became a republic once more, and for the next ten years her rulers had too much trouble at home even to think

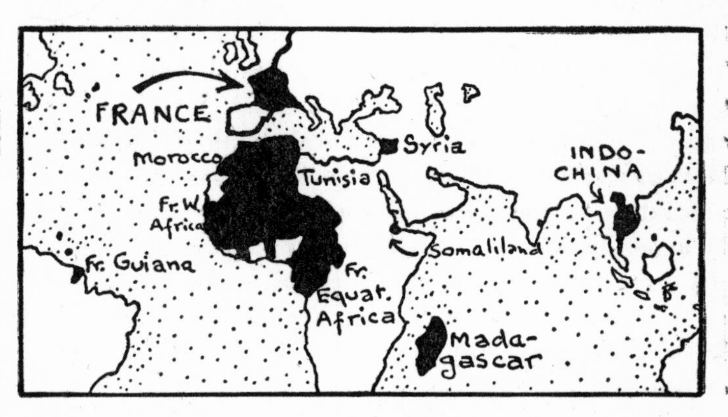

THE FRENCH EMPIRE
They called it "la mission civilisatrice."

of promoting adventure overseas. No sooner, however, did the country pull itself together again, than it began shakily to return to the prowl. The move was not entirely a matter of choice. The French politicians saw the desperate need of recouping what had been lost in the War of 1870—land, wealth, and above all pride—and they also saw that this need could not possibly be fulfilled by striking back at Germany. Such a course would have spelled suicide. So instead they decided to strike out in Africa and Asia. That at worst entailed mere murder.

Naturally, they did not call it murder, or even think it such. They described it as "*la mission civilisatrice.*" In the language of Premier Jules Ferry: "The superior races have the duty of civilizing the inferior ones." So the French became dutiful.

First they marched eastward out of Algeria to carry civilization to Tunisia. That accomplished, they turned southward to conquer the Sahara and all that was available of the Sudan. Simultaneously they deployed inland through the fever swamps on the African west coast to lay hold of Senegal, Dahomey, much of Guinea, and all of the Northern Congo. A titbit was filched in Somaliland on the east coast, and this was followed up with a real mouthful consisting of Madagascar in the south. At the same time they took the precaution of "regularizing" their position in the Far East by annexing Annam, Tonking, and Indo-China.

Within little more than twenty years the French politicians were able to boast that—all in the line of duty—they had acquired an empire approximately the size of the whole of Europe.

In the meantime, however, half a dozen other nations had become fired with "*la mission civilisatrice.*" The passion was kindled even in Russia, a country which was in most material respects completely barbarous. But the Russians themselves insisted that those respects, being merely material, were really immaterial. They felt they had a right to go a-missionizing because they were supremely advanced in spiritual ways. They had a unique Soul, and were therefore in duty bound to let its effulgence shine on others.

Not even the wisest or wordiest Russians seemed able to describe that Soul with any precision; but that, it was argued, merely proved how unique it was. Most authorities on the subject were content simply to say that it was Slavic.

Curiously, few Russians had known that they were thus endowed until well into the Nineteenth Century. By that time they had already devoted three hundred years to territorial expansion, pushing westward out of Muscovy far into Poland, northward to the Arctic, southward to the Caspian, and eastward actually to the Pacific. They even crossed to Alaska and set up block-houses as far south as California. But their motives during all that period had been admittedly selfish. They had needed some occupation for their generals, more land for their barons, better seaports for their merchants, and larger revenues for their Tsars.

Eventually, however, something began to itch inside them, and when they scratched—a task at which they had developed marked proficiency—lo, out came that Soul of theirs! They immediately decided it had been there all along; but this is more than doubtful. All the evidence indicates that it was an importation from Western Europe, where the manufacture of national souls had just become a major intellectual industry. Being neither animal, vegetable, nor mineral, that foreign notion had entered Russia duty-free.

And it began to flourish there like the cholera. First the notion was taken up by the few liberals in the land: the advanced intellectuals, the more imaginative bureaucrats, and the most enterprising merchants. These professed themselves very proud of their Slavic Soul, but wanted to tuck in its shirt-tail and make it look a bit more "Western." Before long, however, even the reactionaries succumbed to the fad, and then it was given a new twist. These reactionaries insisted that the Slavic Soul needed no "Westernizing"; it was perfect as is. And in the end their attitude prevailed. Almost everybody who was anybody in Russia learnt to call himself a "Slavophil," and took to talking far into the tea-soaked night about something called "Pan-Slavism." Ostensibly this was an idealistic project to unite all peoples who spoke a Slavic tongue into one Soul-conscious family headed by the "Little Father" who ruled from St. Petersburg. Actually it was nothing but the old Muscovite imperialism with its beard combed.

For the Tsarists were still eager for conquest. Though their empire already included more than a sixth of the habitable land on earth, they still lacked safe access to navigable water. And that, one suspects, was why they began to make such a to-do now about "Pan-Slavism." It gave them a perfect excuse for hewing a corridor through the Balkans and hacking out a door on the Mediterranean. The Balkans were largely Slavic in population, yet they were dominated almost entirely by Turkey and Austria-Hungary. So the Tsarists could say it was their sacred duty to free their "little brothers."

They did say that. Year in and year out they fomented sedition and war in the Balkans. They stirred up the Bulgarians, the Bosnians, the Moldavians, and the Herzegovinians; they intrigued with the Czechs, the Croats, the Slovaks, the Slovenes, and the Serbs. That, they said, was what their Soul required of them. It was their Mission.

Now, if even so backward a people as the Russians could afford a mission, surely no advanced one could do less. Take the Belgians, for example. True, they were a very small people occupying what was no more than a sliver of country. But they had made it a great center of industry, and had acquired therewith much pride. No sooner did they learn about "*la mission civilisatrice*" than they felt that they too ought to take it up.

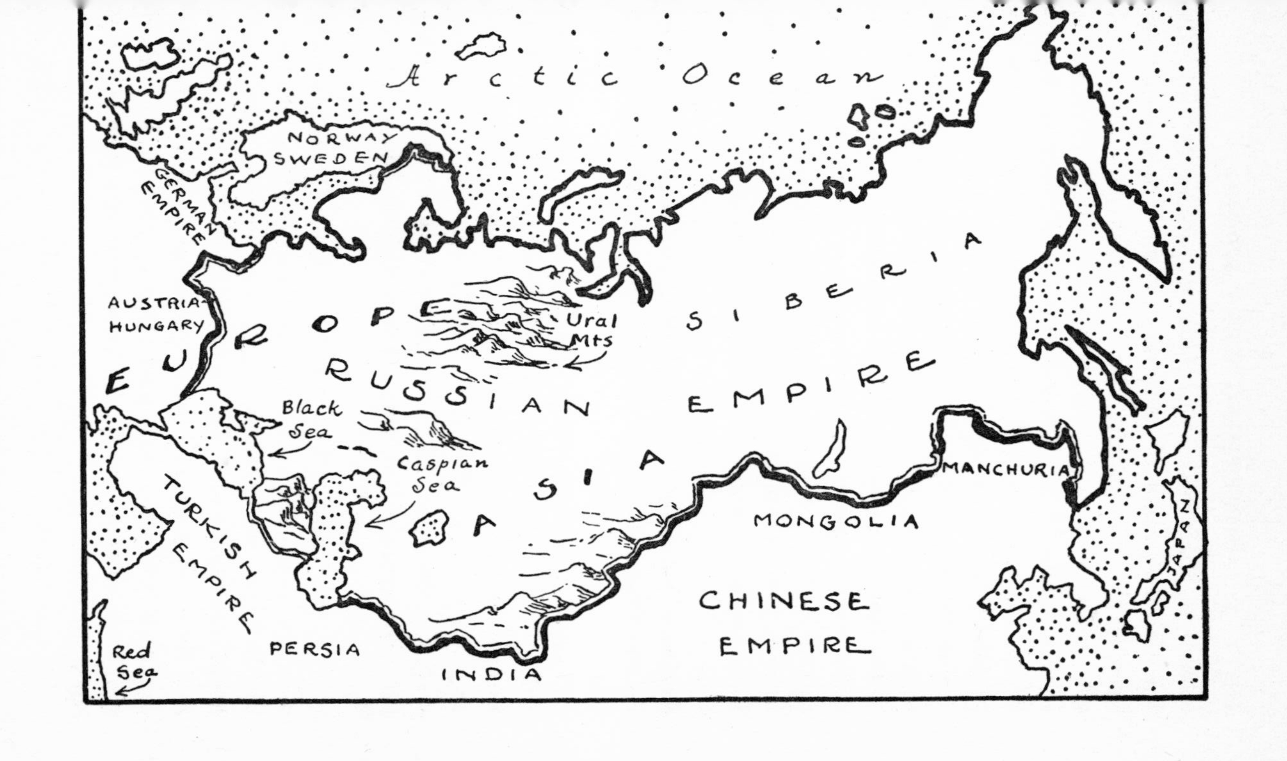
Arctic Ocean
NORWAY
SWEDEN
GERMAN EMPIRE
AUSTRIA-HUNGARY
EUROPE
RUSSIAN EMPIRE
Ural Mts
SIBERIA
Black Sea
Caspian Sea
ASIA
TURKISH EMPIRE
PERSIA
INDIA
Red Sea
MANCHURIA
MONGOLIA
CHINESE EMPIRE
JAPAN

To take it up, however, was not enough. One had to have some place to carry it—and Belgium had no place. Unlike some of the other minor European nations, Belgium had not even existed during the earlier period of colonial expansion. Holland still retained much of the territory seized during that period, especially in the East Indies. Portugal could still boast vast dependencies in Africa, and fragments all over the seven seas. Spain, too, had remnants of an empire, and so had even Denmark. But Belgium had nothing.

This naturally distressed the little country, and especially her ruler, Leopold II, who was a man of large ambition as well as piety. He realized two things: first, that his country deserved to have colonies, and second, that she was too weak to fight for them. Accordingly he set out to get them as a gift. That took brains, but he had them; it also required influence, and he had that too. He was related to the crowned heads of England, France, and Austria, and in addition enjoyed high repute as a patron of religion, science, and the ballet. So when half a dozen of the larger nations fell to squabbling over which had a prior claim to the Congo Basin, he was able to persuade them to leave it all to him.

His sole desire, he assured them, was to do the high-minded thing, and bring light into that "heart of darkness." He talked of sending in an army of explorers, engineers, and teachers, and of establishing a great network of hospitals and missions. To some people this sounded perhaps a shade *too* high-minded. As the Prince of Wales (later Edward VII) declared: "Philanthropy is all very well, but unless [Leopold's program] is practical, and gives a practical result, it will not find that favor in the eyes of the English public that it deserves." These misgivings, however, were soon dispelled.

Once the Powers agreed to let the Belgian idealist take the Congo, he proved himself almost disconcertingly practical. The region measured nearly a million square miles, and Leopold at once decreed that every uncultivated inch of it was state property. Since he was the state, and virtually all of the region was uncultivated, he thus made himself the personal owner of an area about *ninety* times the size of Belgium. He called it the "Congo Free State."

To prove his heart was in the right place, he first got rid of the Arab slave-traders. Then, to show his head was there too, he proceeded to fill the place with his own slave-drivers. Agents were stationed in the jungles to buy up ivory and rubber on a commission basis: the less they paid for the stuff, the higher was their bonus. If the natives would not sell, the agents were left to devise their own methods of persuasion.

They did devise them, and the results were as bloody as they were lucrative. The natives were literally hounded to death. Between forced labor, forced migrations, and recurrent pillage and massacre, half the entire population of the Congo Free State was destroyed within fifteen years. But the gain to King Leopold was impressive. One of the many corporations which he organized to exploit the region made a net profit of 1800% during the first four years. A second made 1700% in six years. A third which he owned outright yielded him a personal income estimated at $1,500,000 a year. By the turn of the century he was one of the richest men in Europe.

Nor was he the only one to gain. He had had to call on the Belgian capitalists to help him finance the Congo developments, and these got their due compensation. So did the thousands of Belgian valiants who went out to do the actual developing: the explorers, soldiers, engineers, administrators, and agents.

Even the Belgian masses came in for a share of the gain. Not financially, of course. The Congo Free State might have belonged to King Tutankhamen for all that the average Belgian got out of it financially. (Could he buy even a tiny patch for his bicycle tire at a discount?) But the masses did gain in other ways. First of all, they could feast their eyes on the new splendor that their country was acquiring. King Leopold was littering it with a glorious array of palaces, fountains, theaters, monuments, museums, and gambling casinos. Secondly, they could take pride in the thought that their nation was doing its duty. Was it not bringing light into the "heart of darkness"?

The yearning for colonies, it must be admitted, was motivated by more than mere desire for pelf. One can tell that from the way the masses reacted in every land that rushed to imperialize now. Consider, for example, the case of the United States. The citizens of that republic certainly did not need more territory. They already owned an area almost as large as the entire continent of Europe. Nor did they lack opportunities for capitalist exploitation. They had barely begun even to sample the resources buried in their own soil, and they had a home market for immeasurably more than they could produce. Nevertheless, they too became possessed with the notion that they must go adventuring overseas.

They got the notion primarily from the British, with whom they had not alone financial but even closer spiritual ties. When Rudyard Kipling published his brassy poem about the "White Man's Burden," the Americans immediately assumed that he meant it directly for them. It became a standard recitation piece at their church socials and school assemblies, and every sentimental and audacious soul in the land began to crave to go a-burdeneering.

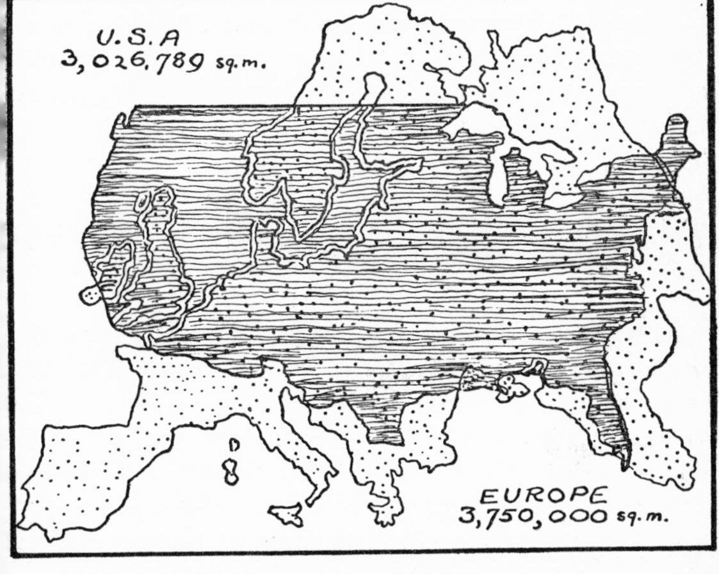

U. S. A. = EUROPE

. . . they certainly did not need more territory.

Of course, there was plenty of opposition. The leaders of the Democratic Party went so far as to condemn imperialism in their official platform. As one of those leaders exploded, "Uncle Sam ought to know better than start shooting everybody who doesn't speak English." All the sanest elements joined in the opposition, and so did some of the meanest. Parodists cut loose and sang—

"Take up the White Man's burden,
Send forth your sturdy sons,
And load them down with whiskey,
And Testaments and guns.
Throw in a few diseases
To spread in tropic climes,
For those poor healthy niggers
Are quite behind the times. . . ."

But such sentiments were generally branded ignoble. Americans with red blood in their veins preferred to listen to handsome young Senator Albert J. Beveridge, who on the tenth day of the Twentieth Century arose before the Upper House of the United States Congress and cried:

"We will not renounce our part in the mission of the race, trustee, under God, of the civilization of the world. . . . He has marked the American people as His chosen Nation to finally lead in the regeneration of the world. This is the divine mission of America, and it holds for us all the profit, all the glory, all the happiness possible to man. . . . What shall history say of us? Shall it say that we renounced that holy trust, left the savage to his base condition, the wilderness to the reign of waste, deserted duty, abandoned glory? . . . Shall it say that, called by events to captain and command the proudest, ablest, purest race of history in history's noblest work, we declined that great commission? . . . Pray God the time may never come when mammon and the love of ease will so debase our blood that we will fear to shed it for the flag and its imperial destiny!"

The Senator from Indiana did not pray in vain. That same year the United States annexed the Philippines, Guam, and Eastern Samoa, made a territorial possession of Hawaii, pressed negotiations for the purchase of the Danish West Indies, put out feelers for the Galápagos Islands, and dispatched 2,400 troops to help police the Chinese ports.

As imperialism went, that may not have been much. But it looked like a good start.

XXIII. THREE WHO CAME LATE

NE summer day in 1853 a swarm of half-naked yellow men on an island in the North Pacific stood and stared in awe and anger toward the sea. Four incredible black vessels had just entered the bay, two of them propelled by preposterous revolving fins, and all four belching smoke. A swarm of scows darted out from the beach, and besworded spokesmen shouted up at the monsters to begone. It was against the law, they shouted, for any barbarians—"all same foreigners"—to approach these islands. During more than two hundred and fifty years that had been the law, and what few had dared transgress it had paid with their lives. Therefore, cried the spokesman, "*Ikke!*"—which in their language meant "Get out!"

The barbarians, however, merely patted their cannons and smiled. It appeared that they had a letter to deliver to the Mikado of these islands from the Mikado of the U. S. A. Moreover, they announced, they would not leave until they had both delivered it and been promised an answer.

Six months later they returned for the answer—this time in a squadron of ten smoke-belching vessels—and now there was not even an attempt to shoo them off. Instead they were invited to land and celebrate, for the reply to the request contained in their letter was, Yes. Whereupon there was much mutual bowing, rejoicing, and carousing, and an interchange of presents. The barbarians had brought a miniature steam-train for the Mikado, and also four volumes of the *Annals of Congress*, two volumes of the *Farmer's Guide*, three "10-cent boxes of fine tea," eight yards of scarlet broadcloth, one sheet-iron stove, one keg of whiskey, and many other gifts. For the Empress there was a flowered silk frock and an assortment of perfumery, and for the numerous princes a variety of novelties including clocks, pistols, a list of the United States Post Offices, and a copy of Owen's *Geology of Minnesota* (2 vols.)!

Thus was the fabled Empire of Nippon finally unsealed to world trade. For centuries various nations in the West had been hungering to peddle their goods to the Nipponese. Now, apparently, the way was clear.

But things did not turn out quite as anticipated. Once

the door to Japan was opened, it became not so much an entrance as an exit. The white man did not go in; the yellow man came out. In little more than one generation the Japanese learnt to do almost better than they could be done. They began to sell even more than they could be sold.

This was certainly the most amazing turnabout in history. As late as 1853, Nippon might almost have been on another planet for all it knew of the West and its ways. It was completely a feudal realm dominated by local gang-lords and their armed goon-squads. Life was as orderly as in a prison camp, each man knowing his place, and keeping it. The law prescribed where he might live, what he should plant, how he should dress, and even how much he might spend on festival days. None might leave the land, even as none might enter it. For centuries the population was kept at a dead level of about thirty million.

But then those Yankee frigates poked their guns into Yeddo Bay, and Japan suddenly woke up. Busy-ness became the national obsession. The traders, so long a despised caste in Nippon, began to rush around with new-found insolence. They ganged up on the local gang-lords, took away their swords, and helped revolutionize the government. They encouraged the peasants to grow more rice, nurture more silk-worms, and overspend not alone on festival but even ordinary days. They herded the village craftsmen into improvised factory-towns, and set them to spinning, weaving, and carving by machinery. They bored coal-mines, built railroads, erected stores and docks, and started shipping lines. The Black Life took hold, and urban boils began to break out all over the little country. Overnight Japan became the Land of the Rising Smoke.

And that, of course, led to trouble. The smoke began to get into the nation's eyes, and these, being peculiarly narrow, were acutely sensitive. Problems arose which had been undreamed of in the merry—*i.e.* "short"—old days. Though the main island of Japan was no larger than Great Britain, and very much less fertile, its population leapt from thirty to forty-five millions within a generation. How was the nation to sustain so many millions? By selling manufactured goods in exchange for food? But to manufacture one had to have mineral resources, and Japan lacked these almost as sorely as arable acres. All her coal was buried in narrow seams far beneath the surface, and there was exceedingly little iron. How and where were the Japanese to get more?

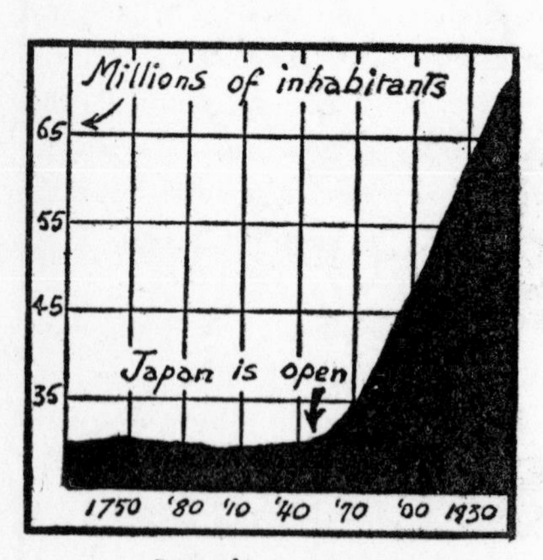

JAPAN'S POPULATION

They soon found out. The little yellow men were smart, and learnt to solve their problems almost as quickly as they created them. To be sure, their solution was not perfect; but it was certainly no more imperfect than any the white men had discovered. How could it be, seeing it was copied from them? Precisely twenty-one years after the first American gunboats arrived to open up Nippon, the first Nipponese gunboats sailed forth to open up the island of Formosa!

Japan started to grab. Having got a toe hold in Formosa, she turned to secure a foothold in all the smaller islands along the way. Then she reached northward to extort trade privileges from the Kingdom of Korea. Finally in 1894 she dared to pick a quarrel with the giant Empire of China, and drubbed it so thoroughly that she was actually able to raise the Japanese flag on the mainland.

But at that point a growl came out of the West. Russia, France, and Germany rose up in white indignation and told

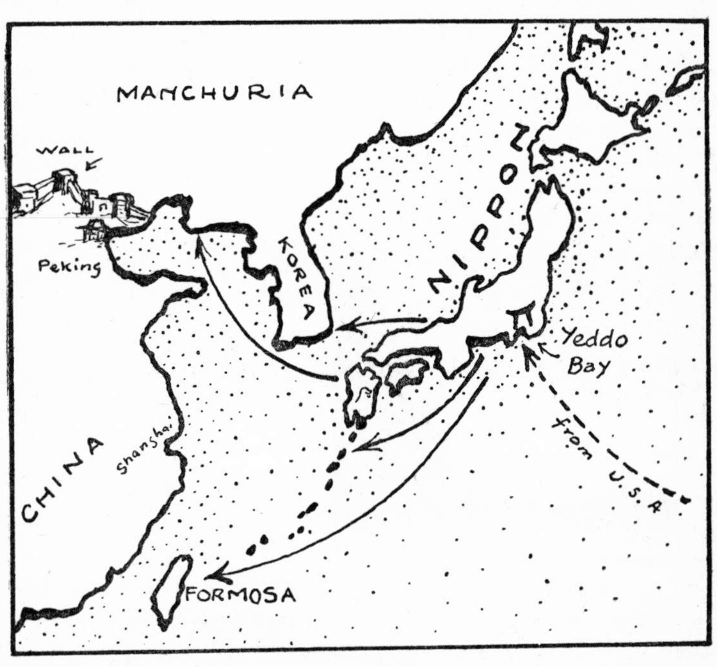

JAPAN OPENS UP

The little yellow men were smart.

Japan she had gone too far. They were willing to let her keep the islands she had snatched from China, and even the gold indemnity—but not the territory on the mainland. This consisted of the southern tip of Manchuria, which besides being fabulously rich in mineral resources, was of immense strategic importance. It commanded the sea entrance to Peking. Japan was "advised" to give it back. She knew better than to refuse.

But thereupon the breath-sipping little yellow men were given a lesson they never forgot. No sooner did they restore what they had filched on the mainland than the great white men turned around and blandly took it—and much more—for themselves. Russia "leased" a broad corridor through South Manchuria, Germany "leased" Shantung, France "leased" Kiaochow Bay, and Britain "leased" Wei-hai-wei. Whereupon a great bitterness entered the heart of Japan—and stayed there.

But Japan was not unique in that respect. A similar bitterness had already invaded the heart of Italy, and for much the same cause. It so happened that Italy had been only a little less belated than Japan in throwing off feudalism. Moreover, she had encountered no less hardship in trying to take on industrialism. As late as the 1860's Italy had still been a collection of rival kingdoms, principalities, and vassal states, most of them ruled by men as hostile to progress as the Nipponese samurai. Not until 1871—three years after Tokyo was named the capital of a revolutionized Japan—did Rome at last become the capital of reunited Italy. King Victor Emmanuel II, who had spent more than twenty years scheming and warring to accomplish that feat, arose then and cried: "Italy is now united and free; it remains for us henceforth to make her great and happy." But, as his people were soon fated to learn, greatness and happiness were easier to wish for than achieve.

Geography was against the Italians. Their country lacked coal and iron and most of the other raw materials essential for large-scale industrial development. At the same time, owing to the exhausted condition of the soil, there was little room even for agricultural development. All that Italy produced in abundance was bambinos, and this served only to complete the nation's plight. There were so many mouths to feed that nothing could be saved to start the factories which might have provided the means to feed those mouths more generously.

A considerable portion of the population had long been compelled to feed itself abroad. Millions had to drift off annually to the neighboring countries, or to America, and though some returned with their savings, the net result at home was sad. Those emigrants were mostly laborers, and their savings were slight. The real profit went to their foreign employers—and remained with them. Nor was that all. The majority of the emigrants never returned at all, which meant that Italy was being steadily drained of much of her finest human material.

Now, being in a sense a new nation, Italy was all prickly with patriotic pride, and the thought of her plight distressed her unendurably. She decided there was only one thing for her to do: lay hold of colonies. Where? Obviously in North Africa, which was close at hand, and Italian by right of hoary title-deeds. Had not Rome owned the entire North African coast fifteen hundred years earlier? Unfortunately, much of it had recently been seized by France and Great Britain; but not all. Tunisia was still unappropriated, a quite sizable land—actually almost half as large as all of Italy—and fairly fertile. Also it was rumored to contain excellent mineral resources. Incidentally, it was the site of ancient Carthage, and therefore in an historical sense Rome's very own footstool.

Italy reached for it. Not brusquely, of course; she did not dare. First she made—and paid—advances to the bankrupt Bey who ruled Tunisia in the name of Turkey; then she encouraged hundreds of her landless peasants to migrate there and start small farms; finally, she bought off the British by purchasing—at far too high a price—the bit of railway they had built between the city of Tunis and the shore. Then the rulers of Italy felt they had everything ready to make the snatch.

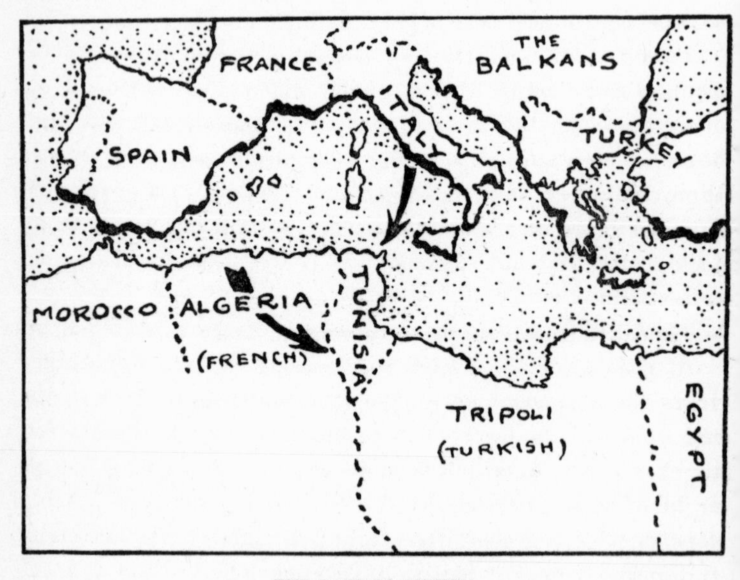

THE RACE TO TUNISIA
The Italians came too late.

But the rulers of France had precisely the same feeling—and moved faster. No sooner did the Italians acquire the Tunis railway than the French provoked an "incident" across the border, in their own Algeria. It was not the first time trouble had occurred there. The Colonial Office in Paris could point to a list of 2,364 occasions on which Tunisian warriors had raided the Algerian frontier during the preceding decade. But now the French declared their patience was at an end. They ordered their troops to march forth and punish the raiders—and then keep on marching. The troops obeyed.

And thus the Italians were robbed of what they had so carefully planned to steal. Tunisia became a French "protectorate," and the approximate heirs of the Caesars had to look elsewhere for a colony.

To look, however, was not enough. One had to have sufficient guns to point at the quarry and also to shoo off all other hunters. Italy lacked them. For a while she had high hopes of bagging Ethiopia, a handsome expanse almost three times the size of Italy, and alluringly undeveloped. But again she was foiled, this time by the native ruler. In 1896 Italy sent out an army of 12,000 men to bring him to heel; but the black king mustered 90,000, and in a single battle killed or captured more than half the invading host.

After that Italy waxed exceedingly bitter. For thirty years she had spent herself to create an empire, yet in the end what did she have? Here a flea-bitten port, there a few rocky isles, in a third place an expanse of rotting jungle or blistering duneland. At the end of a generation all her dependencies together were failing to shelter half as many Italians as had died merely to conquer them. Italy felt she had a right to feel bitter.

And much the same was true of Germany. Like Japan and Italy, Germany had started late as a nation. Unlike them, however, she had started strong, and might easily have gone on the prowl when colonies were still plentiful. But Bismarck held her back. There were certain elements in Germany—missionaries, explorers, and overseas traders—who were wild with eagerness to see their country follow right on Great Britain's heels. But Bismarck did not like the look of those heels: they were too heavily shod. Besides, he considered overseas possessions a luxury. "A colonial policy for us," said he, "would be just like the silken sables of Polish noblemen who have no shirts." Even when he was offered colonies practically as a gift—for example, the Sulu Islands, Mozambique, and Indo-China—he still shook his head.

That was his attitude throughout the 1870's, and even into the 1880's. Finally, however, the tugging became too much for him, and he was forced to slip the leash. But that was all he would do. He absolutely refused to emulate the statesmen of England and France, and shout encouragement to his pack. If individual Germans went out and grabbed colonies, he would back them up; but he certainly would not lead them.

So the Germans came out poorly in the scramble for

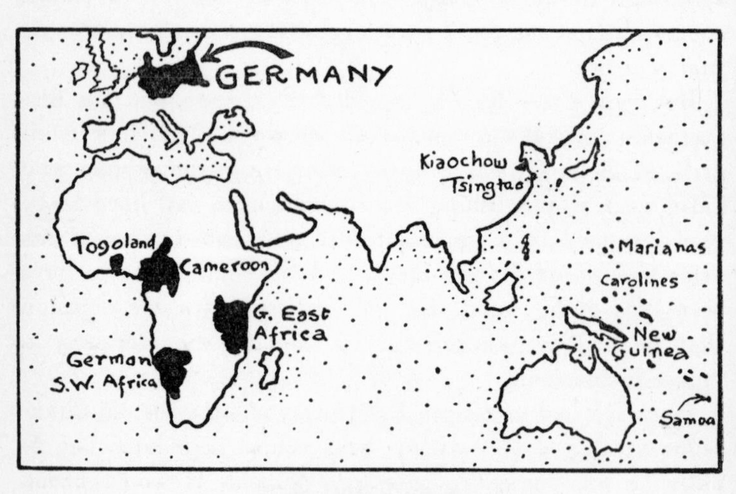

THE GERMAN EMPIRE

. . . relatively mean pickings. . . .

colonies. They did manage to sink their teeth into the flanks of Africa, and also to bolt a number of islands in the Pacific; but these were relatively mean pickings, both in size and quality. They consisted almost entirely of stinking jungle or parched wilderness, and were as widely scattered as they were wretchedly peopled. By 1890 the French possessions were more than three times as extensive as Germany's, and contained almost five times as many inhabitants. The British ones were twelve times as large, and contained thirty times as many people.

To make matters even worse, most of the races that fell into Germany's hands seemed to be peculiarly unmanageable. This, to be sure, may have been in part her own fault: she was too prone to use her hands as fists. Her colonial administrators had a way of confusing officiousness with efficiency. They seemed unable to understand that wild fowl resented being made to step like geese. As a result it looked as though Germany would have to depopulate her wretched colonies before she could start exploiting them. That was no pretty prospect.

But then a new Kaiser ascended the throne, and the Bismarckian policy was summarily dropped. This new monarch, Wilhelm II, was a cocky, blustering young man who hid a weak mouth behind fierce mustachios, and liked to be photographed in a spiked helmet and sword. One of his arms was crippled from birth, and the same seems to have been true of his mind. He was obsessed with the delusion that he had been appointed by God to win Germany a "place in the sun."

Bismarck had to resign. For twenty months the old Chancellor struggled to curb his wild young liege-lord, but finally he was forced to give up. Wilhelm II would brook neither criticism nor counsel. He said he knew precisely what he wanted, and swore he would not rest till he got it. And what he wanted was more and better colonies. Germany, he bellowed, must expand. She must have more room for her people, more room for her trade, more room for her army, more room for her pride. True, her total domain already comprised fully one and a half million square miles. But the French owned four million square miles. Russia owned more than eight million, Britain could boast twelve million. Was that just? The Germans, after all, were no longer a mere peasant folk content to produce fodder, beer, and poetry. They had become one of the greatest industrial nations on earth. They had already outstripped all the others in the production of chemicals, toys, and cathartics. They were rapidly outstripping them even in the production of coal and iron. So they had to have more room. And he, Friedrich Wilhelm Victor Albert, by the grace of God ninth King of Prussia and third Kaiser of Germany, was going to get it for them.

But that, he soon discovered, was easier to say than do. He had come too late. All the desirable room in the world seemed to be already either occupied or spoken for. Gone was the day when one could acquire colonies by merely lighting matches to scare poor natives. Now one had to brandish guns against other white men. And that was risky, especially when those other white men had as big or bigger guns.

Here was the sort of thing the Kaiser found himself forced to suffer. For years he kept casting covetous glances at the Spanish-owned Philippines, but no sooner did he think it safe to reach for them than the Americans and English intervened. That happened in 1898, when the United States, having picked a quarrel with Spain over Cuba, sent a squadron racing into Manila Bay. By "chance" a German squadron was already on the scene, and for a moment it looked as though there might be a battle. But a British squadron was also there, and it maneuvered itself into such a position that the Germans could not possibly shoot without precipitating a war with England as well as America. Result: the Kaiser did not get the Philippines.

It was much the same wherever else he turned. No matter how strenuously he blustered, or how slyly he connived, nearly always he was balked or bilked. And that made him sore all through. It made his people sore, too. The incessant frustration rowelled their swollen pride. Worse still, it cramped their swelling economy. So Germany, like Japan, like Italy, became a country with a rancor in its soul.

That boded ill for the peace of the world.

XXIV. DEATH FOR SALE

IT BODED ill for all mankind that so many nations wanted to become empires. There wasn't room enough. The earth, after all, was not the expanding universe. It was no more than a fifth-rate planet dancing like a midge around an nth-rate star. And that fact, long considered merely true, began to grow unpleasantly real now. Even as late as 1870 the earth had seemed inexhaustibly vast. At that time fully half of it had not yet been even explored by Europeans. But by 1900 virtually every last corner of it—with the exception of the Polar regions—had been not alone explored but claimed.

Where were the nations to go grabbing after that? For none, not even those that had grabbed most, felt they had grabbed enough. If you had colonies, you had to have safe access to them, and that meant you had to have fortified coaling-stations all along the route. Once you had such coaling-stations, you had to acquire the valleys behind them, and the highlands commanding those valleys. Imperialism was like money: to keep what you already had, you always had to get more. But where under the sun were so many nations to get more?

Cecil Rhodes had a suggestion. Said he,

> "Think of these stars that you see overhead at night. . . . I would annex planets if I could. I often think of that. It makes me sad to see them so clear and yet so far."

But Rhodes was not typical. He could afford to talk like that, poetically, whimsically, since he had already done more than his bit in practical ways. He had plastered his name across a region larger in size than all of France, Germany, Belgium, and Holland combined. Other imperialists, having been less successful, were less inclined to gaze at the stars and sigh. Instead they glared at the earth and fumed.

That spelled trouble. Too many hands had been plunged into the one small grab-bag which was the earth. Now that almost all the prizes had been seized, there was nothing left but for the hands to start grabbing from each other. That spelled lots and lots of trouble.

The nations took to snarling at each other like tigers over a dismembered carcass. More and more they snarled, and every once in a while they pounced, or at least lashed out. We have already seen how Japan pounced on China in 1894, and the United States on Spain in 1898. That same year Britain lashed out at France because the latter sought to snatch the Egyptian Sudan, and the next year Germany

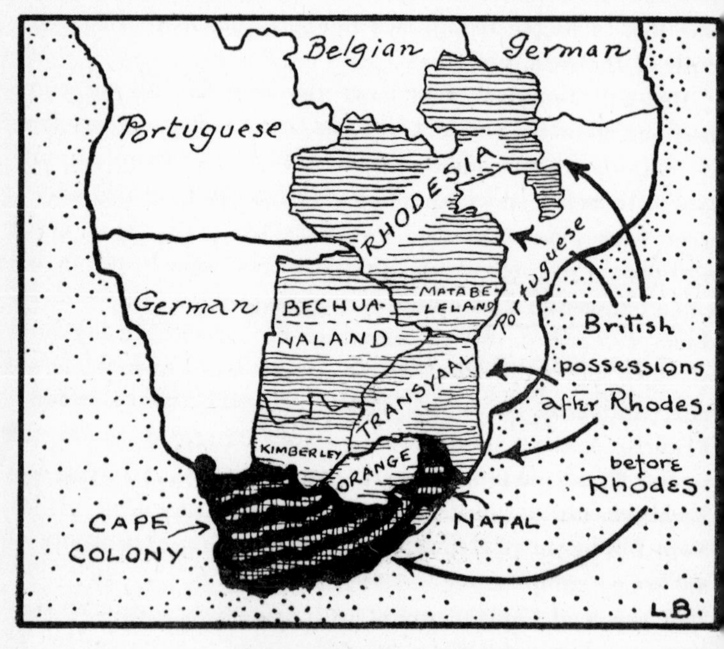

BEFORE AND AFTER RHODES
He could afford to talk poetically.

bared her teeth because Britain had begun to rend the Boer Republics. So it went year after year.

But it could not go on so forever. Sooner or later one of those tigers was bound to lash too far, or pounce too wildly, and then—? Even the most rabid of the tigers could see what that foreboded. War would ensue, and then all might be lost to the jackals. The tigers did not relish that prospect, and decided to gang up to prevent it. They formed themselves into teams which were bound by treaties both open and secret. Germany, Austria, and Italy joined fangs for mutual protection; so did France, Russia, and Great Britain. The smaller nations, not knowing which alliance was less to be trusted, joined now one, now the other, now both at the same time.

But this served only to make the situation all the more perilous. Now the entire world was likely to become involved if—no, when—war finally did come. Such was the plain outlook even before the close of the Nineteenth Century, and it grew ever plainer as the Twentieth unfolded. So a fierce agitation arose for more "preparedness." Each nation became convinced that unless it armed itself to the teeth, its doom was sealed. All of them therefore rushed to lay hold of more and mightier weapons. Great Britain doubled her war equipment between 1895 and 1905, and Germany, France, Austria, Italy, and Japan, struggled to do the same. Even piddling powers like Portugal, Greece, and Serbia began to gird themselves against the Day of the Sword. The entire civilized world took on the appearance of an armed camp.

It was mad—stark, raving mad. Each nation claimed that it was arming solely to preserve its own sovereignty. In other words, it was wasting its substance in order to preserve the right to be compelled to waste its substance. Could anything have been madder than that?

Yet there seemed to be no way to stop it. Some individuals, indeed, did not want to stop it. Take Basil Zaharoff, for example. Just where he came from is still shrouded in mystery. (Pious people claim there is less uncertainty as to where he finally went.) He seems to have been born of Greek parents in Asia Minor, and he is said to have started life as one of those shabby "guides" who offer to procure lively diversions for lonely travelers in Constantinople. If that story is untrue, the more's the pity. Certainly Zaharoff could not have found a fitter apprenticeship for his life-work. Eventually he became a munitions-agent.

He proved his worth shortly after he got his first job. The firm he represented, a German concern named Nordenfelt, had developed a new type of fighting-craft for which it seemed unable to find any customers. It was a submarine, and the naval experts of the major powers had declared the contraption hopelessly impractical. The directors of Nordenfelt began to fear that all the cunning, labor, and money they had put into the device would go to waste. But then Zaharoff came to the rescue. Sidling up to the authorities in Athens, he patriotically offered to deliver a submarine to the Greek navy at a bargain price. On easy terms, too. Those authorities could hardly have been ignorant of the ancient adage about Greeks bearing gifts; but they were themselves Greeks, so the point of that adage was lost on them. Instead of showing Zaharoff the door, they begged him to show them where to sign.

With that deal consummated, the rest was easy. Rushing off to Constantinople, Zaharoff presented himself before the Turkish authorities and inquired how they would like to wake up some fine morning and find Greek torpedoes zipping about in the Dardanelles. They granted they would not like it at all—and ordered two submarines.

Then the race was on. If Turkey had under-water ships, obviously Russia had to have them too; if Russia, also Germany; if Germany, also Britain and France. Before long the diving monsters became standard equipment for all navies the world over. Zaharoff became one of the owners of his firm.

There was no holding him down after that. He had talents, and he knew now just how to use them. His tongue was glib in many languages, his voice was gentle, his mind was sharp, and he could pass a bribe faster than you could say Basil Zaharoff. Before the close of the century he was in control of the English firm of Vickers, the greatest armament concern on earth. He became a British subject then, and proved so loyal a one that eventually he was awarded a knighthood.

His loyalty, however, remained broad. During the war in South Africa he sold arms not alone to the British, but also to the Boers. Breadth of loyalty was a matter of principle with him. He sold arms impartially to the French, the Germans, the Austrians, the Serbs, and every other people that needed them. He even went out of his way to see to it that they did need them. He bought up newspapers, generals, cabinet ministers, occasionally even kings, and through them stirred up all sorts of war alarms.

Zaharoff's wealth and power grew legendary. Wherever his lean, ferret-eyed, goat-bearded visage appeared, it was recognized as that of the "Mystery Man of Europe." He was universally hated, yet almost as universally fawned on. France gave him a Grand Cross of the Legion of Honor, Oxford certificated him a Doctor of Civil Law, Monte Carlo hailed him as its patron saint. However, to the very last—he died in 1936 at the age of seventy-seven—he was never awarded the Nobel Peace Prize.

What shall we say of Sir Basil Zaharoff, G.C.B., G.B.E., D.C.L. (Hon.)? That he was a rascal, a villain, a demon who fed on human blood and bones? Perhaps. But in all fairness we ought to add that he was merely a businessman. He was a merchant, and like any other merchant, he tried to sell all he could, for as much as he could, to as many customers as would buy. That was what he was there for. It was none of his concern whether the goods he sold were harmful. That was up to the customers. *Caveat emptor!*

Had Zaharoff refused to sell munitions, plenty of other men would have been glad to oblige. As a matter of fact, plenty of others did oblige. If they never became quite so notorious as he, it was because they were less elaborately mysterious, or less annoyingly successful. The Krupps in Germany, Sir Hiram Maxim in England, Eugène Schneider in France, Alfred Nobel in Sweden—all these munitioneers, together with all their associates, bankers, salesmen, and press agents, were in principle just as guilty as that sinister Greek. And just as innocent.

They were simply businessmen trying to earn an honest penny by supplying a commodity in general demand. If, incidentally, they did what they could to increase the demand, it merely proved they were good businessmen. Ribbon-makers went out of their way to aggravate feminine vanity; hair-oil manufacturers deliberately excited masculine pride. Why then should not munition-makers do their bit to inflame international hatred? A good businessman had to see to it that the penny he earned was pretty as well as honest.

Therefore, just as Zaharoff was no guiltier than any other dealer in arms, just so were all of them no guiltier than the dealers in almost anything else. Take the case of a man who sold quicksilver. In earlier times his work had been distinctly beneficent, since quicksilver had been primarily a medicine. Now, however, that element had become essential in the manufacture of shells. Though mercury was still used to repair the damage done by Venus, it was being used even more to increase the havoc wrought by Mars. Consequently, all who dealt in mercury were to some degree henchmen of Mars. The same was true of all who dealt in steel, copper, oil, nickel, glycerine, brimstone, and a thousand other commodities. Even the producers of so innocent a stuff as cotton were implicated in the armament industry. Without cotton there could have been no smokeless gunpowder.

The armament industry had become an integral part of the entire industrial system, and though it was obviously a cancer, there appeared to be no way to cut it out. Indeed, the very fact that it was a cancer made it seem all the more valuable. Armaments were superbly destructive. They destroyed not alone themselves, but also whatever came near them. Therefore, in a perverse way, they were extremely useful. They quickened consumption, and thus blasted room for more production.

In addition, armaments were peculiarly salable, hence highly profitable. Other wares had to be marketed to the public, and the public was chronically short of cash. But slaughter-goods were sold to governments, and governments did not need cash. They could issue bonds—that is, mortgages on the lands they ruled—and thus raise ample credit.

So the armament industry, though a curse to humanity, seemed a blessing to business. Even in times of peace it seemed a blessing. Whenever business began to limp, it could reach for the bloody crutch of armaments. Whenever there was a slump, and ordinary goods became hard to sell, some businessman began to raise a clamor for more "preparedness." That was one way to keep the factories going. The unemployed could be put to work making guns and shells and battleships. It would certainly have been wiser had they been put to work making shirts and shoes and baby carriages. But those businessmen could not afford to be wise; they had to be smart. They had to look out for their profits.

So they kept raising war-scares—and got their profits.

XXV. THEY CRY PEACE, PEACE!

IT WAS mad. The whole situation was nightmare mad. Here was a world ready for peace, a world that needed peace; yet it kept preparing for war. No one in his right mind wanted the sort of war for which the powers were preparing. A little skirmishing out in the colonies—yes! Raids on remote frontiers, jungle battles—fine, splendid! Most good folk rather liked that sort of thing. The average citizen found it cheery to sit by his fireside and read how "his" army had just done in a lot of Moros, Tuaregs, or Fuzzy-Wuzzies. It made him feel strong and proud—yes, and civilized. But a real war? That he definitely did not want.

He knew that he himself would have to fight in a real war; and unless he was very young, or burdened with an insufferable wife, he did not really care to fight. This does not mean that the average citizen had suddenly gone soft. He had been soft for centuries. The proof of it is that not in centuries had he willingly gone into battle. He had left that to professionals. Ever since Roman times almost all battling had been done by mercenaries. That was why they were called "soldiers": they fought for *solidi*, "coins." But the situation had changed in the Nineteenth Century. The rise of nationalism had made every citizen a soldier, and had turned fighting into a public duty instead of a private privilege. Professional armies still existed, but they were used largely to guard the frontiers or police the colonies. In the event of real war, conscript armies were expected to go into the field.

Virtually all the great powers, and most of the minor ones, had made conscription the rule since the 1870's. Britain was an exception, because it could rely on naval defense. The United States, too, was an exception, because it was too remote from powerful enemies. But even in these countries it was understood that, should the need arise, every fit citizen would be expected to join the colors. So the situation amounted to this: all able-bodied males throughout the civilized world were now potential cannon-fodder.

That was one reason why there was little eagerness to let the cannons go off. Here and there one might come across isolated individuals who still talked of war as something virtuous and desirable; but they were almost as rare now as pacifists had been a century earlier. Even in Prussia, the most militaristic land in Christendom, the apostles of "war for war's sake" were considered extremists. Elsewhere they were commonly regarded as psychopaths. All right-minded people had become convinced that war was stupid, wasteful, and wicked. The very men who sold the cannons did not want to see them go off. They realized that if that happened, their own sons might get killed. Besides, those cannon-venders were as a rule quite decent and humane men. The same was true of most of the generals who ordered the cannons, and of most of the politicians who signed the vouchers. As for the taxpayers who footed the bill, they most emphatically did not want the cannons to go off. Their heads were stuck in the muzzles.

What they wanted was peace.

And they had peace. Incredibly, more than thirty years elapsed after 1871 without one major conflict. Of course, there were many minor ones; too many. But these, being confined to the colonial regions, were considered merely colorful incidents. Within Europe itself, indeed throughout all the "civilized" world, there was approximate quiet for one entire generation.

That was good. It gave certain healthy forces a chance to assert themselves. Science was one of those forces, decency was another, common-sense was a third. Such forces had long been at work in the world, but largely underground. They had seeped into hidden caves whence they had tunnelled stealthily, breaking to the surface only here, there, in a third place. But now these breaks began to connect; the welling waters flowed together. Men awoke to discover that despite all the frontiers between nation and nation, common ideas had begun to spread over the entire earth.

Not all men discovered this, nor most, nor even relatively many. But some did. In every land some people discovered that they had comrades abroad. And they went out to meet them. Like cells responding to some chemical attraction, people with common interests began to collect and connect. For, in addition to the will, they had the means now. Transportation and communication had become so vastly improved that distance was no longer a hindrance.

All sorts of international societies came into being. Believers in political democracy formed an Inter-Parliamentary Union, agitators for economic democracy organized a Socialist International, feminists established a World Alliance of Women for Suffrage. Protestants from various lands created a Young Men's Christian Association, and Catholics from the ends of the earth gathered in periodic Eucharistic Congresses. Even the Jews, chronically a divided lot, began to meet and squabble in Zionist conclaves. Scientists travelled thousands of miles to convene in person with their fellow-specialists, or at least subscribed to international journals which published reports in several languages. Educators did the same, and so did philanthropists, spiritists, stamp-collectors, even athletes. The ancient Olympic meets, the last of which had been held in A.D. 394, were revived on a world scale in 1896.

The trend was so strong that even governments had to yield to it. Formerly they had rarely convened save to divide the loot after a war. Now they took to collaborating on the everyday needs of life in peacetime. In 1875 some twenty-three governments agreed to adopt the French metric system. A permanent International Bureau of Weights and Measures was set up in Paris to decide the standard length of the meter and weight of the kilogram. That same year thirty governments founded a Universal Telegraph Union, and by 1882 twice that number had joined a Universal Postal Union. The following year nineteen nations bound themselves to respect each other's patent regulations, and in 1887 fifteen adopted uniform copyright laws.

All this was good. It showed that the world was ceasing to be a collection of cages, and that the word "foreign" might ultimately lose its hoary meaning. Thus far that word had had a hateful ring, for it had connoted a person on the other side of what the Romans called the *foris*, the "door." But now all doors were swinging wide.

The Machine was responsible. It could not tolerate closed doors. The world had to be clear and open so that the mounting flood of goods might flow unchecked. We have already seen how the Machine levelled the provincial barriers in countries like Germany and Italy. Now it was beginning to do the same to national barriers everywhere. It was making all men neighbors, and insisting that they behave as such. So the sudden flush of cosmopolitan activity was good indeed.

But it was no more than a flush. Only on small issues would any governments agree to collaborate; on all grave ones they felt they must keep jealously apart. For they were suspicious of one another—and they had a right to be. Each nation knew that every other was armed.

There was but one solution: disarmament. Unless all nations agreed to beat their swords into plowshares, none could trust that war would be no more; and without that trust, none could truly prosper. One did not need to be a sage to see that. The fact was so obvious that it could impress even ordinary minds. And it did—gradually. In one land after another a persistent agitation got under way now to call a final halt to warmongery. The movement was started, naturally, by eccentric folk: pietists, anarchists, feminists, and the like. But eventually it began to attract quite respectable people. Several minor statesmen took up the cause, and so did many major clerics, educators, and philanthropists. Here and there even a retired munitions-maker gave himself to it heart and purse. For example, there was Alfred Nobel, a Swede who had made many millions out of high explosives. Also there was Andrew Carnegie, an American who had amassed a quarter of a billion out of steel. Cynics might sneer that such men were merely paying hush-money to their consciences. All the same, it was negotiable money, and bought results. The dove's nest may indeed have been feathered with guncotton and steel-shavings—but it *was* feathered.

Pacifism became almost fashionable. By 1895 nearly four hundred different societies were devoting themselves to it all over the world, and between them they began to create a quite impressive stir. Special trains were chartered to carry delegates to periodic congresses at which extra wire-facilities were installed to telegraph resolutions to cabinets and kings. Huge printeries were kept busy turning out pacifist booklets, leaflets, posters, and subscription blanks. Pacifist oratorical contests were subsidized in colleges, pacifist sermons were supplied free to preachers, pacifist lobbies were installed in all the major legislatures. A fierce crusade was launched to teach children never, never to play with toy soldiers.

The net effect, however, was disappointing. It was almost as though the pacifists were setting mouse-traps to catch the hounds of war. No matter how they pleaded, how they protested, how they whimpered, how they stormed, never for an instant were they able to halt the growth of armaments. Not until 1898 was even one little gesture made in that direction, and then it was initiated by the ruler least troubled by their agitation. Nicholas II, Tsar of all the Russias, suddenly came out that year in favor of a world agreement to check the military race. He had his reasons. Russia had fallen behind in that race. For nearly a decade she had been struggling to build up an industrial plant, and most of the money the country could scrape together had gone into railways, mines, and factories. Now her ruler woke up to the fact that in the event of war Russia was lost. Her armaments, especially in the artillery branch, had become hopelessly antiquated—and there was no money on hand to buy fresh equipment. The populace was already seething with sedition because of the crushing taxes. And that was why Nicholas II turned suddenly idealist. What could he lose?

But the pacifists did not ask why Nicholas II took up their cause. All they cared was that he had done it. The moment the Tsar issued a call for an international "Non-Augmentation of Arms Conference," their enthusiasm waxed so strident that twenty-six sovereign governments—including Siam—felt constrained to respond. On the 18th of May, 1899, one hundred plenipotentiaries gathered at The Hague and proceeded to confer.

For ten weeks they conferred and conferred. Then, slightly hoarse, they went home. The Russian delegates, however, did not go straight home. They stopped over in Paris to see about raising one more loan for their country. They knew that the new military equipment would have to be bought after all.

The Hague Conference had failed. Almost all that the delegates had been able to agree upon was a pious resolution that "the restriction of military expenditures . . . is extremely desirable for the increase of the material and moral welfare of mankind."

So the race for "preparedness," already mad enough, grew even madder. Formerly it had been largely confined to preparations for land conflict, but after 1899 its scope was widened to include the sea. Germany was chiefly responsible for that, or rather the man who had become Germany's Kaiser. On

January 1, 1900, this might-drunk defective barked to the world:

> "The first day of the new century sees My army—in other words, My people—gathered around its standards, kneeling before the Lord of Hosts. . . . Even as My grandfather labored for His army, so shall I in like manner relentlessly carry on and carry through the reformation of My navy, to the end that . . . the German Empire may at last be in a position to win the place which it has not yet attained."

He was as bad as his word. Then and there he ordered his Reichstag to vote him nearly half a billion dollars to build the largest navy afloat. This naturally perturbed the British, for they felt that *theirs* must always be the largest navy. Unless they absolutely ruled the waves, how could they permanently hold their far-flung shores? They had no illusions as to what the Kaiser was up to. He might protest until his mustachios wilted that "every German warship launched is one more guarantee of peace on earth." They knew better.

So a contest started between the two nations to see which could outlaunch the other. Soon France joined in, and also Russia. Japan, too, got busy, and that spurred the United States to follow suit. Even Brazil and Austria, countries which had formerly given little thought to heavy battlecraft, began to spend millions now for what were called "dreadnoughts."

The peace-workers grew frantic. They organized mass protests, circulated mass petitions, and camped in the anterooms of embassies all over the earth. What they wanted was another conference of the nations. Failing that, they warned, civilization itself would be destroyed. It would sink and drown in debt if not in gore.

And finally, in 1907, they got another conference. Again

it was Tsar Nicholas II who sent out the call, and again the meeting-place was The Hague. This time, however, eighteen additional governments sent delegations, and the sessions lasted not ten weeks but sixteen.

Yet again nothing real was accomplished. The second Hague Conference, like the first, generated much fine sound and fury; so far as concrete results were concerned, however, it got barely halfway to nowhere. The most hopeful thing it did was pass a resolution to reconvene—in 1915. . . .

XXVI. AND THEY CRY HAVOC!

SOMETHING had gone wrong. Here was a world that hungered to thrive, that deserved to thrive; yet all the time it kept racing toward suicide. It was surely a better world than had ever existed in the past, a cleaner, healthier, more orderly world. Never before had men exerted such mastery over nature; never had so many children of men enjoyed as much abundance. Slavery and serfdom were already things of the past, and brutality of every sort seemed to be waning. The demented were no longer kept in chains, and transgressors were rarely subjected to public floggings. In many lands there were laws forbidding cruelty even to animals. Religious dissenters were ceasing to be commonly persecuted, and racial minorities were being less and less oppressed. Travel was increasing, for it no longer connoted travail, and even common people were sloughing off the provincialism that had so long kept them doltish. Women were acquiring a new legal status and social dignity. The masses were achieving unprecedented political importance. The dream of universal Liberty, Equality, Fraternity, and Prosperity appeared to be growing a near reality at last. With all its faults, this machine-turned, gilt-edged civilization of the early Twentieth Century was certainly the best that mankind had ever known.

Nevertheless it seemed doomed, for a cancer was eating at its vitals. By 1908 Europe alone had 4,000,000 men under arms, and another 6,000,000 ready to snatch them up at a moment's notice. By 1914 fully *ninety per cent* of all national taxation throughout the world was being used to pay for past or future wars. Even in the richest lands the governments were spending a thousandfold more money on battlecraft than on scholarships. Everywhere life had to be deprived of nourishment because so much had to be squandered on means of dealing death.

Something was radically wrong here, and even the most gullible pacifists should have sensed as much. No matter how trusting they might be, how soft and sentimental, at least a little suspicion should have wormed its way into their minds that more than mere perversity was at the bottom of it all. But if such a suspicion did occur to them, few dared follow it through. The rest recoiled, stabbed by a dread which was all the deeper because it was repressed. They could not bring themselves to face the fact that militarism had become an integral part of the economic system, that war had somehow become a natural function of business—indeed, that it *was* business. Most pacifists, it must be realized, were proper middle-class folk who took the capitalist system so much for granted that they did not even know it had a name, let alone a fault. They were therefore quite incapable of seeing the connection between profit and slaughter.

This blindness, however, was not universal. There were some people who were well aware that warmongery had economic causes. And though these too called themselves pacifists, they were such only incidentally. The most vocal among them insisted that before all else they were—socialists.

On a chill, gray day in March, 1883, a small group of foreign-looking mourners might have been seen gathered about a fresh grave in a suburban London cemetery. One, a lean bespectacled man wearing a fierce goatee, made a brief speech in German. A second did the same in French. Then a third stepped forward and launched into a formal eulogy. Solemnly, with the air of one addressing all the ages to come, he made known that the man here laid to rest had been precisely the greatest thinker of his generation. "His name and his works," declared the eulogist, "will live on through the centuries."

It took faith to utter such words, for the buried man was Karl Marx, and by 1883 even the police had half-forgotten his existence. But the speaker was Friedrich Engels, and his faith was abundant. That is easy to understand, for during nearly fifty years Engels' life had been completely wrapped up in that of Karl Marx. The real wonder lies in the fact that Engels' faith was soon to prove justified. Hardly had the flesh in that grave turned to mold when the ghost of Karl Marx began to haunt half the countries on earth.

For socialism began to flourish then. It struck root like a weed wherever industrialism had plowed up the soil, and began to flourish uncontrollably. See what happened in the land where Marx was born—and whence he had had to flee. By 1890, barely seven years after his death, nearly 1,500,000 Germans were voting a Socialist ticket. True, most of them did not know just what that ticket stood for; but all of them had at least become convinced that that ticket had most to offer them. By 1912 some 4,250,000 had arrived at that conviction—fully a third of the entire German electorate.

That was not typical, since in no other land did socialism advance as spectacularly. Yet it was symptomatic, for the movement did make headway almost everywhere else. By 1911 it managed to attract a million votes in Austria, and by 1913 almost as many in Italy. In the French elections the following year it carried one-sixth of the total poll. Even in Russia the movement took hold. Even in Japan. Even in the United States.

And Karl Marx, more than any other one man, was responsible. To be sure, this that was spreading was hardly his own kind of socialism. No longer was it a bramble of blood-red thorns; instead it had become a bower of pinkish blooms. Yet the roots were one; and, since Marx had done most to nourish those roots, packing them tight in a rich humus of theory and dosing them daily with the elixir of zeal, he most of all deserved credit for their flowering.

He got it, too. The term Marxism came to be very nearly a synonym for socialism. In some circles this identification was of course bitterly resented. At one extreme there were certain strict disciples who insisted that the Master's teachings were being shamelessly betrayed. At the other there were certain skeptics who insisted that the movement would be better off if those teachings were completely ignored. But neither of these groups seemed able to recruit a mass following. The successful socialist leaders were those who steered a middle course, following Marx only where they thought he was right, and for the rest going their own way.

Here was their argument. Marx, they said, had written as a scientist, not a soothsayer. Though he had ventured to predict what must happen, he had done so solely by sighting along the line of that which had already happened. He had observed society become increasingly split into two unequal classes, and from this he had deduced that the process would continue until the inequality became too monstrous to endure. So much wealth would be concentrated in the coffers of so few, and so much misery would be pent up in the bellies of so many, that—*smash!* With one swift and terrible heave, the oppressed would rend their chains and roll over on their oppressors.

That, it had seemed to Marx, was the fated program. The main social trend, he had insisted, pointed straight and inexorably toward revolution.

But was this still true? Hardly. It was plain to see that the trend had changed since the time Marx made his first observations. The rich were no longer growing fewer and more despotic, nor were the poor sinking ever deeper in despair. The bourgeois order, far from developing fatty degeneration, seemed to be waxing hardier all the time.

Marx had spoken too soon. Certain developments had occurred during the latter part of the Nineteenth Century which completely spoiled all his neat extrapolations. One was political democracy: the laborers had acquired the right to vote. A second was industrial democracy: the laborers had learnt to organize and strike. As a class they were therefore no longer impotent. They were still the bottom-dogs; but, whereas once they had been able to do nothing but whimper and whine, now they could rear up and bite.

Nor was this all that had occurred. The middle-dogs, too had failed to suffer according to schedule. The ranks of the small proprietors, far from dwindling, had swelled prodigiously. So had the ranks of the salaried employees and the professional people. All the petty exploiters—they who were themselves exploited—had so increased in numbers and influence that they had become the very backbone of bourgeois society. It was these middle-dogs now who believed most ardently in the principles of "rugged individualism"; it was they who labored most obstreperously to preserve "free enterprise." That was why they fought tooth and nail against the unions below, the trusts above, and the tariffs all around. They wanted more competition, not less. For they were still on the climb.

Marx had not reckoned on that. He had taken it for granted that, as time passed, such people would give up all idea of climbing. They would join the bottom-dogs and snarlingly wait for the day when, as one pack, they could turn and make a meal of the top-dogs. But had that happened? Had even one little sign appeared that it might happen? No. On the contrary, those little fellows were clambering with more zest now than ever. Even those nearest the bottom, the so-called "white collar workers," even they were still doing that—or at least trying. In an economic sense these white-collared folk were almost worse off than the muffler-wearing laborers, for though their pay might be a little higher, they had to spend much more on laundry. Yet would they fall in with the laborers, join unions, strike? Not likely. They had their pride! Laborers, they insisted, worked for mere wages; but *they* received salaries.

Yes, Marx had apparently spoken too soon. All but the most slavish of his followers could see that now. Apparently there never would be a revolution. The top-dogs would not invite one, the middle-dogs would not allow one, and the bottom-dogs would not start one. Capitalism would pass, of course. There, it was felt, Marx had been correct, infallibly correct. Capitalism was inherently so planless, so wanton, so self-destructive, that it would just have to pass. Moreover, socialism would certainly take its place. But the transition would be gradual, not sudden. It would be achieved by means of votes, not volleys.

That possibility, as a matter of fact, had been entertained by Marx himself before he died. In a speech delivered in Amsterdam on September 8, 1872, he had said: "There exist countries like America, England, and . . . Holland, where the workers may well be able to attain their ends by peaceful means." Engels had lived long enough to go much further: he had conceded that a peaceful transition might even be a probability. No wonder, therefore, that many socialists should be moved now to go the limit, and say that a peaceful transition was a certainty.

Such a conviction began to be voiced first in England, where a number of gifted intellectuals—among them George Bernard Shaw and H. G. Wells—joined an organization called the Fabian Society, and began to urge a more "realistic" approach to the whole problem of economic change. Fabianism soon found its approximate counterpart in Germany, where it was called Revisionism, and in France, where it was known as Possibilism. Eventually the heresy invaded every other land where Marx's teachings had attracted a following. And in each it swept the field.

There was one exception: Russia. That, however, was easy to understand. Industrialism had not reached the Tsar's domains until the 1890's, and the succeeding years saw conditions develop there which were almost more appalling than those in England in the 1840's. Consequently the Russian socialists could read the *Communist Manifesto* as though it were written in and for their own day. Only a minority of them—in their own language, the *Mensheviki*—dared question what it foretold. The majority—the *Bolsheviki*—remained devoutly sure that the only conceivable outcome was revolution.

But that one exception went almost unnoticed. Most of the socialists elsewhere in the world hardly knew that their movement had even penetrated Russia. Certainly none imagined that its career there would ever amount to much. The destiny of socialism, they were all convinced, would be decided entirely in the more advanced lands.

And immediate events seemed to prove them right. The Russian radicals actually did attempt a revolution in 1905. A stocky, broad-cheeked, bald-headed man who called himself Lenin, suddenly showed up in Moscow and began to shout: "Comrades, to the barricades!" A younger firebrand who operated under the name of Trotsky, set up a "Proletarian Government" in St. Petersburg. For months there was mutiny, pillage, arson, and murder everywhere from Poland to the Caucasus. But in the end nothing was accomplished. Soon the revolutionists fell out among themselves, the Tsar's knout fell on them all, and the whole mad fire was drowned in the blood of those who helped start it.

The moral seemed plain. It had been all very well for Marx to call violence "the midwife of every old social order pregnant with a new." But the world had changed since his day. Midwives were no longer in good standing.

If the moderate socialists needed proof that they were right, they felt they got it in 1905. Revolution had failed;

therefore, they argued, the one hope for their cause lay in evolution. There was no sense in outright radicalism—that is, trying to tear up capitalism by the *radices*, the "roots." It was wiser to try to trim the branches and graft healthier growths into the trunk.

That became their official policy now. They entered politics, got their representatives elected to the various legislatures, and started to trim and doctor with a hot and unrelenting zeal. It was not long, however, before they began to see that the task before them was tougher than they had anticipated. Their tender grafts kept dying in the seed, or else got corrupted the moment they sprouted. And the trimmed branches kept growing back. Worst of all, they discovered a parasite grown around the whole tree which seemed proof against any surgery. This was militarism.

The extreme socialists were equally aware of that parasite, but they were inclined almost to relish its presence. They rarely said so publicly—they realized how shocking it would sound—but among themselves they gloatingly whispered that militarism was in a perverse way their stoutest ally. The more the nations armed, the surer were they to go to war—and, therefore, the sooner would come The Revolution. The moderates, however, recoiled from that line of reasoning. In the first place, they had no appetite for revolution. In the second, they argued that war was as likely to bring on something even worse; namely, reaction. A major war, they argued, was almost sure to do that, since it would give the old fighting caste a chance to get back into power. Capitalism might go under, but only to restore feudalism. That would make the goal of socialism even remoter than it was right now.

So the moderates were all for peace. They made its preservation one of the chief planks in their party platform, and began to hammer on it hard. Their campaign, however, was quite unlike that of the conventional workers for peace. The latter kept appealing to the rulers of the world, and this, said the socialists, was silly. All the rulers, whether crowned or merely heeled, had a direct stake in capitalism. Did not their very life depend on accumulating profits? To get profits, they had to have markets; to get markets, they had to have empires; and to get empires, they had to fight. So what sense was there in begging them to be good and lay down their arms?

The only hope for peace lay not with the rulers but the ruled. Only the common folk, they who got nothing out of war save debt and pain and bloody anguish, they alone could be expected to put an end to war. The one sensible course, therefore, was to arouse the common folk.

Thus argued the majority of the socialists; and they did more than argue. They organized. As early as 1889 they called an international congress in Paris which sought to frame a program of action for the workers everywhere. Marx had convened a similar body twenty-five years earlier, but his prime purpose had been to foment the class war. This "Second International" was more interested in world peace, and said so. It demanded the abolition of all standing armies, laid a curse on all armed preparations, and insisted that in every instance the people must be consulted before war could be declared. The fact that no government paid heed to these demands did not disturb the socialists. Their aim was to be heard by the governed.

And, as time passed, they began to tell themselves that they actually were being heard. One proof was the growing tendency of the workers to elect socialists to the various national legislatures. That, it was felt, was more than a straw in the wind. It was the thunder presaging the storm that must some day drown all the fires kindled by the "bourgeois warmongers." Socialist deputies were the sworn opponents of all military adventures.

But there was another and even more impressive proof. This was the increasing willingness of some of the workers to go right over the heads of their governments. For example, when France and Britain fell out over the Sudan in 1898, the trade unions in both countries publicly joined hands to prevent hostilities. Much the same thing happened when France and Germany seemed about to come to blows over Morocco, when Austria and Italy quarreled over Trieste, and when Sweden was on the point of invading Norway.

Here was something new in the world. The fact was made positively melodramatic at the Socialist Congress in 1904, when the delegates from Russia and Japan, two countries then actually at war, solemnly embraced in the presence of the wildly applauding assembly. It began to look as though Karl Marx had been right on at least one score. The workers of all countries *were* uniting.

But not fast enough. The workers were not uniting nearly fast enough. As a matter of fact, most of them were not uniting even slowly. They were too patriotic. The cult of nationalism had got hold of them like a drink, like a drug. It had crept into their blood, their bones, the very marrow of their bones. They were all swollen with nationalism, all fevered and acraze with it. The fact that they were workingmen seemed to them incidental, even accidental. First and last they were countrymen.

If only the socialist leaders had seen that! Not that they could have done much about it even if they had; but at least they might have tried. Instead they lunged at shadows.

They were too cocksure of the rightness of their own attitude, too blinded by the glare of rationalism in which their own minds basked. Like Marx, they took it for granted that man was primarily a creature of reason, not emotion. Therefore, said they, the primary forces in society were those which the intellect could comprehend—in other words, those rooted in material interests. Now, nationalism seemed to spring from non-material interests. By its own boast, it was something "spiritual." Did it not logically follow, therefore, that nationalism, being non-material, must be *im*material?

Thus reasoned most of the Marxists, and it is hard to see how they could have been more in error. First of all, nationalism was by no means entirely non-material. Did it not create jobs for some people, and profits for others? Did it not spell power to politicians, circulation to publishers, glory to military men, and wealth to munitioneers? Secondly, even if nationalism really were non-material, that did not necessarily make it immaterial. The "spiritual" still had a tremendous hold on the average man. The time had not yet arrived (would it ever?) when he could live by his head alone; he had to follow what he called his heart. Thinking required effort; but to feel, to believe, to sink into the womb-like embrace of faith—that was sheer delight. And nationalism provided that delight to the point of delirium.

All that, however, was largely lost on those fine intellectuals who so optimistically hoped to arouse the masses against war. They seemed as blind to the fell influence of nationalism as were the conventional pacifists to that of capitalism. Consequently their efforts were equally futile. Forces had been let loose on earth which neither they nor any other mortals could curb now. The seed of capitalism working in the loins of industrialism had helped to litter the earth with nationalism. This in turn had cross-bred with both the others to whelp imperialism, which in further turn had cross-bred to bring forth militarism. Catastrophe was therefore inescapable.

Finally it came.

XXVII. THE FIRST WORLD WAI

HE miracle of it was that catas trophe did not come sooner. Th stage was all set for it as early a 1907, and from then on it wa touch-and-go before some blunder ing hand would ring up the cur tain. There was a narrow escap in 1908, when the Austro-Hun garian Empire suddenly darte into the Balkans to snatch the Slav-speaking provinces o Bosnia and Herzegovina. That enraged the Slavophils in St

Petersburg, and had Russia not been so weak at the moment—she had not recovered from her defeat at the hands of Japan in 1905—she might have mobilized. Instead Russia did no more than growl.

But three years later there was another crisis. France made a lunge to seize Morocco, and now Germany flew into a passion. However, Britain threatened to come to France's aid, so Germany cooled off. The Kaiser knew that his navy was not yet large enough to take on that greatest of all adversaries.

But the next year there was a whole series of crises. Italy had declared war on Turkey in the hope of grabbing something in North Africa. That gave all the small Balkan states—Serbia, Rumania, Bulgaria, Albania, Montenegro, and Greece—a chance to turn on Turkey. Before they were through, however, they were turning on one another, and such a bloody scramble ensued that for months the peace of all Europe hung on threads. Austria prepared to invade Serbia, Russia got ready to attack Austria, Germany warned that she would go after Russia, and France seemed bound to fall on the flank of Germany. At the twelfth hour a compromise was somehow arranged, and a treaty was solemnly signed.

It was no more than a truce. Every nation knew it, for each became panicky to add to its armaments. Germany enlarged her standing army to 870,000 men. Belgium adopted conscription, and France lengthened the term to three years. Russia voted millions for more armaments, and England hastened to build additional battleships. Even Australia and New Zealand started to stock up with weapons.

Yet, despite all these frantic preparations—indeed, because of them—most people believed that war would never come. They lulled themselves with the thought that they were making war too terrible to be possible. Even the rulers of the nations seemed to cherish that delusion. As late as the spring of 1914 the Kaiser and the Tsar were still exchanging letters couched in the most endearing terms. Right into the summer of that year the diplomats of England and Germany were amicably negotiating a secret agreement to divide up what was left of the Portuguese Empire.

Amazing! The writing was all over the wall, yet even those who were putting it there failed to understand what it said. So finally the wall fell in on them.

In the year of grace 1914, on the 28th of June—St. Vitus's Day according to the Christian calendar—a handsome, stoutish, middle-aged couple arrived in a flea-infested Bosnian town called Sarajevo. They were splendidly arrayed, especially the man, who looked rather like a prosperous baker dressed for a guild-masters' parade. Actually he was the Archduke Franz Ferdinand, heir-apparent to the Austro-Hungarian throne, and this was a state visit. The town had been heavily beflagged for the occasion, and arrangements had been made for great crowds to line the route of the procession and cheer. These arrangements, however, had apparently been imperfect, for only children, stragglers, and gawking peasants stood in the muddy streets, and these barely opened their mouths. Nevertheless the imperial visitors bowed and beamed as they drove past. They knew their duty. This was a newly acquired province, and its surly Slavic populace had to be won over somehow. They bowed and beamed unremittingly.

But then all at once they became frozen. A black object thrown from a roof-top was falling straight down on the royal car. Just in time the Archduke reached out, caught it, and flung it to the road. There was a blast, and two of his adjutants in the next car slumped in their seats. After that there was no more bowing and beaming.

When the procession finally reached the Town Hall, and the red-faced mayor launched into the official speech of welcome, he found His Imperial Highness unreceptive. "Enough of that!" the latter barked. "I pay you a visit, and you greet me with bombs!" Then he stamped out, followed by his wife, and clambered back into the open car. "Direct to the hotel!" he snapped. The chauffeur hastened to obey, but in his overeagerness he mistook the direction. Seeking to return to the right course by means of a short cut, he blundered into a blind alley, and had to back out. In doing so he almost ran down a bedraggled, hollow-eyed youth who stood on the curb and stared. And then it happened.

That youth was one of the band of conspirators who had tried to kill the Archduke an hour earlier. Since then he had been hiding in back streets, too scared to make a second attempt. But now all fear suddenly left him. He knew that Destiny was on his side. Destiny had decided that he, Gavrilo Printsip, was to be the avenger of Serbia's wrongs, and forever a hero in Serbia's history books. Reaching into his pocket, he pulled out a pistol, levelled it wildly, and fired twice.

Nineteen million people fell dead.

That assassination started the First World War. No one expected it to do that, least of all the assassin. Gavrilo Printsip was an ignorant, shiftless, half-crazed lout who had been told that if the Austrian Archduke was killed, all the rest of the Austrian imperialists would run to cover. But instead they leaped up in rage. They suspected—rightly—that the Serbian government was behind the crime. Serbia had long been hoping to play a rôle in the Balkans like that which

Prussia had played in Germany. Its politicians yearned to create a great Yugoslav nation stretching from Italy to Greece—if not farther. The Austrians, however, had their own plans for that region. They dreamed of making all of it part of the Hapsburg Empire. And now, seeing a chance to realize their dream, they drafted an ultimatum giving Serbia just forty-eight hours to come crawling. This, they hoped, would provoke the pugnacious little country to mobilize, and thus sign its own death-warrant.

The trick worked—but not quite in the way the tricksters had anticipated. Serbia did mobilize, but so did her "big brother," Russia. At this, Germany rushed to Austria's side, whereupon France felt bound to join up with Russia. Seeking to get at France, Germany invaded Belgium, and that was the last straw for Great Britain. Then Turkey got dragged in, then Japan, Portugal, Italy, Rumania, Bulgaria, Liberia, and also the United States. Before the war was over, twenty-seven sovereign nations and five dominions got dragged in.

Men began to kill one another. All over the world millions of men put on special clothes and went out to kill one another. They left the farms, the factories, the offices, the schools, and marched off into the trenches to kill one another. Moreover—this is the grimmest touch—they went rejoicing. They had somehow been made to believe that in this grave moment the sin of killing was no sin at all, but an act of grace. So the slaughterers sang as they marched to the slaughter-grounds, and their women and children strewed flowers and cheered. That happened almost universally. The voice of the people suddenly became the voice of Mars—and it was not all done by ventriloquism. True, there was an enormous amount of artificial stimulation. Glory-starved politicians did put many a word into the mouth of the mob, and profit-seeking businessmen certainly pulled many a string. But had the mob not been amenable to such influences, it would never have reacted as it did. Incredibly, the wild rejoicing that broke out when the War first started was at least in part actually spontaneous.

Even those who had once been the most vehement pacifists joined in the rejoicing. The very people who had formerly stood out as the noblest tribunes of world fraternity now became the loudest shouters for world fratricide. Of course there were exceptions. The Quakers, the Mennonites, and a few other religious dissidents held fast. Here and there isolated radicals held fast. But the rest of the erstwhile pacifists were swept away like leaves in a whirlpool. This was true not alone of the "sentimental" capitalists who had financed the great peace societies; it was almost as true of the "realistic" socialists. For years the latter had sworn that they would never fight in any "bourgeois" war. They had even threatened to call a general strike against any government that dared ask them to fight. But, once put to the test, they succumbed with hardly a struggle. Their vaunted "class consciousness" turned out to be no more than skin-deep. One little prick, and patriotism came rushing out like blood from a stuck artery.

Let me repeat: there were exceptions. The extremists, the so-called "orthodox" Marxists, inveighed against the War with enormous passion. That, however, was largely a matter of tactics with them. Secretly they welcomed the conflict, for they believed it could end only in revolution. They believed that eventually the sheep would sicken of the slaughter, and then they themselves would be able to ride herd. They would be able to turn then to the masses and cry: Did we not warn you? Did we not say you were being duped? Now follow us!

But there were some also among the moderate socialists who stood out against the carnage, and in their case the motive seems to have been less tactical. For example, there was a gaunt, bent-kneed, lovable old sinner in America named Eugene V. Debs who dared to stand up when the war-hysteria in his country was at its height, and proclaim: "I have no country to fight for! My country is the earth! I am a citizen of the world!" He, however, was a rare soul—and went to prison for it. Most of the other moderate socialists proved less intractable, and showed an eagerness to end up in office rather than jail. Nor was this because they were knaves. On the contrary, most of those capitulators appear to have been honest to the core. At the core, however, they were common clay, so they were friable.

All those men had been conditioned in childhood to believe in their country. The schools they had attended had conditioned them to believe in that; so had the storybooks they had read, the songs they had sung, the games they had played. And, once the war-crisis came, that early conditioning broke loose and overwhelmed them. Suddenly they found themselves believing not merely in their country, but even in those of its statesmen for whom they had formerly professed the most hateful contempt. If they were English socialists they cheered to the welkin when they heard Mr. Asquith proclaim: "We are fighting for the moral forces of humanity!" If they were German socialists they roared themselves hoarse when Herr Bethmann-Hollweg clarioned: "We must and will fight our defensive war for right and freedom!" It was the same if they happened to be French, or Russian, or Japanese socialists. Despite all their boasted self-emancipation from "bourgeois patriotism," almost invariably they fell to applauding the most bourgeois of their own country's patriots. They could not help it.

And if such men, avowed socialists, were impotent to withstand the hysteria, what chance was there for conventional folk? The latter had never even attempted to outgrow their early conditioning. Never in all their lives had they so much as questioned the rightness of nationalism. Therefore, no sooner did the war tide begin to flow than they flung themselves into it like fish out of a broken net. To most of them the net was everyday existence, the monotony and gray dreariness that had somehow overtaken ordinary life. War seemed to open up a way of release. In time of peace each day was like every other day, except perhaps Sunday —and that was like every other Sunday. Each day a man had to get up, go to work, come home, go to bed, and then sleep till it was time to get up and return to work. Not much fun in that! A man wanted something to look forward to when he got out of bed in the morning, something exciting, something adventurous, something new. He wanted to feel that he counted in the world, that he had a reason for living, a reason for dying. He seemed to lack that in time of peace.

Industrialism, it must be realized, had made existence almost too orderly for most people. It had so mechanized life that many a man had the feeling that he was hardly a man at all any longer. He seemed part of a machine. He seemed a mere thing hooked up to an engine or a workbench or a counter or a desk. And he could not stand that. He was made of flesh, not wood or pig-iron; he had blood in his veins, not ink or oil. He was a man, not a thing, and he wanted to act up like a man. He wanted to go places, see marvels, laugh, fight, and raise hell.

And that may have been the real reason why the masses proved so avid for war now. True, they had not asked for war; on the contrary, they had hoped it would not come. Fundamentally they were as averse as ever to getting themselves blown to bits. But, once the die had been cast, once that war was already declared, most of them felt a sense almost of release. The average man was starved for a bit of excitement. So long as his betters had insisted on quiet, he had meekly swallowed his want and acted tame. He had tried to vent his lusts in dreams and secret reveries. He had pored over the reports of murder trials in the daily press, or revelled in scenes of violence on the stage and in the movies. But now he could dispense with those surrogates, for war promised him the real thing.

War set him free at last. It set him free to hate and curse, free to shoot off guns and tear down cities. Moreover, he was free to act thus out of duty. The very people who had formerly told him he must be polite and full of loving kindness now urged him to go out and shoot and kill. The silk-hatted statesmen, the sag-bellied bankers, the clever chaps who wrote for the newspapers, the holy men who thundered from the pulpits, the poets, the philosophers, the college presidents, the movie stars—all the great folk whom the average man had been taught to respect and revere—these suddenly began to tell him that his highest duty now was to shoot and kill. Was it any wonder that he exulted when war was declared?

And thus it came about that the earth was turned into a slaughterhouse. During four years there was carnage and destruction beyond any true reckoning. To say that the War caused so and so many people to die is to say next to nothing. One must know *how* those people were made to die, in what bloodiness and horror, after what retching and pain. Some were killed instantly, being torn to shreds by shells, or pierced through with bayonets, or swallowed up in icy seas. Those were the lucky ones. Far more died only after hours of thrashing about on barbed wire, weeks of hunger in burnt-out villages, months of despair in prison camps. Millions upon millions died thus. They died of wounds, poisons, sunstroke, freezing, thirst, exhaustion, and a dozen kinds of plague. Some were young men with weapons in their hands; more were women and children caught between the lines. Never before in all of recorded history had so many humans been destroyed so cruelly in so short a space of time.

Yet even when all that is set down, the real cost of the War is still untold. Many millions were killed, but they would have died anyway in time. It was what the War did to the living that left the lasting scars. It took millions of healthy and reasonably decent youths, and set them to maiming and killing by the clock. In addition it compelled whole populations to concentrate on supplying the means for maiming and killing. No one can say just what psychological effect that must have had; but who can doubt that it was profound and evil? For centuries the race had been slowly building a living tissue of inhibitions to bind down the beast in man. Now that tissue was clawed to shreds.

But there was also a material effect, and concerning this we have concrete facts and figures. During the first three years, the direct cost of the War was $123,000,000 a day. During the fourth it was $10,000,000 an hour. During the last month alone . . . But why continue? Figures so astronomical are meaningless. It is enough to say that the four years of fighting brought more material destruction, and resulted in sharper material impoverishment, than the world was ever quite able to repair. This was not true, of course, of the damage done right in the battle-zones. Actual combat was confined to relatively small areas, and the loss in crops destroyed, forests burned, ships sunk, roads and bridges blasted, towns and villages gutted, was made up in a very short while. The real hurt was done behind the lines, for there the war disrupted the entire economy.

During four years the world failed to produce nearly as much as it destroyed. Luckily, enough had been stored up during previous years to keep civilization going on the planet. Even so, the going became hard, especially toward the last. This business of mass-murder was costly as well as savage. Someone has estimated that it required $21,000 of labor and material to kill a soldier in this war. (In Caesar's time the cost had averaged 75¢.) To kill some nine million soldiers consumed so much substance that in many places the living were left nigh destitute.

The civilian population found itself forced to forego first luxuries, then conveniences, finally even necessities. Rationing of one sort or another became universal in the belligerent countries. In some there was acute famine, and in most there was chronic want. All over Europe, and down into Asia Minor, millions began slowly to starve to death. Scurvy broke out, typhus raged, and a new plague called influenza became epidemic.

It was beyond bearing. People were no longer inured to such concentrated wretchedness. A century of progressive betterment had made them less tough than their forebears. They could still tolerate a certain amount of hardship, a certain amount of insecurity, a certain amount of cold, hunger, sickness, and general misery. Indeed, up to a limit such evils were considered normal and inescapable. But what people had to suffer in the course of the War so far exceeded that limit that finally their spirits rebelled.

By the time that happened, the initial rejoicing was hardly even a memory any more. The surge of elation at the outset of the War had long since petered out, for the populace had discovered that warfare was no fun at all. Gone was the day of pitched battling, wild charging, and heroic hand-to-hand combat. The soldiers had to spend most of their time fighting boredom in muddy trenches. For months on end they had to sit around in dark and stinking dug-outs, their eyes bleared, their bodies numb, and their chilblained hands scratching for fleas. Rarely did they catch so much as a glimpse of the enemy. When they fired, it was usually at unseen targets; when they went "over the top," it was usually to fight barbed-wire and piled sandbags. Mathematicians somewhere in the rear worked out the objectives with the aid of logarithm tables, and then transmitted the orders over telephone-wires. The entire pursuit of mass-murder had become almost as dull as running an abattoir.

The idea that war would bring relief from the tedium of machine existence had turned out to be a fraud. The men at the front very soon discovered that it was a fraud, and eventually so did the people at home. The civilians found themselves forced to build more factories than ever, and toil in them right around the clock. It was all very well to sing, "Keep the home-fires burning." The real need was to keep the factory-boilers going. The entire population had to let itself get caught up in an endless whirl of clanking machinery. Oldsters and women and children had to go into factories and make shells by machinery, pack food by machinery, wind bandages by machinery, nail coffins by machinery. All life had to be run by machinery. For war was no longer the sport it had been—or seemed—in former days. It had become a bloody industry.

That was why the initial delirium was so short-lived. People discovered the truth about war, and the truth made them sick. For a while they steeled themselves, gritting their teeth and swearing to stick it out. But as year followed year without sign of an end to the slaughter, the will began to weaken

—*on both sides*—and resolution gave way to revulsion. The gritted teeth parted in a snarl. Faces drained of blood by hunger and fatigue turned ominously livid with disgust. Soldiers began to mutiny at the front, and civilians rioted in the capitals. We've had enough! they cried.

So then there was an armistice. Neither side had won—can you win an earthquake?—but one side was a little less late to see that it had lost. Sullenly that side dragged out a white flag and offered to call it a day.

After that came the night.

XXVIII. THE RED DAWN

FTER the War came revolution. It broke out first in Russia, where the established order began to crack at the end of little more than one year of military strain. The Slavophils had miscalculated in 1914. Like the imperialists in most other countries, they had expected the War to be brief and for their own side profitable. When these expectations failed, all Tsardom collapsed.

It deserved to collapse. The Tsar himself was a weakling, and the Tsarina a neurotic witch. Their chief mentor was a lousy monk named Rasputin, who was as coarse and lecherous as he was pious and mad. The entire government had the quality of aged carrion. Most offices were held by men who were not even the best whom money could buy. They were lazy men, grossly incompetent as well as corrupt. The military authorities sent troops into battle without enough ammunition, often without even enough guns; and the civil authorities were no less culpable. A regime so rotten could not possibly fight a long war.

Rioting broke out in the capital as early as the spring of 1917. The transportation system had stalled, and there was no flour in the bakers' shops. Twelve hundred locomotives which had been allowed to freeze up during the hard winter were still standing on the sidings like lumps of ice. Fifty-seven thousand trucks which should have been feeding Petrograd were buried in snowdrifts. Women began to march in the streets, famished children at their breasts. "Give us bread!" they howled. They called their men out of the factories, and these too started to march and howl. A million marching stomachs, all hungry, set up a howl that waxed each hour more ominous. The government, taking fright, summoned a division of Cossacks from the front. They were leathery Mohammedan Cossacks who could be relied on to fire when commanded. They did fire—but on the police. Then the Tsar abdicated.

That, however, failed to still the howling. Not the Tsar but all Tsardom had to go now. It did. A new government was improvised, a volubly liberal goverment headed by a benevolently broad-minded prince. Too late. Even liberalism would not do now, especially under the egis of a prince. So a socialist was put in command. He was a typical moderate socialist by the name of Alexander Kerensky, earnest, honest, eloquent, but a lawyer. Despite this, he might have brought some order out of the chaos had he been given a chance. But that chance entailed halting the War, and Britain and France would not hear of that. He pleaded with them to support the calling of an international conference of socialists to negotiate a reasonable peace. Food riots had already occurred in Germany and Austria, and there was considerable reason to believe that such negotiations might succeed. But the Allied rulers, having just drawn in the United States on their side, were in no mood to treat with the enemy. Nothing would satisfy them short of complete victory.

Had those rulers listened to Kerensky, you who read these words, and I who write them, would be living in a different world today. But they did not. Instead they ordered him to continue fighting; and he obeyed. His country had entered into a contract with the Allies, and to him a contract was sacred. Was he not a lawyer?

That proved his undoing. The Russian state was beyond the ministrations of a lawyer. What it needed was an undertaker.

It got one on November 7, 1917. His name was Vladimir Ilyitch Ulyanov, but he was better known to his followers—and the police—as N. Lenin. He was a scrappy, red-bearded, undersized man with a bald oversized head that bulged above the brows like a gourd. He came of respectable middle-class parentage—his father had been a provincial schoolmaster—but from his youth he had been a fanatical Marxist. At the age of twenty-one he had seen his older brother go to the scaffold, at the age of twenty-seven he himself had been condemned to Siberia, and at the age of thirty he had had to flee abroad. At the age of fifty-seven he returned to take over the country.

As an exile he had lived first in Germany, then in England,

then for years in Switzerland; but never even for a day had his mind been away from Russia. All the while that he had lived abroad he had kept printing revolutionary propaganda which was smuggled into the Tsar's domains and there distributed underground. His chief medium had been an inky sheet which he called *Iskra*, "The Spark," and with this he had dreamed of setting all Russia afire.

That was what set him apart from a man like Kerensky. As early as 1903 Lenin had drawn the line, for in that year he had deliberately split the tiny Russian Socialist Party into two splinters. The extremists, those who believed in total revolution, and who were ready to give their lives to hasten it, followed Lenin into his red *Bolshevik* camp; the rest, the make-haste-slowly compromisers, the romantic sympathizers the discreet fellow-travelers, all these became the pink *Mensheviki*. At first the distinction had been vague, but it sharpened after the fiasco of 1905, and grew lurid in 1914. The beating of the war-drums made the Mensheviks blanch, but turned the Bolsheviks redder than ever.

Lenin from his G.H.Q. in a Geneva attic sent forth the command: "Convert the imperialist war into a civil war!" And his followers inside Russia hastened to obey. They were few but stealthy, disciplined, and boundlessly zealous: picked men and women who were ready to die, let alone kill, in the name of Marx. They fomented mutiny in the barracks, organized sabotage in the factories, and provoked riots in the slums. Finally in March, 1917, when Tsardom collapsed they came out into the open and demanded that their leader be allowed to come home.

Mobs greeted Lenin with bands and banners when he arrived at the Petrograd railway station. They led him to the Tsar's own waiting-room, handed him a bouquet of wilted red roses, and then waited for his words of praise. Instead he brandished his little fist in their faces and heaped them with scorn. "This new government which you have accepted," he roared, "is not a people's government. It is a petty-bourgeois oligarchy. . . . It does not bring peace, it cannot bring bread, it dare not bring freedom. . . . It must be turned out!"

Seven months later it *was* turned out.

Perhaps only a Lenin could have managed such a feat. His chief accomplices were wordy fellows, and his mass following was slight. The entire Bolshevik Party did not include a quarter of one per cent of Russia's population. But Lenin had faith, will, insight, and a genius for timing. He knew when to wait and when to spring; moreover, once he sprang, it was with both feet. All through the summer of 1917, and into the autumn, he waited. He wanted to give Kerensky a chance to lose out with the mob. Finally, late in October, he passed the word to his lieutenants that the zero hour was drawing near. Some demurred. They argued that their Party was not yet nearly strong enough to take power. Lenin would not listen. "If one hundred and fifty thousand landlords could govern Russia in the interest of the rich," he snapped, "cannot two hundred and forty thousand Bolsheviks do the same in the interest of the poor?" That silenced the doubters—that and also the knowledge that though their Party was small, its influence was great. Everywhere hot-eyed throngs were shouting its slogans. Everywhere they were marching in the streets and screaming: "Peace to the Soldiers, Bread to the Workers, Land to the Peasants, all Power to the Soviets!"

So the authors of those slogans girded themselves for violence. They still continued to harangue the mobs and squabble with Kerensky, but these were ruses to conceal their real moves. Behind the scenes they organized a "Red Guard" of disaffected soldiers, and equipped them with munitions stolen from the arsenals. They won over key workers in the telephone exchange, the power plant, the police stations. They arranged for mutinous sailors to bring a cruiser up the Neva and hold its radio in readiness. Then, during the icy night of November 7, 1917, they struck.

Twenty-four hours later, Petrograd was all theirs. Hardly a shot had been fired, yet the Menshevik government had collapsed, Kerensky was in flight, and the newspapers, the barracks, even the banks had capitulated. The Red Flag was flying over the capital of one-sixth of the planet.

The next day a little man who had been an outlaw for more than twenty years was proclaimed head of a new Russia. Rising in his shabby clothes before the crowd of henchmen who were now his government, he peered through the frosty steam rising from their mouths, paused for their throaty cheering to cease, and then quietly announced: "We shall now proceed with the building of the Proletarian Socialist State."

That was characteristic of Lenin. In the midst of roaring chaos he could stand calm, sure of himself, for he was not a man. He was a theory made flesh. He believed that the root of all social ill was private property, and this belief was so firm in him, so pervasive, so absolute, that he could serenely contemplate overturning the world to prove it true.

But the world, as we shall see, was unwilling to be overturned. Even Russia proved reluctant. The abolition of private property entailed more than mere economic change. It entailed the demolition of all that had sustained private property, and all that was sustained by it. Religion, education, morals, manners, sex relations, class relations, race relations: these had all been molded by the traditional concept of ownership. To abandon that concept meant to scrap all that was familiar in life—and most people recoiled from doing that. Even the poorest of the Russian poor, those to whom the familiar had never been anything but harsh and miserable, even they quailed before the prospect of starting life anew.

Lenin realized this, and was ready to act on the knowledge. He reasoned that the masses could not be expected to desire communism until they had tried it; moreover, they would not try it unless *forced* to do so. He had read that in the writings of Karl Marx—what had he not read there?—so his course was clear. Following Marx to the letter, he set out to create a "Dictatorship of the Proletariat."

What he achieved, of course, was at most a dictatorship *for* the proletariat. Lenin himself was no proletarian, and neither were most of his collaborators. They were typical intellectuals, sedentary and bookish men with faces pallid from long nights of argument over tea and cigarettes. Trotsky, Zinoviev, Kamenev, Bucharin: these, like most of the rest, were university men. Even Stalin, who eventually put so many of the others to death, was the product of at least a seminary. But here again Karl Marx offered justification. Had he not prophesied, seventy years earlier, that "when the class struggle nears the decisive hour . . . a portion of the bourgeois intellectuals . . . will go over to the proletariat . . . and lay the foundation for its sway?"

So Lenin felt that he and his band had every right not merely to seize power, but also to wield it. They called an immediate halt to the war and ordered the soldiers home. They confiscated all the private business enterprises and gave them into the keeping of the workers. They expropriated all the great estates and partitioned them for the use of the peasantry. "Comrades," Lenin cried to the people, "take the land, the grain, the factories, the goods, the railroads, and protect them as the apple of your eye—all these are henceforth your common property." All hereditary titles were abolished, and all who believed in them were threatened with death. The Orthodox Church was disestablished, and any religious indoctrination was frowned on. Prostitution was forbidden and free love declared quite all right. Divorce was made as easy as marriage, and abortion as free as vaccination. Women were given complete social and political equality with men, and the order went forth: "Every housewife must learn to run the government." Finally, all racial prejudice was proscribed.

It was a clean sweep. Apparently nothing was to remain of the "bourgeois" past. Henceforth there was to be neither rich nor poor, neither grand nor lowly, neither oppressor nor oppressed. All alike were to bask in the sun of science, all were to fill their lungs with the ozone of culture, all were to wallow in the comforts produced by machinery. This new Russia was going to be heaven on earth. And whoever dared to say otherwise was given hell.

Nevertheless many people dared to say otherwise. Most of the poor who were pious refused to accept the new order, and so did all of the rich, whether pious or no. The Tsarists refused, the Liberals refused, the Mensheviks refused, even the Anarchists and Nihilists refused. Lenin and his band found themselves forced to resort to ever-increasing violence. They organized a pitiless Red Terror, and flung people into jail, or stood them against the wall, on the least suspicion of "counter-revolutionary leanings." There were months when they sentenced almost as many people to death as were being slaughtered on the fields of Flanders each and every hour.

Still the opposition persisted. Counter-revolutionary armies collected everywhere from Odessa to Vladivostok, and a White Terror was pitted against the Red. Foreigners joined the crusade, for the entire capitalist world had decided that Bolshevism must be crushed. First came armies of Germans and Turks, and then regiments of British, French, Czech, Polish, Rumanians, Japanese, and even American troops.

But in the end Bolshevism won out. Despite that the armed crusade against it lasted nearly three years, and was pressed on more than thirty fronts, Bolshevism managed somehow to survive. Its chief savior was the man who took command of the Red defense, Leon Trotsky. His real name was Bronstein, and he entered on his duties with absolutely no military experience. He was a Jew by birth, a writer by profession, and a revolutionist by inclination. However, he had colossal nerve, vitality, and talent for organization, and these more than made up for his ignorance of the manual-at-arms. Throughout those three awful years he virtually lived in an armored train, dashing from one front to another and exhorting his tattered troops to stand their ground. They did do that—and more. By the close of 1920 they were driving the last of the counter-revolutionary armies into the sea.

Capitalism had only itself to thank for the defeat. It had invited defeat by failing to give ground in time. Had the Allies permitted Kerensky to take Russia out of the war, Lenin might never have been able to seize power, let alone retain it. And on the heels of that error, capitalism committed another. Having agreed that Bolshevism must be crushed, the capitalist nations failed to cooperate and launch a united offensive. They did not know how. Being capitalistic, they knew only how to compete. Each of them feared to let any other go very far in Russia lest it go too far and decide not to leave. The British invaders devoted more thought to thwarting the French—and the French, the British—than either gave to fighting the Reds. The American troops spent almost all their time getting in the way of the Japanese. Ostensibly those forces were all joined in a holy crusade; actually they were rivals. So in the end all of them were sent packing.

By the beginning of 1921 the civil war was virtually over. The Bolsheviks had won out, and all that remained for them now was to make Bolshevism work out. But that task, they already knew, was going to take time—and something else. The inscrutable logic—or was it caprice?—of history had loaded the dice against them. It had enabled them to get to power under conditions which seemed precisely the least favorable for the accomplishment of that for which they wanted power. The day Petrograd fell into their grasp, they had boasted to the world: "We, the Soviets of Worker, Soldier, and Peasant delegates, are on the point of making an experiment that has not had its like in history." But by the time they had taken the rest of the land, they were inclined to use a soberer tone. Though still sure that the experiment ought to work, they were not so sure that it would.

It had finally dawned on the less impervious Bolsheviks that they had perhaps gone at the experiment in the wrong spirit. Their approach had been that of doctrinaires, not scientists. Communism had been to them an immaculate conception, and Marx a sort of Holy Ghost. They had not said: Let's try collective ownership and see if it works. They had set out with the fixed notion that it *must* work. And now they could see all too plainly that it hadn't. Though the bourgeoisie had long since been expropriated, and only sworn devotees of the proletariat were running the economy, living conditions were getting worse all the time. The workers were arguing more than they were working, for they had been told they were the bosses now—and what was the good of being a boss if you couldn't take time off to argue? But argument didn't produce goods. Less coal and iron were being mined in a month in 1920 than had been delivered in a day in 1913. So little leather was being tanned in 1921 that people even in the cities were going barefoot. And, as a direct result, food too was getting desperately scarce. The peasants were refusing to grow more than just enough to feed themselves. What was the use of producing a surplus when all you could get in exchange for it was worthless paper-money? Nor did it help much if the government sent armed agents to collect food by force. The railways were in such disrepair that half the time the loot went to rot before it could be delivered to the cities. The fetid breath of hunger gathered like a pall over the entire land, and such a howl went up as even Russia had never heard before. For a generation the revolutionists had sung: "Arise, ye pris'ners of starvation!" Well, here they had arisen, and what had it got them?

The fact was plain: total communism had failed. The Bolshevik surgeons had apparently been over-zealous. They had hacked out the capitalist gland with such hammer-and-sickle thoroughness that now the whole economy refused to function. With wages virtually abolished, and all profit-making officially suppressed, the common man felt no incentive to strive and contrive and bring forth plenty.

What to do? Should the Bolsheviks admit they had erred, and restore the unspeakable gland? Many of them flew into a rage at the very suggestion. All that was needed, they stormed, was more terror. A little more violence, they insisted, a little more pummelling and pounding, and the body would simply have to come to life again. But there were others who knew better. These could see that they had already exhausted the potency of terror. Even the agents on whom they had to rely to wield the terror, the soldiers and sailors and militiamen, even they were beginning to balk. The only way out, therefore, was to relent. Lenin himself became convinced of that, and made open confession of the fact. Whereupon a "New Economic Policy" was adopted.

That happened in 1921. Private enterprise was permitted to return—though only on its knees. Whoever could scrape together the necessary cash was permitted to open a store of his own, or start a small factory, or hire laborers to till rented land. Foreign capitalists were invited to lease concessions, and native engineers were given contracts on a commission basis. All the go-getters who still remained in the land were once more allowed to man the pumps at the well of plenty. To be sure, they could no longer pump as they pleased. They had to confine themselves to the smallest spouts, and hand over most of what they got out of them. They were carefully watched and severely restrained and remorselessly taxed. However, they were permitted to retain at least a portion of the profit, and that seemed incentive enough. Despite that the risks they ran were as great as the rewards were small, they pumped with all their might. Like the go-getters everywhere else in the world, their minds were filled primarily with horse-sense. To get them going they had to be shown a bag of oats.

Slowly the economy began to revive. Communism had brought it within an inch of rigor mortis. Now, after the merest whiff of capitalism, it was stirring again.

The Bolsheviks heaved a sigh—and then scowled. They were relieved, enormously relieved; yet at the same time they were sore. It made them sore to think that they had saved the Dictatorship of the Proletariat only by dint of yielding to the bourgeoisie. But there was one consolation: they *had* saved that Dictatorship. Now they could afford to wait awhile. They were still in power, so nothing was lost except perhaps pride. And what was pride to good revolutionists? All that counted was principle, and in that direction the Bolsheviks felt they had not yielded an inch. For they still believed in communism, and they were still determined to make it work.

Their initial effort, they told themselves, had been doomed from the start—and not simply because they themselves had been over-zealous. That, they were convinced, was more an effect than a cause. They had failed primarily because they had been compelled to launch their experiment in the wrong country. Marx had looked for communism to come only after capitalism had gone to seed. But in Russia capitalism had never even properly sprouted. The Black Life had not reached that country until around 1890, and even then it had been unable to raise more than a few microscopic pocks on the map. The native bourgeoisie had had little chance to equip the realm with machines, and no chance at all to teach the masses how to run them. Without an abundance of machines and mechanics, there could not be an abundance of goods; and without an abundance of goods, what could be communized except the lack of them?

Nor was that all. Fate had condemned the Bolsheviks to try their experiment not merely in one of the poorest places, but also at the very poorest time. The Tsar's war had left Russia bankrupt, and no sooner had Lenin tried to set up his receivership than the civil war had come along and wiped out most of the surviving assets. The shops had been looted, the granaries were bare, the transportation system was all but paralyzed, and the entire industrial plant lay in ruins. Had there been any gold left in the national treasury, fresh supplies might have been brought in from abroad. But there was no gold. Nor, in the circumstances, was there any chance of getting credit. The Bolshevists were left to raise their country by its boot-straps—and it had no boots. Was it any wonder that they failed?

But that did not mean they were through. On the contrary, they felt they had barely started. The next step was to import aid, and that meant they must export trouble. They must spread communism abroad, for thus alone could they hope to establish it at home. The whole world must be revolutionized.

This, of course, had been their dream from the start. The very day Lenin arrived in Petrograd in the spring of 1917 he had cried: "Soldiers, Sailors, Workers . . . already we see the dawn of the *world* revolution!" And from that day forth he and his comrades had tried to claw at the clouds which persisted in obscuring that dawn.

During the first two years they had had to confine their clawing to the sky over Russia, but after that, as much out of desperation as desire, they dared to extend their reach. In March, 1919, they invited sympathizers to come to Moscow from the four corners of the earth and organize a "Communist International." This, it was announced, would be the "general staff of the world revolution," and its first task would be the creation of communist parties in all the capitalist lands. Each of these parties would be expected to perform a twofold task: undermine the bourgeois government in its own country, and seek to protect the proletarian one in the Soviet Union. None save out-and-out revolutionists could become members, and the discipline among them would of course be absolute. The rank-and-file comrades would have to obey the leaders of their local "cells"; these in turn would have to obey the leaders at the national headquarters; these in further turn would have to obey the men in control of the "Comintern" at Moscow. And thus, from China to Chile, from Iceland to Tasmania, there would be one resolute effort to hasten the Red Dawn.

The whole conception was typically Bolshevik in its vastness and bravado, and when it was made public it created terrible alarm all over the earth. Protestants swore that this Comintern was more sinister even than the Order of Jesuits, and Catholics branded it a double-damned Freemasonry. Responsible statesmen like the Right Honorable Winston Churchill made the welkin crackle with their denunciations of "a poisoned Russia, an infected Russia, a plague-bearing Russia." The boast Karl Marx had uttered in 1848 had come true with a vengeance: the "specter of communism" had begun to haunt not alone Europe, but all the world.

And the Bolsheviks were elated. The greater the scare they could throw into the capitalists, the more publicity they got for themselves. And they believed in publicity. Once the "New Economic Policy" began to yield revenues, the heads of the Comintern actually took money from the Soviet Treasury to buy publicity. They subsidized communist newspapers in all the leading capitals, and created a world-wide network of distributing centers for their literature and films. They organized strikes in the industrialized lands and fomented sedition in the colonial regions. Wherever there was a break in the social tissue they wormed their way in and planted bacilli of mutiny. For their only hope now lay in more revolution. They felt that one-sixth of the planet did not provide scope enough for their experiment, especially when it was so backward and ravaged a sixth. If Bolshevism was to succeed, it would have to spread. Farther and farther it would have to spread.

Otherwise Bolshevism seemed doomed.

XXIX. THE PLAGUE OF NATIONS

UT Bolshevism did not spread. Despite all the efforts of the Communist International, no other country would go the way of Russia. Many revolutions followed in the wake of the War, but few of them were directed by Moscow, and those few were all ill-fated. The Hohenzollern Empire collapsed, the Hapsburg Empire flew to pieces, the Turkish Empire sank out of sight. The rulers of virtually all the defeated countries were pushed from their thrones and sent packing. But though their successors did not dare assume crowns, neither would they stoop to wearing caps. They preferred to put on silk hats.

That was symbolic. Those successors did not want to be taken for proletarians. They had resorted to revolution only in order to establish better bourgeois governments. Therefore they insisted on dressing like proper bourgeois gentlemen. Their idol was not Lenin but was a man named Wilson.

Mr. Woodrow Wilson was the most powerful man on earth when the War came to an end. He was that not alone because he was the head of the world's richest nation, but even more because he had made himself the oracle of the world's most ardent hope. He was a tall lean man with a long lean face that seemed to break in two when he smiled. He was a great idealist, a great humanitarian, a great liberal, and a great talker. He believed in God, Truth, Justice, Free Trade, Democracy, Peace, Prayer, and his own conscience. He came of a long line of Presbyterian ministers.

At the outset of the War he had done all in his power to keep his country neutral. "We are too proud to fight," he had proclaimed. Even after the conflict had entered its third year he had still insisted that "the objects which the statesmen . . . on both sides have in mind are virtually the same." But then, having meanwhile been reelected to the Presidency, he suddenly reversed his stand.

The reasons are not too obscure. One was the pressure of popular sentiment. Native sympathy coupled with foreign propaganda had at last persuaded the majority of Americans that the Allies deserved to win. Another was the pressure of national interest. Germany was a brashly aggressive power, and there were good grounds for fear that if she triumphed in the Old World, she would soon be reaching toward the New. A third reason was the pressure of financial anxiety. American industry had supplied the Allies with enormous stores of munitions on credit. Finally, and perhaps most potent of all, there was the pressure of Mr. Wilson's sense of personal consecration. He felt it was his bounden duty to bring about a "just" peace, and he belatedly realized that to fulfill this duty he would first have to decide the War.

In effect he did decide it. Once America threw its enormous weight on one side, the other did not stand a chance. For America's weight was made up of more than sinew and fighting gear. It included a promise. Mr. Wilson had sensed that the swiftest way to end the War was to promise the people on the other side that they might really win if they surrendered. Accordingly he had announced that, so far as his own country was concerned, this War was being fought not for loot, not for glory, but solely to establish a new order among the nations of the earth. This new order, he had gone on to particularize, would be one guaranteeing eternal peace and universal freedom, for it would proscribe all secret diplomacy, abridge all restraints on world traffic, reduce all armaments, emancipate all subject peoples, and unite all nations in one common fellowship. These principles, together with their corollaries, he had called the "Fourteen Points," and in the end they accomplished what ten times as many army divisions could not have done. On the strength of those "Fourteen Points" the people on the other side did surrender.

An armistice was signed, and then Mr. Wilson set sail for Europe to arrange the peace. Never in all history had any man been received there with as great acclaim. People wanted to kneel in his presence; they wept for joy wherever he appeared. He had become more than a mere man to them: he was the Messiah. Did he not bring assurance that a New Day was about to dawn? Millions of people *on both sides* had endured the War solely in the hope that peace would usher in a better world. Now, they told themselves, President Wilson would see to it that the hope was not betrayed.

That was one reason why they refused to succumb to Bolshevism. Mr. Wilson, they discovered, did not like Bolshevism. What he liked, and what he wanted his fellowmen to like, was liberalism. The root of all evil, he insisted, lay in the realm of politics rather than economics. What the world needed, therefore, was merely more "democracy." If every government would become like his own, a government of the people, by the people, and for the people, then universal peace and freedom would ensue as a matter of course. He was convinced of that with a conviction as lofty as it was innocent. And a populace grown sick of war and oppression was only too ready to agree.

But this readiness, it turned out, was due largely to a misapprehension. Most people in Europe, or at least those who spoke for most people, seemed to think that the beginning and end of liberalism was nationalism. They were obsessed with the belief that all would be well merely if each folk with an apparent identity of its own were given absolute sovereignty in a country all its own. The War was in part to blame for that. The belligerent governments had done all in their power to exacerbate nationalistic pride and prejudice. They had done this not alone at home, in order to bolster the fighting morale of their own people, but also abroad, in the hope of wrecking that of the enemy. Each side had sent out agents to stir up the subject peoples behind the other's lines. Germany had promised national independence to the Finns and Letts and Poles if they would revolt against the Tsar. Britain had sworn to heap all sorts of glories on Arab sheikhs if they would rise up against the Turks. Every oppressed folk was encouraged to believe it would become free and sovereign if only it would turn on its current oppressors. Even the Jews were offered that bait.

So when the War was over, the world was left one mass of nationalistic rashes. What might otherwise have been a mild affliction, like acne in adolescence, had been aggravated into a disfiguring plague. For let us be clear on one point: nationalism would have spread even without the War. It was one of the inescapable consequences of the spread of machinery. Let us be clear also on a second point: this consequence had definite social value. Nationalism spelled progress. It blasted the shells of provincial clannishness, and set men free to acquire broader loyalties. It forced sullen tribes to merge, and encouraged subject races to rebel. All of which was good, for it engendered growth.

But the War overstimulated the growth, and in doing so, made it poisonous. It led people to believe that their new horizons must necessarily be frontiers, and that the love they felt for the folk inside them could be measured only by the hate they bore toward all who belonged outside. It taught people to equate cultural freedom with political sovereignty, and national independence with the right to have an army and a diplomatic corps. Though it educated many backward races, it left them unenlightened; though it quickened their minds, it also envenomed their hearts.

Mr. Wilson found that out before long, and the revelation caused him much grief. In principle he had no objection to nationalism. On the contrary, he considered it an essential element in the new world order which he had planned. No fewer than eight of his "Fourteen Points" dwelt on what he called the "self-determination of nations." And all went well so long as he continued to make speeches, for the "self-determination of nations" was a fine mouth-filling phrase. Once he had to get down to business, however, he swiftly discovered that the phrase was hard to digest. The more he chewed it, the more it kept regurgitating. For just what was a nation? Moreover, just how was it to determine itself?

Many answers were forthcoming, but no two of them quite jibed. Whole throngs of theatrical-looking personages, some in rented frock-coats, some in turbans and robes, queued up in front of his office to tell him the "facts." They piled his desk high with books, maps, and handsomely embossed resolutions proving that the Armenians were a nation, and also the Croatians, the Assyrians, the Moldavians, and the Bessarabians. Apparently the Wends too were a nation, and the Livs, the Letts, the Kurds, the Esths, the Jews, the Basques, and of course the Irish. One delegate arrived from the Pontus on the Euxine Sea with a documented plea for the restoration of the kingdom of Mithradates the Great, which had been destroyed in 47 B.C. . . .

To have accepted all these claims would have meant carving the map of the Old World into a jig-saw puzzle. The claims were too numerous, and also too conflicting. The various nationalities did not merely crowd each other; they overlapped. Ruthenians lived in the midst of Poles, Poles in the midst of Czechs, Czechs in the midst of Hungarians, Hungarians in the midst of Rumanians, and Jews in the midst of all. It was obvious that complete national self-determination could be achieved only through international extermination.

In these circumstances there was but one way out for Mr. Wilson. He had to compromise. Even had his task been less impossible, he would still have had to compromise. After all, he was not the sole arbiter of the peace. A certain Mr. David Lloyd George had some say in the matter, and so did an even more certain M. Georges Clemenceau. Bteween those two gentlemen, one as smart as a fox and the other as fierce as a tiger, the American could do little save play the mule. They were infinitely wilier men than he, and unencumbered with his fine visions. They had no thought of trying to set the world to rights. All they wanted was to buttress certain imperial wrongs. Lloyd George wanted to preserve Britain from ever again being challenged on the sea, and Clemenceau wanted to do the same for France on land. So they went to work on their stubbornly righteous colleague and bluffed, huffed, blandished, and bargained till they got him around to what they called "reason." After that it was the old, old story of the voice being the voice of Jacob while the hands were the hands of Esau. Mr. Wilson talked on and on about how the map ought to be redrawn, and meanwhile those other gentlemen redrew it.

They redrew it badly. Though many changes were made, and all at the expense of the defeated nations, none seemed to satisfy even the victors. The number of sovereign states in Europe was increased from twenty-six to thirty-five, but that merely meant seven thousand extra miles of frontier to stumble over—and fight about. The new boundaries were intended to serve political expediency, so they failed to conform even to racial demands. The sovereign state of Poland was allowed to include regions inhabited primarily by Ukrainians, Lithuanians, or Jews. Czechoslovakia was made to include compact minorities of Germans, Hungarians, and other volubly non-Slavic folk. To make matters worse, economic needs were almost entirely ignored. An industrial center would be left on one side of a frontier, and its agricultural hinterland on the other. Here would be the iron-mines, and over there the coal-beds. Moreover, the lines running between them would be no mere marks on the map. They would be a solid chain of forts, custom sheds, and passport offices.

So there was trouble. The new pots of political sovereignty

began to seethe and boil over with nationalistic rivalries. Greece invaded Turkey. Rumanian, Czech, and Yugoslav armies looted Hungary. Poland seized Wilno from Lithuania, and Lithuania seized Memel from Germany. Italy tried to take Fiume from Yugoslavia, and Yugoslavia did take Montenegro from Montenegro. Everywhere there was contention over boundaries, everywhere agitation against minorities.

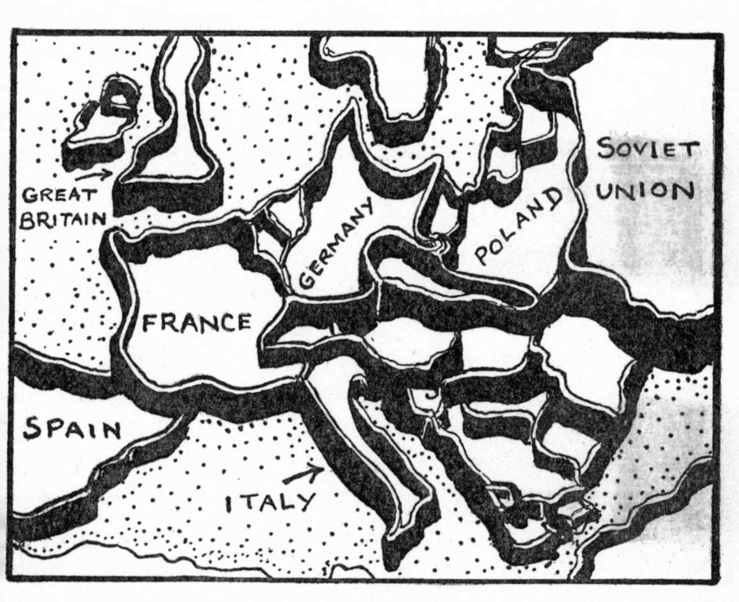

THE NEW EUROPE
. . . 7,000 extra miles of frontier.

This, however, had one supposedly redeeming feature. It kept the people so excited about nationalism that they had no chance to succumb to communism. Take the Poles for example. Had the masses among them not been distracted by patriotic passions, they would almost certainly have emulated their neighbors to the east. They were equally poor and downtrodden, and no less hungry to vent their spite. But instead of venting it on the real wolf in their midst, they vented it on scapegoats. They raged because Jews were too active in the cities, and fumed because Ukrainians were too numerous in certain rural parts. They swore at the Czechs for "stealing" half of the Teschen area, and glared daggers at the Lithuanians for having dared to "usurp" the city of Wilno. It made no difference that the Jews had helped create those cities, that the Ukrainians had first tilled those fields, that Teschen was at least half Czech, that Wilno was almost all Lithuanian. Nothing seemed to make any difference except the accident of racial, cultural, or national differentness.

Such blindness was as menacing as it was perverse. Nevertheless it persisted. Why? For at least three reasons. First of all, the masses apparently preferred to be blind. The longer they could keep their eyes closed to baffling facts, the freer were they to revel in exciting fictions. Secondly, the leaders of the masses failed to recognize that it was a blindness. Most of those leaders came from poor but bourgeois homes, and they had been schooled to accept none save thoroughly bourgeois ideals. And by now nothing was more bourgeois than nationalism. Thirdly, Great Britain and France deliberately fostered the blindness, for they seemed better able to get what they wanted if those from whom—or through whom—they took it could not see.

So the blindness persisted. Even the Germans remained blind, and they were one people who should surely have learnt to see through nationalism by this time. If the War failed to open their eyes, the subsequent peace ought to have done the job. Mr. Wilson had promised them that if they put down their arms, and put out their Kaiser, they would be given an equal voice with the victors in drawing up the final settlement. But no sooner did they comply with these demands than they found themselves treated like felons. For seven months they were kept on tenter-hooks before they were permitted even to show up officially at Versailles; and then, when the permission was finally granted, it was only to learn that the peace terms had already been settled.

Old Clemenceau presided at that historic session, and the story of how he behaved was not soon forgotten in Germany. Leaning back in his chair, he raised stony eyes to the German delegates, and snapped: "Messieurs . . . the time has come when we must settle our accounts. You have asked for peace. We are ready to give you peace." Whereupon he handed them a 230-page document, and told them to sign within three weeks.

Clemenceau had his gloves on at the time—he almost never appeared without them—but nevertheless his fingerprints were all over that document. So were Lloyd George's. Like the staunch patriots they were, they had done their duty well. Here were some of the stipulations set down in that document. First, Germany was to acknowledge full responsibility for starting the War, and for causing all the consequent loss and hardship. As partial penalty she was therefore commanded to surrender 15% of all the arable land she owned in Europe, 10% of all her population there, 10% of her industrial plants, 12% of her livestock, 20% of her coal reserves, 50% of her lead, 60% of her iron ore, 70% of her zinc, and also "the skull of the Sultan Mkwawa which was removed from the Protectorate of German East Africa." She was further ordered to hand over all her colonies, and virtually all her investments and holdings in foreign lands. Her navy, formerly second only to Great Britain's, was to be completely wiped out, and her merchant marine reduced by

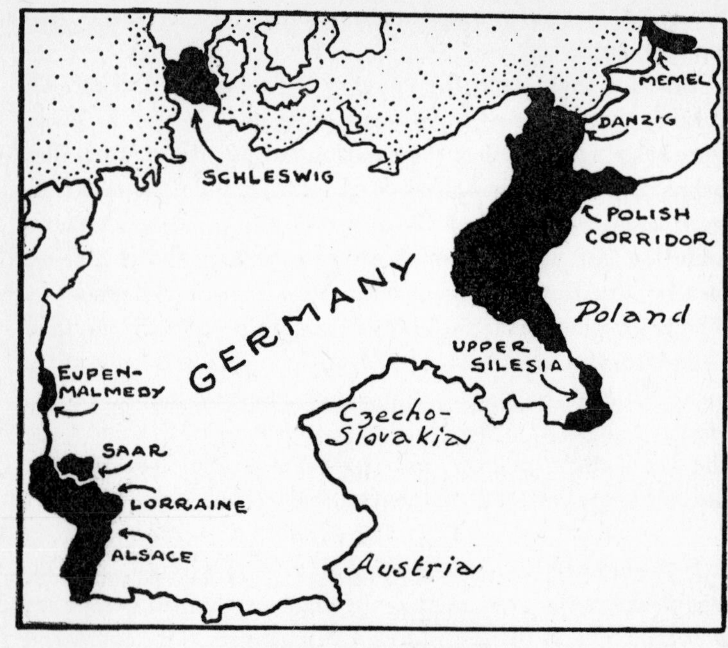

WHAT GERMANY LOST

. . . also the skull of the Sultan Mkwawa.

nine-tenths. Her army was to be hacked down to one-seventh the size of that of France, and her munition plants were to remain under Allied control. Finally she was ordered to pay five billion dollars in cash or commodities by May 1, 1921, and also sign a blank check for the still unestimated cost of repairing "all damage done to the civilian population of the Allied and Associated Powers and to their property."

Such was the "Treaty of Versailles," and it well deserved the name. The word "treaty" is derived from the Latin *tracto*, meaning "drag violently," and rarely had it been employed with greater aptness. On June 28, 1919, five years to the day after a half-demented Balkan lad fired a pistol at

Sarajevo, Germany was dragged violently to Versailles and made to sign.

But did that teach the country a lesson? It did not. Of course, there were *some* Germans who got the point. There were *some* who saw that their nation had landed at Versailles primarily because it had started out from Potsdam. There were some who realized the utter insanity of nationalistic ambition in a world in which machinery commanded that all men be kin. But these were few, and without solid influence. The Kaiser may have fled, but his generals were still on hand —and so was a certain one of his corporals. The government changed, the flag changed, even the style in moustaches changed; but the outlook of the people remained in one sense the same. Now as ever, now indeed more than ever, their dearest slogan was "*Deutschland über alles!*"

So here was still another thing that went wrong—and this was perhaps the gravest thing of all. Nationalism swelled up poisonously and turned into rank chauvinism. This happened not alone in Germany, but throughout Europe, indeed throughout most of the world. People in any number of lands became persuaded that to be true patriots they must be jingoes. They completely failed to realize that the progression from family to tribe to province to nation must go on till the scope of a man's loyalty encompassed all the earth. *The nation seemed to them the culmination.* What they should have recognized as a stage, they took to be a terminus. Instead of using nationalism as a thoroughfare, they made it a blind-alley.

To be sure, this did not happen universally. In many places there were leaders who could see what plague was spreading, and in at least one immense region a sharp effort was made to root it out. That region was the Soviet Union. Lenin and his comrades were blind to many things, but never to the menace of chauvinism. Their domain contained at least a hundred and eighty different peoples who spoke almost a hundred and fifty different tongues. To fight the plague of clan bigotry was therefore utterly imperative. Those diverse groups had to be taught to live together in peace and work together in comity; otherwise there was no hope for communism. The Bolsheviks had known that all along. (One of them, a Georgian called Stalin, had written a thesis on the subject as early as 1912.) Furthermore, they had realized that coercion would never accomplish their aim. The Tsarists had used coercion, and it had brought them nothing but grief. The more they had labored to enforce uniformity on Russia's subject peoples, the more passionately had these remained diverse. So the Bolsheviks had decided to try another method. Instead of seeking to crush diversity by force, they set out to undo it by dint of kindness. They granted each national group complete cultural autonomy, and actively encouraged it to speak its own tongue, enjoy its own folkways, conduct its own schools, theaters, and even police courts. But —and this was the big but—no such group was permitted to have its own army, or its own foreign office, or its own domestic economy. All the soil and its resources, all the factories and their products, had to belong to all the Soviet nationalities in common. Thus, it was hoped, none would find cause to envy another, and none would feel impelled to try to take away what another had. All groups would enjoy an equal right to live, and therefore none would be tempted to go out and kill.

That was the Bolshevik scheme, and it was succeeding. Russians and Tartars, Cossacks and Jews, Armenians and Georgians and even Ukrainians were becoming neighborly. Just because all the Soviet nationalities were allowed to remain different, most of them seemed increasingly inclined to merge. The Bolsheviks had apparently discovered a sure antitoxin for nationalism. It was comradeship.

But this served only to make the Bolsheviks appear all the more monstrous to the outside world. The average citizen in the capitalist lands did not want to be cured of nationalism. It had somehow become part of his being, part of his very reason for being. Nationalism had become his religion. If that went, what was left for him to live for?

XXX. THE LITTLE CAESARS

HE World War had been fought for two different sets of reasons: *real* ones and *good* ones. The real reasons were concerned primarily with real-estate, and they did not come clearly to light until the terms of peace were announced. The good reasons, on the other hand, were given intense publicity from the very start, but once the conflict ended they inevitably dropped out of sight. These good reasons—on the side of the Allies—were voiced by Mr. Wilson, and they centered around two supremely noble aspirations: the world must be saved from belligerency, and the world must be made safe for democracy. Neither was even remotely realized.

Belligerency suffered only a token defeat, and even that only for a moment. It is true that the chief defeated powers were stripped of their arms. It is true also that nearly all the victors and neutrals formed themselves into a "League

MILITARISM: 1913 *vs.* 1930

of Nations" to prevent any further resort to arms. But both stratagems proved of small avail. The world merely demobilized; it did not demilitarize. How could it when there were more sovereign states now than before the War, and therefore that much more room for rivalry and cause for conflict? Not until after 1924, by which time some of the worst errors of the Treaty of Versailles had been partially corrected, did the caldron of hate in Europe show signs of beginning to cool. But it was a fleeting respite. The fires were merely banked, and that only because the governments seemed to need time to store up fresh fuel. By 1930 France had 3,000,000 men in her first-line reserve and another

1,000,000 in her second line. In that year Italy had a reserve of 2,500,000; Poland had 1,700,000; Czechoslovakia had 1,000,000. By 1935 the nations of the world were spending nearly four times as much on armaments as in 1913. It was plain to see that the interlude of peace was being used solely to prepare for more war.

And just as belligerency was not halted, so democracy was not furthered. It is true that the World War wiped out four imperial autocracies. It is true that the ensuing truce saw six new states emerge as republics, and also five old ones. It is true that by 1919 there was not a single monarch left in all Europe who dared claim to rule as had his ancestors—by divine right. But it is equally true that, despite these marks of apparent progress, the political tone throughout the Old World actually retrogressed.

The myth of the divine right of kings was torn down only to make way for a reality that was worse. That reality was the demonic might of thugs. It emerged first, as we have seen, in Russia. The Bolsheviks were precisely thugs, for like the Hindu fanatics who bore that name originally they tyrannized only out of a sense of righteousness. No matter how noble Lenin's ends may have been, many of the means that he employed were unspeakable. It may be argued that he was hardly to blame for that. He had learnt those means from the Tsarists, and was simply employing them more efficiently. Perhaps he even deserved a measure of praise, since he sincerely intended to abandon those means so soon as he had attained his ends. Neither he nor any other responsible Bolshevik regarded the Dictatorship of the Proletariat as more than a makeshift. They all hoped to establish complete democracy in the Soviet Union—eventually. In their own view, indeed, that hope was already better than half-realized. The formula for complete democracy, they liked to argue, was comparable to that of water: two parts of the hydrogen of economic equality, to one of the oxygen of political liberty. Well, they had already provided the first—and that was more than any capitalist government had ever done. As for the second, they would provide that too—as soon as it seemed safe. And this promise was more than a ruse. From all indications, the Bolsheviks really meant it. Moreover, had they themselves been less fallible, and the world around them less hostile, quite conceivably they might have carried it out.

But it is vain to speculate on what *might* have happened. All we know is what did happen, and it amounted to this: the trend in the technique of government was thrown into reverse. Thus far the prevailing tendency in politics had been toward more and more freedom. Ever since at least the Eighteenth Century there had been increasing revolt against the ageless dogma that some people were fitted to rule and the rest must necessarily be ruled. Now that dogma reasserted itself—and not in the name of reaction, but revolution. Lenin insisted that only those men and women who had proved themselves worthy of enrolment in his Communist Party could possibly know how the country ought to be run. Therefore they had not merely the right but the absolute obligation to assume absolute dictatorial powers.

They did assume them. Moreover they managed to retain them. And the lesson was not lost on the world.

The War, it had been hoped, would make the whole world safe for democracy. Instead it made much of it ripe for tyranny. This was not evident at once. Most devotees of democracy were inclined to raise their brows when they first heard of the dictatorship in Russia. After all, they sighed, what else could one expect in so backward a country? But before long strange reports began to come out of Italy, and then the sighs turned to gasps. Was it possible . . . ?

Yes, it was possible, all right. Proof? It actually happened. Italy, which had had a parliamentary government ever since its rebirth as a nation, had suddenly succumbed to a dictatorship.

This is how it came about. Of all the victors, none emerged from the War with less glory or loot than did Italy. Perhaps that was no more than just, since no country had gone into the War with less honor or passion. Nevertheless the adventure had cost Italy dearly—fifteen billion lire and seven hundred thousand lives—and when the time came for the spoils to be divided, she felt she deserved her promised share. She did not get it.

That made her people sore. Their hearts were sore, and also their bellies. The country had been poor enough even before the War; now it was virtually bankrupt. Commerce and industry were at a standstill, and the cities were crowded with jobless men. Agriculture had been neglected, and now the peasants roamed the marshes for food. Before long the currency began to lose its value, and then the government lost all prestige. Italy seemed ready to sink into chaos. "The sheeted dead did squeak and gibber in the Roman streets."

It was probably no more than a passing phase, but there were many in the land who would not wait to find out. Roughly these were of two kinds: dislocated workers looking for jobs, and demobilized soldiers spoiling for trouble. Had the two combined, Italy might possibly have gone the way of Russia. But they did not combine, so the country went a way all its own.

That way became known as Fascism, and it was blazed by a tragi-comic character named Benito Mussolini. He was the son of a violent village Marxist, and had been born in 1883, the year Karl Marx died. His childhood was bitter, and the taste remained with him throughout his life. As he himself wrote years later:

> "Poor, dreadfully poor was my home, poor and wretched my whole existence. Where could I learn tenderness? At school, in the cloister, in the world? Nowhere! Why then should people wonder that I am taciturn, secretive, harsh, and stern?"

He managed to pick up enough education to become a country school teacher, but his weakness for brawling and incendiary speech soon forced him into a career of vagabondage. For ten years he wandered about as a political agitator, eating regularly only when in jail. Finally, at the age of twenty-nine, he became the editor of a socialist newspaper in Milan.

Comrade Mussolini was ill-informed but opinionated, unsound but vehement, so he quickly attained wide fame as a radical journalist. He attacked capitalism, nationalism, imperialism, monarchism, clericalism, and militarism with exemplary comprehensiveness and abuse. When the War broke out, he was all against Italy's going in. As late as September 1, 1914, he waved his clenched fist at the "bourgeois war-mongers." Then, four days later, he suddenly joined them.

When next seen he was editing a newspaper of his own. He had become an all-fustian jingo; so much so that when his country did finally enter the War, he was nearly one of the first to enlist. But a bout of stomach trouble followed by an accident in a rear trench forced him to accept an early discharge. "I take my place as a fighter in my newspaper office," he then declared.

The Armistice found him still clinging to that battlement, but with guns shooting straight into the void. Now the conflict raged within Italy, and he could not decide which side to join. First he thought the workers stood the better chance. They were launching strikes and riots throughout the land. In the industrial north they were actually seizing the factories, and in the agricultural south they were demanding division of the great estates. But, perhaps because the masses had no Lenin to lead them, their assault soon bogged down; whereupon Mussolini's mind became clear. ("I am like the beasts," he once said of himself. "I smell the weather before it changes.") He sensed that the people on top and the people on the bottom were deadlocked. The issue therefore lay with the people in the middle. These were the small businessmen, the salaried managers, the minor professional people, the white-collar workers, and the farmers who still owned a little land: what Marx had called the "petty bourgeoisie." That class had long cherished a will to power, but had not known how to assert it. Mussolini decided to show the way.

He already had a small following of patriotic young roustabouts who hawked his sheet on street-corners and in cafés. To these he now added fresh recruits from among the demobilized soldiers, dressed them all in formidable-looking black shirts, and organized them into *fasci*, "bunches." He gave them an ancient insignia consisting of a bundle of rods tied around a battle-axe, and ordered them to salute with outstretched arm as in ancient Rome. Then he turned them loose to slug the "red workers" and curse the "war profiteers."

The government lacked not alone the might but also the will to intervene, and this encouraged the "bunches" to grow increasingly violent. Finally, in October, 1922, Mussolini ordered them to march on Rome and demand political recognition. He himself, though their *Duce* ("leader"), remained behind. He barricaded himself in his newspaper office in Milan, and directed the "offensive" by telephone. Not until word reached him that all was safe did he himself start to march—by Pullman car.

The next morning, clad in his black shirt, he presented himself before the King. "I beg your Majesty to forgive me for appearing in uniform," he puffed. "I have just come from a bloodless battle which had to be fought." The King, a bewildered little man, gave a bewildered little smile, and formally appointed Mussolini his Prime Minister.

In 1912, Comrade Mussolini had written: "Imagine an Italy in which thirty-six millions should all think the same . . . and you would have a kingdom of utter imbecility." Ten years had elapsed since then, and his mind had apparently changed. What he had once considered imbecility, now impressed him as the only sanity.

His first objective was to imitate Lenin, and set himself up as absolute dictator. This proved not over-difficult, since he too had a pack of henchmen sworn to do his bidding. The Fascists in Italy, like the Bolsheviks in Russia, formed no more than a tiny minority of the population; but they were hand-picked, disciplined, and determined. In addition, they had the guns—right from the start they had infiltrated into the army—so they were irresistible. Officially and otherwise the Fascist Party became the "Black Guard" of the realm.

Mussolini took over completely. He smashed the trade unions and thus routed his former comrades, the "Marxian" socialists. He outlawed Freemasonry, and thus closed a vital channel through which the "Liberal" capitalists had been accustomed to wielding influence. He ordered the priests to stay out of politics, and thus spiked any chance of effective opposition by the Church. He made Fascist house-organs of all the newspapers, personal mouth-organs of all broadcasting stations, turned Parliament into a sounding-board, and the King into a ventriloquist's dummy. He set out to regiment public speech, private trade, personal habits, and communal traits. Whoever dared protest was clubbed, jailed, banished, or murdered. "To remove rebels from circulation," said Mussolini, "is merely national prophylactics." In this, as in so much else, he was still imitating Lenin. "There are those," Mussolini thundered, "who must be crushed by the truth before they can understand it."

The Duce's "truth," however, was quite unlike that of the Bolshevik leader. He was not interested in creating a new world, but in reviving an old country. He yearned to turn the clock back and restore the Roman Empire.

But such a miracle could not be accomplished by force alone. Suasion was necessary. Accordingly Mussolini resorted to the tactics of the ancient Roman demagogues, and set out to give the rabble "bread and circuses."

He found it easy to provide the circuses. He was a born actor, and knew just how to stage a show. He organized monster patriotic gatherings which he usually addressed from balconies, thus lending height to his chunky frame, and bringing out all the massiveness of his prognathous jaw. He caused his likeness—usually set in a fierce scowl—to be displayed in shop-windows, pasted on hoardings, flashed on cinema screens, and hung in all public buildings. He ordered that the first spelling-lesson for children should be devoted to the text: "The Duce is always right." He further ordered that all loyal citizens should swear allegiance by reciting this credo:

I believe in the State, apart from which I can never attain full manhood.

I believe in the Sacred Destiny of Italy, which is to exert the greatest spiritual influence on the world.

I believe I must obey the Duce, for apart from obedience there is no well-being.

He encouraged the young and the old to keep marching, singing, saluting, and obeying, and thus sought to make all life one round of joy.

But the task of providing bread proved more difficult. Having seized power on the excuse that Italy must be saved from communism, he could hardly turn around and adopt the communist economy. At the same time he realized it was impossible to save the country by means of old-fashioned capitalism. He therefore improvised an economy of his own which, if neither fish nor fowl, was at least good red herring. He called it the "Corporative State," and its apparent intent was to distract capital as well as labor by diverting both from their own wants to those of the nation. The rich were allowed to keep their property, but with the stipulation that the nation had first claim on the profit. The poor were expected to keep their place, but on the understanding that the nation would raise it to glory. As for the in-between people, these were going to run the nation. Italy's government was to be a Dictatorship of the Salariat.

Here was something new under the sun. Thus far it had been taken for granted that the bourgeoisie could be overthrown only to raise the proletariat to power. Conservatives and radicals alike had believed that a modern economy must necessarily be either capitalistic or socialistic. Now a third possibility had emerged: a nationalistic economy. What that foreboded, Mussolini himself did not know—yet. He was essentially a careerist, and worried more about the *how* of his going than the *where*. Having flung himself on the bosom of Fame, his fiercest concern was to hang on.

And this which was true of Mussolini, was equally true of his imitators. For he acquired many imitators before long. In one country after another wilful men set themselves up as dictators: Kemal Pasha in Turkey, Horthy in Hungary, Primo de Rivera in Spain, Pilsudski in Poland, Smetona in Lithuania. . . . And not any of these little Caesars knew where they were going. They were just going.

And more and more of the world went with them.

XXXI. STILL THE MACHINE GROWS

OLITICALLY the world had begun to retrogress. There were more frontiers now to divide mankind, and behind most of them there was less freedom, less independence, less understanding. In one country after another men seemed deliberately bent on turning back the clock of civilization.

As yet, however, all they moved was the hands. They had not thought—yet—to reach behind the dial to stop the works. Therefore, though the world retrogressed politically, it still continued to forge ahead industrially. The War had wound up the springs of production, and enormously enlarged the wheels. The ravening demand for more and still more armaments had forced all the advanced countries to expand their factories to the limit. Even then they had not been able to produce enough, so they had had to recruit the help of the backward ones. Spain was induced to open up her mines. Egypt and India were encouraged to build modern mills. Giant processing plants were started in Malaya, Bolivia, Alaska, and Manchuria. Industrialism exploded and littered the entire globe with machinery.

And this machinery continued to function after the War ended. It even expanded then, for that was the way of machinery, always to feed on its own growth. By 1928 Japan was producing five times as much cotton print as in 1914, six times as much steel, and seven times as many woolen goods. China had 3,500,000 textile spindles by 1930, and India nearly 8,500,000. The industrial population of South Africa more than tripled. Palestine, where production had formerly been confined almost entirely to religious relics, suddenly developed into a land flowing with orange juice and potash.

That was good. Not perfect, certainly, but at any rate good. Immediately it might cause severe affliction, robbing the old industrial countries of their established markets, and blighting many former agrarian ones with the Black Life. Immediately it might—and did—provoke vast dislocation and distress. But ultimately it gave promise of bringing plenty to regions which in the past had never known anything but want. That was indisputably good.

And another thing happened now which was even better. Industrialism did not merely expand; it immensely improved.

Its whole character matured, and so prodigiously that observers began to say a "third" Industrial Revolution had got under way. The first had been ushered in by the clattering steam-engine, the second by the spluttering electric-battery, and now the purring dynamo was heading the parade.

All the established sources of energy—water, wind, fire, and lightning—were being harnessed with a new effectiveness. Hydro-electric plants were being erected which could feed power to motors hundreds of miles away. Single turbines were built that were capable of yielding as much energy as three million men straining with all their might. The gasoline engine was brought to a new stage of perfection, and so was the oil-burning Diesel engine. An accounting made in 1930 revealed that every human being on earth had been invested with the power of four hundred slaves.

Yet even more striking than this increment of physical energy was the accession of mechanical efficiency. The dream of many an early inventor became realized at last: machines appeared that worked almost automatically. Human beings needed merely to press buttons, and steel forged itself, dough turned into bread, ships steered precise courses, cows gave their milk, and eggs nestled tenderly in crates. Raw wool fed into one end of a machine was washed by it, combed, fluffed, spun into yarn, dyed, woven into cloth, cut into lengths, rolled into bolts, wrapped, labelled, and stacked ready for shipment. Raw tobacco was similarly metamorphosed into packaged cigarettes, and ambiguous foodstuffs into canned soup or bottled sandwich-spread.

Any number of once complicated, arduous, and monotonous tasks had somehow become magically swift and simple. Man was now removed by two degrees from the actual burdens of toil. In the beginning he had had to wield tools, and then he had had to tend machinery. Now motors and photo-electric cells did both. Moreover, the motors never wearied, nor did the "electric eyes" ever wander or blink.

The processes of industry began to take on a new nature. They grew not merely more efficient than ever in the past; they became hushed, clean, almost dreamlike. That was what helped to make them so much more efficient. The great technicians had always known this, but the little industrialists had never believed them. The latter had imagined that cleanliness was a luxury, and silence a sign of impotence. James Watt tells us—

"I have once or twice trimmed the engine to end its stroke gently . . . but Mr. —— cannot sleep unless it seems quite furious. . . . Horrible noise serves to convey great ideas of power to the ignorant, who seem to be no more taken with modest merit in an engine than in a man."

But now the ignorant were no longer in command of industry. Though they might still claim to own the machines, they had long since ceased to run them. That task had been taken over by salaried experts, and these were in a position at last to enforce their own standards. The one thing they most abominated was waste, any kind of waste—waste motion, waste noise, waste smoke, waste space. See, for example, what feats of thrift they performed in connection with refuse. They gathered up the cottonseed which had formerly been thrown away at the gin, and used it to produce felt, rope, flour, lard, writing paper, salad oil, fertilizer, face cream, roofing tar, laxatives, and nitroglycerin. They took the maize that had once been thrown to the hogs and turned it into oil, soap, glue, laundry starch, breakfast food, tanner's sugar, and—again!—nitroglycerin.

All that was good—to a degree. Unhappily, however, the

degree was insufficient. The improvement was too largely confined to the *processes* of industry rather than its *purposes.* The men who wrought the improvement were interested solely in technology, not sociology. They were just as eager to increase the production of nitroglycerin as soap. A good plant, in their eyes, was merely one that worked well, regardless of whether it produced mustard plasters or mustard gas. They were scientists, they insisted, not world-savers. Theirs not to reason why, theirs but to do—and earn their salaries.

That was, of course, a tragic limitation, and it contributed eventually to world disaster. The technologists were penny wise but pound foolish. Immediately, however, their penny-wisdom brought rich rewards. For one thing, it increased the supply of goods. For another, it decreased the blight of squalor. For a third, it created a new kind of loveliness. Boiler-rooms began to take on the air of cathedral naves; machine-shops acquired the look of well-run laboratories. In part that was because there was no longer any effort at prettification, no longer any passion for sticking iron posies and curlicues on machinery. Now the commanding urge was to simplify, to let the Machine be itself, to let it fulfil its function without apology or pretense. The gain was twofold. Now the Machine was able to become a thing of beauty as well as a source of goods.

Production billowed like smoke from a volcano, and the whole earth filled up with merchandise. This was due not alone to the existence of more machines, but also to the presence of more people to tend them. Women had entered industry in unprecedented numbers ever since the War. In addition, thanks to the declining death-rate, a larger proportion of the population was adult. The world-production of coal and iron and silk almost doubled between 1910 and

1930. Every other commodity from aluminum to zinc increased in abundance. Meat became more plentiful, fruit and vegetables more variegated. The yield of wheat leapt from 3,250,000 bushels in 1910 to 4,500,000 in 1930.

And what was true of raw-stuffs was truer still of manufactured wares. Completely new products appeared on the market: synthetic fabrics, plastics, metals, lacquers, and dyes. At the same time familiar products acquired a novel charm and cheapness. Clothing increased in quality as well as quantity. Mass-production brought the styles of Paris within the means of typists and shoe-clerks' wives. Housing improved, and sanitary facilities began to flush the world. There was actually a beginning of slum clearance in several lands. The automobile became commonplace all over the globe, and also the tractor, the airplane, the telephone, the cinema, and finally the radio. Arabs began to cross the desert in air-conditioned busses, and Thibetans learnt to tune in Moscow on their crystal sets. Books multiplied, microscopes multiplied, vaccines, insecticides, spectacles, safety razors, tooth brushes, sewing machines, and refrigerators multiplied. Contraceptive aids, those supreme labor-saving devices, began to be produced so cheaply that they found a market even in China.

At last the promise born with the Machine was being surely realized. Thus far the world had seen no more than the first faint glimmer of the Day of Plenty.

Now the sun was out.

XXXII. THE BIG BOOM

HE sun was out, and it warmed one land especially—the United States. The First World War had served it much as the Napoleonic Wars had once served Great Britain. The Americans were able to turn the apple of discord into hard cider and go on a spree. Thus far they had always been on the receiving end in their commercial dealings with Europe—and had had to pay for it at heavy interest. Now the tables were turned. Not America but Europe had to do the buying and borrowing; and not Europe, but America, raked in the profits. Even before the United States came around to entering the War, it had already ceased to be a debtor nation. Eventually it became the world's record creditor.

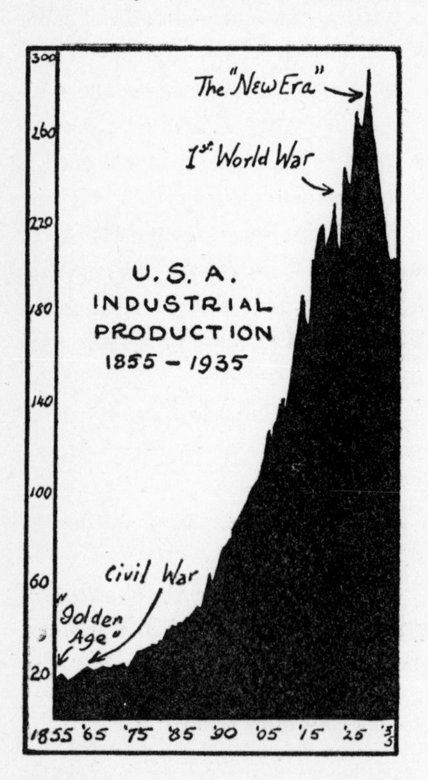

And it remained that. The country had not alone managed to collect the richest store of gold; it had also succeeded in erecting the mightiest hive of industry. This gave it an unbeatable advantage once a battle-battered Europe began to try to mend itself. The War Boom, after a sickening post-war slump, gave way to a peace boom. Europe needed food, Europe needed clothing, Europe needed machinery, Europe needed credit. America sold her food, America sold her clothing, America sold her machinery, America gave her credit.

That was how America's peace boom got under way—on a gust of foreign trade. Once launched, however, it caught a domestic wind, and then it went higher than a kite. That wind was caused by many factors, but the chief was probably the explosion of the automobile industry. A crotchety manufacturer whose name has already been mentioned, Henry Ford, got the notion that the surest way to profit by the "horseless carriage" was to make it not bigger and fancier, but simpler and cheaper. As early as 1908 he decided to concentrate on a single model which could be assembled out of standard parts with a minimum amount of fumbling and fitting. To speed up the process—and speed was his abiding obsession—he borrowed an idea from the Chicago meat-packers. They used an overhead trolley to swing the carcasses down a line of butchers, so he introduced a "conveyor belt" to carry the automobile parts to his mechanics. That saved time, and time was money. By 1914 Henry Ford was able to turn out 700 cars a day. Even then he was not satisfied. He kept improving and extending the assembly lines until by 1922 he was producing 4,000 cars a day, and by 1924 as many as 7,000.

Other automobile makers began to imitate him. By 1929 one firm in Milwaukee was turning out a complete chassis every eight seconds, fully 10,000 in a day. That year the total output of automobiles reached a peak of 5,000,000 units.

This alone would have been enough to create a surge of prosperity, for it stimulated production in a hundred auxiliary industries: tin, rubber, petroleum, glass, timber, upholstery, and first-aid kits. Roads had to be built, and also garages, gasoline stations, hot-dog stands, hotels, motels, and morgues. Mechanics had to be supplied with overalls, insurance agents with calling-cards, and traffic-cops with throat lozenges.

Yet even greater than the direct effect of the automobile itself was the influence exerted by the way in which it was manufactured. Ford made America "mass-production conscious." Every up-and-coming industrialist sought to standardize his product, and turn it out on an assembly line. Every conceivable article from a pin to a locomotive began to be fabricated with the aid of conveyor belts. The United States began to wallow in something no country had ever achieved before: actual *abundance*. By 1929 it was able to boast nearly as many automobiles as families, almost as many telephones, twice as many daily newspapers, five times as many monthly magazines. There were enough shoe factories to make seven pairs of shoes for every man, woman, and child in the land. The tobacco factories were actually producing 97,000,000,000 cigarettes a year.

Americans had been proud of their productivity in 1914, for their industrial plant had been able to turn out twenty-three billion dollars' worth of merchandise that year. By 1929 it was turning out more than three times as much.

The merchandise was not all good, of course. On the contrary, some of it was harmful, more was tawdry, and much was worthless. There were worms in many of the canned foods, toxins in most of the patent medicines. The cheaper furniture was held together by glue, and the cheaper textiles by starch. Most of the newspapers were full of lies, many of the magazines were full of filth, and almost all of the movies were full of imbecility. More often than not the shoes pinched, the shirts shrank, the clothes shredded in a season, and the stockings tore in a day.

Nevertheless they sold. The very shoddiness of such wares helped to make them sell. People were forced to keep buying because so little that they bought would last. And of course there were other compulsions. Advertising goaded people to want things, more and more things. Poets like Stephen Vincent Benét might lament that—

"... when the last moon-shiner buys his radio,
And the last, lost, wild-rabbit of a girl
Is civilized with a mail-order dress,
Something will pass that was American
And all the movies will not bring it back."

But those who had goods to sell were not interested in bringing anything back. Their one aim was to push everything forward. That was why they advertised.

They persuaded people to replace not alone the articles that didn't last, but even those that could and did. This was not too difficult: the sellers merely extended the fashion-craze. No matter how durable an object might be, invariably a way was found to make it swiftly obsolete. An automobile that would run at all had to be built stoutly enough to run for six or eight years. So the body-styles were changed annually. Any radio that would really work was likely to keep on working until even Amos 'n' Andy ran out of breath. So the cabinets were built differently each season.

A thousand stratagems were employed to stimulate people to buy, stratagems as old as Christmas and as new as Mother's Day. And people bought.

Not that they had the cash. How could they have the cash when the bulk of them were workers? True, wages had gone up somewhat, especially in the mass-production industries. As early as 1914, Henry Ford had astounded the world by announcing that henceforth the least he would pay any of his employees was $5 a day. By 1926 he had raised the base-rate to $7. But the work was seasonal, and unless his employees could find other jobs when he laid them off, their earnings barely averaged $150 a month. That, obviously, was not enough to provide cash for luxuries. It was not even enough for ordinary necessities. A government survey re-

vealed that in 1929 a "standard" Ford worker's family wa
able to spend *throughout the entire year*—

$7.69 for amusements
4.23 for laundry
1.66 for literature
1.08 for domestic help
9.62 for religion

Yet such a worker was receiving relatively high wages
The average industrial laborer did not earn more than $10
a month during 1929, and the average white-collar worke
only $117. In July of that year—the best month—the aver
age farm laborer earned barely $50, no board included
Between 1919 and 1927 all the farm families in the countr
had an average monthly income of $63 in cash. In 1929 full
a third of the entire population of the country was livin
on the level of bare subsistence.

Nevertheless goods got sold. How? On credit. What ha
once been the prerogative of the rich became the privileg
of the poorest of the poor now. Almost anybody could bu
almost anything on the "installment plan." And almos
everybody did. The idea of buying goods on the basis of "a
dollar down and the rest when they catch you" proved irresistibly alluring. Consequently, although wages went u
barely 12% during the seven fat years beginning in 1922
purchasing power went up more than 22%. People bought
not alone houses on installments, but permanent waves, ob-
stetrical operations, even funerals. It meant, of course, that
they paid high prices, and steeped themselves deep in debt.
But what did they care? "The Lord is my shepherd," they
sang, "I should worry!" Or else they snickered: "Wouldn't
it be funny if we could afford to live the way we do?"

And thus the land began to heave and rock with what was
said to be prosperity.

The effect, naturally, was soon felt abroad, especially in Europe. Even Germany, the stricken heart of Europe, started to pulse again with what some people took to be prosperity. And there too the secret of it all was credit.

Germany was supposed to pay fabulous reparations for the damage she had done in "causing" the War. These sums were supposed to go to the Allies, who were then supposed to pass them on in payment of their debts to America. But how was Germany to provide the sums in the first place? The War had worn her out, and the peace had left her prostrate. Between economic depletion, political dissension, and monetary inflation, she was reduced to complete bankruptcy. Obviously there was only one way to put her in a position to hand out cash, and that was to give her credit. So it was given.

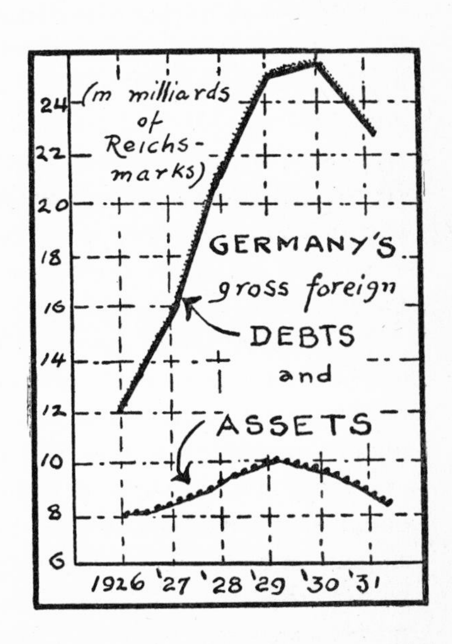

England, Holland, and Switzerland gave part, and the United States gave the rest. It was a case of handouts-across-the-sea. Between 1924 and 1928 Germany received some six billion marks in credit, and returned—mark this!—only five and a half billion in cash. Immediately, therefore, she seemed to profit by the whole arrangement.

Immediately everybody seemed to profit. Germany got credit with which to renovate her factories, France and her satellites got cash with which to expand *their* factories, and the United States got encouragement—at 6%—to advance more credit. It was all mad, of course. What would happen once the process of renovation and expansion was complete, and production got into full swing? There would be no place to sell. The domestic markets would be glutted because the masses within each country would be too poor to buy. Moreover, the foreign markets would be closed because most countries had walled themselves in with tariff barriers. Eventually, therefore, the borrowers would no longer be able to incur new debts, for they would be failing to pay the interest on their old ones. So then the chief lender, Uncle Sam, would have to turn into Uncle Shylock, and the whole crazy merry-go-round would inevitably collapse. Anyone with the wit and will to look ahead could see that that was as sure as . . . shooting.

But very few people had that much wit, and even fewer the will. Why worry about the future? A good capitalist was supposed to let the future take care of itself. Sufficient unto the day was the profit thereof.

So those in charge of the merry-go-round let it go faster and faster. More speed created not alone greater profit but also a stouter illusion of security. It increased the giddiness and thus lessened the temptation to try to think. Even those who were paid to think, the statesmen and economists, even they seemed reluctant to try. They preferred to go round and round with the world, and hope for the best.

This was true in every capitalist land, but most of all, of course, in the United States. There the giddiness grew so intense that people actually began to think it normal. They began to say a "New Era" had arrived. Henceforth there could never again be unemployment, misery, or class-conflict.

True, there were at least a million laborers still out of work in the country, two million families in distress, and never a day without strikes. But these were dismissed as passing phenomena. Between mass production, high wages, installment buying, and a sound Republican administration, this country was definitely assured of more and more prosperity with each new day.

Such things were not merely said; they were believed. Moreover, they were said and believed not merely by common folk, but by the most noted in the land. Even Mr. Herbert Hoover, already the Secretary of Commerce, and soon to be the President, solemnly declared, "The poorhouse is vanishing from among us." The idea that prosperity had been made permanent became a national dogma, and all right-thinking citizens felt it their duty to gamble on it. Of course, they did not call it gambling. They called it "investing in the future." But by any other name, it was still gambling. Some people gambled in real estate, others in dreamy mining ventures, but most gambled in registered stocks and bonds. Wall Street became the National Shrine, and literally millions rushed to lay their offerings on its counters.

The rich and the learned, the righteous and the worldly-wise, all began to worship the Golden Bull. Businessmen took to spending more time in brokers' offices than in their own factories or stores. Union officials grew to find the Dow-Jones averages more enthralling even than the baseball scores. Window-cleaners eavesdropped on financiers for rumors of "pools." Chorus girls sacrificed what was left of their virtue for "inside tips." Shopkeepers, schoolteachers, parsons, and widowed mothers took their life-savings out of the bank to "play the market." People mortgaged their homes and borrowed on their insurance to get more and more money to buy "securities." They borrowed on the "securities" themselves, paying the brokers as much as 9% interest in order to be able to hold shares that had never paid even 5% dividends.

For those people were not thinking of the dividends. Most of them did not expect to hold their shares long enough to get the dividends. They were buying for the rise. Stocks were going up. The "bulls" had broken loose, and it looked as though one need merely grab a tail to get a free ride to Eldorado. Every day, every hour, every minute the stocks kept going up. Not all of them, of course, but most of them, or nearly most. Radio Corporation of America, after knocking about for years at a few dollars a share, leapt to $94 in 1928, and $549 in 1929.

That was the great year—1929. By then every significant index pointed to trouble. Ominous things were already happening in Europe: unemployment was mounting, demagogues were running wild, and governments were finding it more and more difficult to meet their obligations. Even in America the ground was beginning to crack. Most of the billions that had gone into the stock-market had been used to create "capital goods"—that is, to develop factories, mines, and other productive enterprises. Now that those enterprises were beginning to fulfil their purpose, the country was heaping up with "consumer goods." But where were the consumers? Who was going to buy all the automobiles that crammed the warehouses, all the skirts and shirts and shovels and shoes that piled up in the stores?

Purchasing power was not keeping up with production; not nearly. Wages had been rising barely 1½% a year, whereas the output of goods had been swelling at the rate of 4% a year. To be sure, the wage-earners could buy on the installment plan—but not indefinitely. It was all very well to let people get up to their necks in debt, but if they went deeper than that, they were no longer able to pay through the nose. That was why there was a necessary limit to consumer credit—and the limit had already been reached. The proof of it was that merchandise already purchased on consumer credit was beginning increasingly to return. The buyers were failing to meet the monthly payments.

That was a storm-warning, and some who recognized it knew enough to run to cover. They dumped their stocks and ducked into cellars made tight and snug with cash or government bonds. But the few that behaved thus were subjected to general ridicule. They were called fools, old fogies, fellows without faith, fellows without vision, fellows too dumb to understand that a "New Era" had arrived.

The storm-warnings multiplied. Unemployment kept increasing, and so did the case-loads of the charity organizations. Merchants who still found time to look at their shelves began to notice that they were not emptying nearly fast enough. But did Wall Street take heed? It did not. The Republican Party had just been returned to office for the third successive term, and Wall Street knew that the Republican Party was the "Party of Prosperity." Mr. Herbert Hoover had been elected the President, and Wall Street knew that Mr. Herbert Hoover was a millionaire and sound. So why worry?

Stocks continued to rise. All through the summer of 1929 they continued to rise higher and higher. American Can rose to 160, to 170, to 181½. New York Central climbed to 250, yet went on climbing. General Electric hit 396. Too high, brother? Don't be silly! Look at Morgan—he's still buying! Look at Rockefeller, Vanderbilt, Astor, Whitney—they're all buying! And they're on the inside! They *know!* So buy, brother! Buy!

Brother did buy, and sister too. Fish peddlers brought their smelly dollar bills to the brokers to buy "sump'n you tink good, Boss!" Waitresses pooled their dimes and rushed to the brokers to take a "flyer." Everybody bought, and stock quotations rose higher and higher. They rose higher . . . still higher . . . and yet still higher.

And then—

XXXIII. THE GREAT CRASH

THEN came the Deluge. Thunder pealed all through September, 1929, but the great wise men on Wall Street—and even more the little wise guys on Main Street—refused to take heed. The sudden and recurrent breaks in the stock market were dismissed as "technical adjustments." There were further and sharper breaks in early October; but still the speculators remained bullish. One of the high priests at the

National Shrine, Mr. Charles E. Mitchell of the National City Bank, looked up from his altar and pontificated: "The American Markets generally are now in a healthy condition."

Instantly prices rallied—but only to sag again the next week. On October 23 there was a break that carried some stocks down more than ninety points. Knees began to quake then, and faces grayed. The next morning a number of stocks could find no buyers at any price, and then even the high priests became alarmed. They had advanced more than six and a half billion dollars to the speculators. Should they call in those loans and start a panic? Or should they sit tight and risk bankruptcy? A conference was hastily summoned in the Holy of Holies—the directors' room of J. P. Morgan & Company—and throughout the land anxious hearts pounded louder than the tickers. Finally, at 1:15 P.M., word came of the decision. Mr. Richard Whitney, then floor-operator for the Morgan company—later floor-sweeper in Sing Sing—strode into the Exchange and bid for a block of U. S. Steel at twelve points above the current price. Salvation! Immediately stocks ceased to fall. Some even began to climb.

Not for long, however. The public, reassured by the miracle on Black Thursday, started to buy again. But those who had worked the miracle began to sell. Quietly, gently, they eased themselves of their burdens. Four days this continued, four fevered days during which all who were supposed to be in the know talked "long," and all who were behind the show sold "short."

Then, on October 29, it happened.

The storm finally broke, and it tore the bottom right out from under the market. The rush of selling orders jammed the tickers, choked the telephone wires, wrecked the teletype machines. Within half an hour of the opening of the Exchange, more than a million shares had been dumped on the counters. By noon the volume of trading had passed the eight million mark. When the closing gong tolled the end of that stark raving day, nearly sixteen and a half million shares had changed hands. The National Shrine had become the Wailing Wall.

The Big Bull Market had collapsed. The vaunted New Era was no more. What had happened so often before, had happened once again: having begun by losing their heads, the businessmen had ended by losing their shirts. And even their hides, this time. The Panic of 1837 had been bad, that of 1857 even worse, and in 1875 and 1893 others had come which had proved still worse. Yet all those four together did not equal the one that now befell the United States. The investment structure became a shambles. What had so long been called "securities," became mere paper flying before the wind.

At first all authoritative voices insisted on screaming that there was no cause for alarm. "Don't sell America short!" they screamed. The President naturally refrained from screaming; he spoke calmly, as became one in so august an office. But what Mr. Hoover said calmly might just as well have been screamed, for it was no less delusory, and no more effective. Time and again he cleared his throat, moistened his lips, and shakily asserted: "We have now passed the worst. . . . Prosperity is just around the corner." But where was the corner?

The panic deepened and spread. During 1931 alone some 2000 banks had to close their doors; 28,000 business firms went bankrupt. That same year 39% of the largest corporations in the country lost money, and half of the major railroads went into receivership.

And conditions grew even worse in 1932.

People ceased to call it merely a panic; it had become The Depression. A corner had been reached at last, but behind it lurked prostration. Goods would not move. No matter at what price they were offered, they would not move.

By January, 1931, wheat was selling at the lowest price in two hundred and fifty years. Nevertheless, millions of poor people failed to eat more bread. By the end of that year the wholesale price of textiles was down 32%. Nevertheless those millions failed to buy new clothes. It was not that they did not want such things. They wanted them so badly that they were ready to steal them. But they could not buy them. They had always lacked cash, and now the merchants would not give them credit. How could one give credit to people who had no jobs?

For unemployment had increased appallingly. Even before October, 1929, there were already some 2,000,000 jobless people in the country. A year later there were 4,000,000; two years later, 7,000,000; three years later, 13,000,000. The national economy went into a tailspin. More unemployment meant less purchasing power, and therefore still less manufacturing, and therefore still more unemployment, and therefore . . . By the end of 1932 there were 35% fewer people at work in the factories than in 1929. To make matters worse, those who did have jobs were getting lower wages. Factory payrolls had fallen off by 54%. To make matters still worse, agricultural income, which had been low even during the Boom, sank actually lower by some 57%. The net result was that common purchasing power was reduced by some thirty billion dollars—approximately as much as the country had spent to fight the World War.

That was why goods failed to move. The masses lacked the means to get at them. Millions had to spend all they could earn or beg merely to lay hold of enough food to keep flesh on their bones. If they had anything left over—often even if they hadn't—they helped themselves to liquor and tobacco. Of all the major industries, only liquor—despite that it was illegal—and tobacco seemed able to prosper.

Evil days fell on the land, evil days and months and years. Breadlines formed in the cities, and foul squatter settlements—"Hoovervilles," they were ironically called—gathered like scabs over the city dumps. Dispossessed farmers sold their plows and mules, piled their families into old Fords, and started wandering in search of a place where there was food. A horde of ex-soldiers marched on Washington and encamped there in shacks until driven off by fire and tear-gas. Skilled workers became hoboes; bookkeepers became hoboes; teachers, lawyers, even former bankers became hoboes. Boys just out of high school, and girls who dressed like boys, began to rove about in packs. Crime increased everywhere; gangsterism broke all bounds. Evil days fell on the land.

And it was even worse abroad. A good deal of the world had been living off American capital ever since the War. Eleven billion dollars had come pouring out of the United States between 1917 and 1924, and another three billion dollars between 1924 and 1928. Most of the money had gone to Europe, where it had been used first to set the economy back on its feet, and then to keep it moving. Once this support was withdrawn, only one thing could happen.

Europe's economy collapsed.

In a sense it was dragged down, for the Americans did not simply stop lending money to Europe; they began to demand that what had already been borrowed should be returned. They called in their short-term loans, and asked for the interest on the long-term ones. Moreover, they wanted payment in cash. They would not take goods. They already had more goods than they knew what to do with. They wanted gold.

For a while they got gold. But after a year the supply began to give out in Central Europe, and then the situation grew critical. By May 1931 the chief bank in Vienna began to totter, and its collapse threatened to drag the entire nation into bankruptcy. The German banks, being heavily involved in Austria's economy, rushed to the rescue. This, however, left them so weakened that they in turn began to cave in. The British banks struggled to shore them up, only to weaken themselves in further turn. All Europe teetered on the brink of financial chaos. The whole world teetered there.

At the last moment President Hoover took it on himself to propose a year's moratorium on international debts. Too late. In July every bank in Germany had to close its doors. In September Great Britain had to refuse to honor its notes in gold. By the end of 1931 fourteen other nations—among them Sweden, Japan, Siam, Chile, Persia—were off the gold standard.

Half the world had gone over the brink.

The blame was laid, of course, at the door of the United States. Though this country had ceased to demand gold, it was still refusing to buy goods. Formerly it had been the world's largest customer for raw materials, and the second largest for manufactured wares. But now, with the domestic markets glutted, and the foreign ones choked, importation necessarily had to decline. By the end of 1931 the United States was importing less than a third as much as in 1928. That meant unemployment in the tin mines in Malaya, the silk mills in Japan, the rubber groves in Java, the coffee plantations in Brazil. It meant unemployment in the English woolen mills, the German dye works, the Czech glove factories, the Italian felt looms. By the summer of 1932 there were nearly 14,000,000 Europeans out of work. In Germany half the young men between the ages of 16 and 32 were without jobs.

The horror spread from the cities to the villages. Once the urban masses began to pull in their belts, food began to fall in price. Debt-ridden farmers found that interest charges which they had once been able to meet with a hundred bushels of wheat could not be settled now with less than two hundred. That drove them still deeper into debt, forced them to sell their cattle, finally left them bare. The word *mortgage* began to recover its original meaning—"death-grip." Peasants in China had to let their sons become bandits. In Japan they hired out their daughters as whores. In the Balkans they took to wearing animal skins and eating rats.

Despair stalked the earth. Men could not understand this evil that had befallen them. Had it been a famine, they would at least have seen a reason for their hunger. Had there been an earthquake, they would have known why they were shelterless. But food was rotting in the granaries and fields; everywhere shops and dwellings stood empty. Yet millions throughout the world were begging for a crust to eat, millions were sleeping under bridges or in the open fields.

Something had gone wrong. Everybody knew now that something had gone very wrong.

XXXIV. THE BEST LAID PLANS

HE Depression spread like a creeping paralysis over every land on earth—except one. That was the Soviet Union. Lenin had died and Trotsky was in exile, but the government they had established was still in power there. It was dominated now by a man named Dzhugashvili, *alias* Stalin: a hulking, heavy-footed, hammer-fisted Georgian who had been a faithful Bolshevik conspirator from his youth. During all the years that Lenin had directed the movement from Geneva, Stalin had carried on underground at home. He had raised funds—often with a gun—to send to Lenin, and had distributed the smuggled literature which those funds made possible. When the Revolution finally came in 1917, he received his reward. He was made a member of Lenin's cabinet.

Seven years later, when Lenin died, most people expected his mantle to fall on Trotsky. That is almost certainly what would have happened had the question been put to a general vote. But the decision rested with the Communist Party, not the people. It did not rest even with the whole Party, but merely with the head men; and among these Trotsky had many enemies. The chief of them was this Stalin, and he was as shrewd as he was implacable. He had all the gifts of a ward-boss, and he began to exercise them now on a continental scale. By dint of playing on the fears and jealousies of the other commissars, he got them to kick Trotsky down—and finally out.

That happened in 1927, and led swiftly to the inauguration of a new policy. Trotsky, like Lenin and most of the other leading Bolsheviks, had never ceased to believe that what had happened in Russia would soon have to happen elsewhere. Most of them had lived elsewhere during prolonged periods of exile, and no matter how far they had roamed, invariably they had run into revolutionists. Indeed, wrapped up as they were in the radical movement, they had rarely met any foreigners who were not revolutionists. From this they had naturally concluded that the whole world crawled with revolutionists, and that it waited only for a signal before all of them started turning every country upside down.

But Stalin believed otherwise. Only once in his life had he ever set foot outside the Russian Empire, and then it had been only to smuggle himself to Prague to attend a Party conclave. Being so ignorant of conditions abroad, he was less mistaken about them. Peasant that he was, he had a peasant's ingrained conviction that foreign lands and foreign peoples must necessarily be completely unlike his own. And events had seemed to prove his conviction sound.

Despite all the fierce work and fiercer talk of the Comintern, no other country had gone the way of Russia. Hungary had made a lurch in that direction in 1919, but only to be dragged right back. There had been a moment in 1923 when Germany almost lurched, and in 1926 when England was rumored to be almost on the point of lurching; but in both cases nothing had happened. Even China, after having supposedly sprawled over in 1925, somehow recoiled in 1927.

Stalin could draw only one deduction from those facts: the capitalist world was not yet ready for revolution. And from that deduction he could draw only one corollary: if the revolutionary economy was ever to prevail, it would have to be worked out first within the Soviet Union alone. So that became his program now: "Socialism in one country!"

After all, reasoned Stalin, the Soviet Union was certainly big enough a country. It comprised, according to common calculation, fully a sixth of the habitable globe. Its population was almost as vast as that of all North America, and its resources were said to be even vaster. True, the Soviet population was relatively backward, and the Soviet resources were largely buried. But surely there was a way to remedy that.

At worst, according to Stalin, there was the familiar bourgeois way. But Marx, he believed, had long since exposed the folly of that way, and so had history, even though tardily. Wherever a government had encouraged laissez-faire, wherever it had "let 'er go," there invariably the economy had sooner or later come a cropper. The bourgeois way did work, but not beyond a certain point—and even up to that point only in a blind, muddled, and destructive fashion.

Therefore Stalin was all for trying another way, the one that Marx had labelled "proletarian." Instead of relying on rampant individual enterprise, this insisted on employing only collective effort. Lenin had started out with that in mind in 1917, and though he had turned aside in 1921, he had never lost sight of his original intention. His New Economic Policy, with its grudging concessions to petty capitalism, had been no more than an enforced detour. Now, six years later, Stalin felt it was time to return to the high road.

Conditions in the Soviet Union were no longer so dire as they had been in 1921. The wreckage caused by the War and the Revolution had been partially repaired, and there was once more a little capital in the treasury. The New Economic Policy had laid its golden egg, so Stalin decided it was safe to liquidate that goose. All the country needed now, he believed, was a good big incubator to hatch out the egg and bring forth a new kind of gosling.

And it was going to be a better kind. Stalin was still enough of a Bolshevik to be absolutely insistent on that. The same was true of all his henchmen. Nature, they insisted, would have to be taken in hand, and made to do what it was told. No more barnyard anarchy, no more loose cackling and looser enterprise. The Soviet economy would be made to grow as no economy had ever grown before. Why? Because every detail of the growth was going to be thought out in advance. And not the economy alone, but also the culture. All life in the Soviet Union was going to be made to advance *according to a Plan*.

It was a fantastic idea, yet it was undertaken most grimly. A commission of some seven hundred experts was appointed to draw up and execute what was called the *Piatiletka*, the "Five-Year Plan"; and by 1928 the schedules were all complete, the maps and charts all drawn. Within the next five years, it was proudly announced, the output of coal and oil was going to be doubled, that of iron trebled, that of electricity quadrupled. The cost of production was going to be reduced by 33%, and the yield per man-hour increased by 100%. Fifty-five million acres—one fifth of all the peasant holdings—were going to be collectivized and tilled with the latest mechanical equipment. Common schooling was going to be so increased that illiteracy would be practically wiped out, and enough scientific institutes were going to be established to train all the needed technicians. In five years the Soviet Union was going to "take and overtake" the capitalist standard of living!

Naturally, there would be a price to pay. In money-terms the program would cost the equivalent of almost thirty-three billion dollars. And who would provide this sum? The workers, of course. Each worker would have to subscribe at least a week's wages to a State Loan with which to prime the pump, and thenceforth all would have to pump as they had never pumped before. That, after all, was how capital was created in the bourgeois lands. The only difference was that there the workers, though they did all of the actual pumping, got little of the profit. Here, on the contrary, they were going to get every penny of it.

Propaganda of that sort was hard to resist, especially when conducted as the Kremlin did conduct it. Every organ of publicity was in its hands, and all of them were made to blare the same tune unremittingly. Party orators were sent to harangue the workers in the factories, the peasants in the fields, the children in the schools. All the journalists were brought into the campaign; so were all the poets, all the novelists, all the actors on both stage and screen. The average man could no more resist the clamor than he could a tidal wave. It bowled him over, and set him threshing about in a sea of foamy enthusiasm.

There was some dissent, of course. In the fat grainlands of the Ukraine there was some very bitter dissent. Many of the abler, or luckier, or greedier peasants down there had waxed relatively rich under the New Economic Policy. These were naturally loath to give up their riches. They burned their crops and slaughtered their cattle rather than turn them over to the collectives. But that did them no good. If they were outspoken in their dissent they were shot or dragged away in chain-gangs. If they were merely sullen, they were driven into a corner of their lands and left to starve. That, to be sure, did not do the country much good either. Famine swept the grainlands, and the fetid breath of hunger returned to the cities. But it did at least crush the dissent.

Yet terror was only a minor factor in the success of the campaign. The major one was true zeal. It may not have been spontaneous zeal, but once kindled it flamed hot and wild. Millions of workers subscribed not a week's pay to the State Loan, but a month's and even more. Tens of millions worked not alone harder, but longer and for no extra money. They exhausted themselves merely to win a badge, or to carry a flag, or to get their names on honor-rolls. Men and women joined "shock-brigades," and competed to see which team could accomplish most in the least time. Production-contests were voluntarily arranged between factories, between farm groups, between railway lines, even between prison gangs. Work was made a form of sport, but with a touch of war desperation added, and also a touch of religious frenzy.

And prodigies were performed. The oil industry was well on its way to completing its five-year assignment at the end of two. Soon the automobile industry was almost equally ahead of schedule, and so was the farm-tool industry. The whole campaign advanced at such a pace that before long a demand arose for a new goal. More and more people began to urge that the Five-Year Plan be finished in four. Just who gave them that idea, they did not know, and the Kremlin saw no reason to tell them. But once they did get it, they were given no chance to let it go. Wherever they turned they were confronted with the slogan: "The Five-Year Plan in Four!" It was in all the newspapers, on all the hoardings, over every public building, inside every factory hall. People read it on the paper napkins in the restaurants, on the wooden benches in the parks, even on whitewashed walls of the latrines.

The campaign succeeded. Fast as people had worked before, now they worked even faster. Not better, of course. There was no time for that. Merely faster. Sweat poured from them as they toiled faster and faster. The miners sweated, the farmers sweated, the machinists, the clerks, and the bookkeepers sweated. All the rivers in Russia ran with sweat. And the Five-Year Plan *was* finished in four.

True, it was finished very imperfectly. If some industries over-fulfilled their assignments, others did not even approach them. And all achieved their results by forgetting all about quality. The clothes and boots were abominably made out of the most abominable materials. The household wares were as flimsy and crude as any Great Britain had misbegotten in the first days of her own unplanned industrial surge. Many of the machines were faultily constructed, and even more were wrecked by faulty mechanics. Some of the new factories began to crumble even before the scaffolding around them could be removed. One of the largest, an automobile factory at Nizhni-Novgorod that had been expected to turn out 144,000 cars a year, had to be closed within three months of its much-celebrated opening.

To make matters worse, not merely was quality overlooked, but quantity was overstated. Too-zealous bookkeepers had added where they should have subtracted, and multiplied where they should have added. Every total had to be heavily discounted to allow for error or warm-hearted fraud.

Nevertheless the achievement was stupendous. Nearly two-thirds of the agricultural land was collectivized and at least partially mechanized. School attendance was more than doubled, and illiteracy was about decimated. High up in the Urals a monster steel-plant was erected, and around it a brand-new town housing 180,000 people. Way down in Turkestan a former American I.W.W. had carried through the construction of a railway traversing 1,100 miles of desert and rock. A giant dam had been flung across the river Dnieper to provide a head of water for an electric plant generating 900,000 horsepower. The gangrenous slums around the oil-wells at Baku had been supplanted by a garden city on the heights, with clubs, schools, hospitals, an electric railway, and pure water piped from reservoirs ninety miles away. Stalingrad on the Volga was made a little Detroit, Magnitogorsk a potential Pittsburgh, Kharkov another Kansas City. The commissars began to boast that their country had made as much industrial progress in four years as any capitalist nation had achieved in forty.

The idea of drawing a blueprint for economic growth had apparently worked. It had worked so well, or at least so spectacularly, that even before all the figures could be totalled the Kremlin decided to launch a Second Five-Year Plan. This, it was announced, would plug the holes in the

First, and round out the level of progress. More attention would be paid to quality in basic construction, and more to quantity in consumer goods. Prices would be reduced by 40%, real wages increased by 100%, and the trade turnover multiplied by from 250% to 300%. The masses were going to be provided with more and better houses, more and faster trains, more and smoother roads. There were going to be neckties for the men, lipsticks for the women, fountain pens for the students, and rubber dolls for the tots. There was even going to be enough white bread!

And once more the masses fell to with a will. Once more they began to sweat as they labored, and grin through their sweat. They knew they were making progress. Every day now, every hour, life was improving under the Red Star. Goods were multiplying, and with them was coming goodness. That at least was what those masses told themselves. The achieving of material abundance, they believed, would soon bring all sorts of spiritual abundance in its wake. Already there was talk of how Stalin was preparing a new Constitution for the country, one guaranteeing complete freedom and civil liberty. That meant the Dictatorship was about to end, or at least about to begin to end. The Soviet Union was going to taste the joys of full democracy at last.

So there was ample reason for the Soviet masses to grin as they sweated. They were making progress.

XXXV. A NEW DEAL

LMOST everywhere else in the world there was cold despair, but in the Soviet Union people wallowed in hope. Everywhere else unemployment kept mounting, but in the Soviet Union there were more jobs than hands. Everywhere else the economy withered, but in the Soviet Union it appeared to be all buds and blooms.

The contrast was so stark that people everywhere else began to scratch their heads and wonder. Not all the people there did that, nor most, nor even relatively many. But those who did were usually the sort who could attract attention, for they had heads that towered, and they knew how to wonder out loud. Most of them were mettlesome intellectuals, or militant workers, or active humanitarians, and they exercised an influence out of all proportion to their numbers. Some went to Russia to see for themselves what was happening, and of these the most vocal came back with ecstatic reports. Said one of them, a famous American journalist and cynic named Lincoln Steffens: "I have seen the Future, and it works!" And myriads who never went to Russia took such reports as gospel truth. They repeated them, expatiated on them, rhapsodized about them. Thus there was created a tremendous stir.

The general attitude toward communism began to change somewhat in most capitalist lands. At first it had been one of horror, and then one of contempt. Now an increasing number of people started to accord the movement a grudging admiration. Quite respectable people caught themselves worrying whether those crazy Bolsheviks might be right after all. Not in everything, of course. Not, for example, in their advocacy of violent revolution. There they were no better than criminals. Nor in their acceptance of political dictatorship. There they were just plain fools. But what about that idea of theirs about economic planning? That certainly seemed to be working. No matter how one discounted their figures and distrusted their tales, the fact remained that they *had* achieved a triumph. They had hoisted the half-dead Russian bear out of the dust, bound his wounds, cured his mange, put a gleam in his eye, and set him coasting on roller-skates. And all within half a decade. They had taken a region that had never caught up even with the

Nineteenth Century, and in half a decade pushed it smack into the middle of the Twentieth. And all without any financial aid from abroad. That seemed nothing short of a miracle. Yet it wasn't really a miracle, for see how it had been accomplished. No prayer, no mumbo-jumbo. The communists had simply drawn a blueprint of what they wanted, and then had worked like hell to carry it out.

More and more people in the capitalist lands began to argue thus. And more and more began to ask themselves a question. At first hesitantly, then almost with bravado, they began to ask themselves: If the communists can do a thing like that, why can't we?

It was a blasphemous question in a way, blasphemous because it challenged the first principle of capitalism. According to that principle, a plan was already in existence, a perfect one ordained by Nature. All respectable people had believed that for a hundred years or more. They

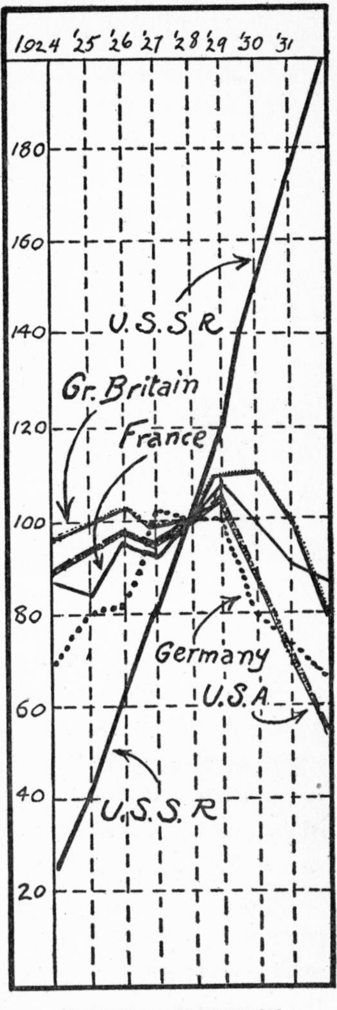

INDUSTRIAL PRODUCTION
1924–1931

In the U.S.S.R. people grinned through their sweat.

had universally taken it for granted that, thanks to the mysterious beneficence of some Inscrutable Force, if each man would only mind his own business, all men would prosper—in the end. But now people were less sure of that. The Depression had made them a lot less sure of that. All along they had let Nature take its course—and look where it had landed them!

That was why many people in the capitalist lands were ready now to indulge in blasphemy. Their faith in the capitalist system had been shaken. All along that system had promised to bring prosperity, and until 1929 it had given proof that it might fulfil the promise. Had it not multiplied the machines that multiplied goods, and flooded the earth with plenty? Had it not humbled the feudal lordlings, and given the common folk a chance to rise? Of course it had! By every gross standard it had improved life for the man in the street, and even for the man in the alley. That was why both had accepted capitalism, and had identified it with civilization and progress. But now? Now they were not so sure. Though they might still believe in that system, they had finally become convinced that it needed to be taken in hand.

Their attitude might be likened to that of vassals toward a king who in his prime had been able to shower them with favors, and who for that reason had been forgiven all his sins. Though he had lied and cheated, though he had often been cruel and always been selfish, those vassals had been reluctant to complain. After all, was he not in his own capricious way making them rich and powerful? Far from complaining, they had hailed him to the skies, and had howled down all who dared do otherwise.

But that was in the past. Since then the monarch's sins had caught up with him. The excesses he had so long indulged in had begun to tell at last, and his prowess had suddenly waned. Proof? Look at his condition right now. He was prostrate. He had fallen all of a heap in 1929, and had not stirred since then. True, he had broken down many times before. Once in about every ten years he had reeled and slid under the table. In the past, however, he had always snored when piled into bed. Now he was barely able to breathe. In the past he had always begun to stir after at most a few months. This time he was still in a stupor after three years. So the truth was out: His Majesty was no longer the man he used to be.

What then was to be done? Should he be dragged out and thrown to the dogs? No, that was neither feasible nor politic. The most powerful courtiers were still faithful to the old reprobate, and these would fight hard in his defense. Besides, what guarantee was there that a new king would prove any better? For that matter, how was there to be any agreement as to who the new king should be? It was wiser, therefore, to do nothing drastic. It was wiser to try reform rather than revolution. First the sick ruler ought to be dosed with stimulants to bring him back to life. Then, once on his feet again, he ought to be told to behave. And *made* to behave. A strict regimen ought to be imposed on him, and precautions taken to see that he kept it. Thus the invalid would not alone be restored to vigor; he might even be made more vigorous than before. And then his vassals would be able to enjoy even greater beneficence at his hands. . . .

That, in crude analogy, was how many people began to feel about capitalism. They did not want to destroy it. On the contrary, their one desire was to keep it from destroying itself. To do that, however, they felt they must rein it in a bit.

And this they began to do now. In Britain a coalition government proceeded to pass "Marketing Acts" and other measures to take some of the spleen out of laissez-faire. In France a little later an avowedly socialist government began to move in on the banks, and nationalize various industries. In the Scandinavian countries flagrantly radical cabinets gave increasing support to the cooperative movement. In Spain a revolutionary government overthrew the monarchy, and formally announced, "The Spanish State is a workers' Republic." And in the United States the old Democratic Party set out to establish a "New Deal."

Of all those developments, the last was the most portentous and impressive. It was directed by a handsome individual named Franklin Delano Roosevelt, who was at once a gentleman and a politician, a sportsman and a paralytic, a man who could keep his gaze on the stars and his ear to the ground. He had stupendous courage, energy, charm, and humor. In addition—and this was decisive—he had a most beautiful voice. The day he took office was perhaps the darkest in his country's history. All the banks had been closed to prevent a total collapse of the financial structure. Industry was threatened with strangulation, and commerce seemed on the point of death. Terror had closed over the entire land, for millions of citizens faced the prospect of losing every cent they had saved. It was a day so fearful that only a Titan could hope to save it. Luckily such a one was there.

Franklin Delano Roosevelt was there, and when he raised his voice, the day was saved. For tens of millions could hear that voice—they had their radios—and there was assurance in it, clear, strong, ringing assurance that made every listener's heart beat anew. Said he:

> "The only thing we have to fear is fear itself—nameless, unreasoning, unjustified terror. . . . This great nation will endure as it has endured, will revive and will prosper. . . . The people of

the United States have not failed . . . [it is] the rulers of the exchange of mankind's goods [who] have failed, through their own stubbornness and their own incompetence. . . . Their efforts have been cast in the pattern of an outworn tradition. . . . *They have no vision, and where there is no vision the people perish."* . . .

That was talking. That was good, plain, knuckle-hard talking. And it was followed at once by just that kind of action. Months earlier Mr. Roosevelt had promised the people a "New Deal," and now he set out to give it to them. During those months a hand-picked group of young advisers—his "brain trust," it was called—had helped him draw up a plan of action.

Four problems had to be solved at once. The first was unemployment, which had become a choking embolism in the blood-stream of the economy. There were perhaps 15,000,000 people who were out of jobs, and most of them had to be staked until they could find jobs. The second problem was farm poverty, which had developed chronic ulcers in the economy's stomach. Agricultural prices were so low that crops were fetching less than they cost to raise. Some 30,000,000 farm-folk were faced with foreclosure on their lands unless the government came at once to their aid. The third problem was industrial stagnation, which was fast crippling the economy's limbs. With so many workers unemployed, so many farmers out of funds, and most of the foreign markets closed, the owners of the machines were naturally refusing to produce more goods. And, most exigent of all, there was finally the problem of the financial breakdown, for that threatened to paralyze the economy's entire nervous system. The banks had to be immediately rehabilitated, the stock exchanges had to be reformed, and the whole monetary structure had to be made over.

A man less brave than President Roosevelt—or more sapient—might have quailed before tasks so tremendous. But he sailed right into them with both fists flying. He set hundreds of thousands, eventually millions, of people to work draining swamps, building roads, painting murals, giving concerts, and carrying out a thousand other good or makeshift projects. He extended loans to the debt-ridden farmers, and paid them subsidies in order to raise farm prices. He tried to end the chaos in business by setting up codes of "fair practice" in commerce and industry. He buttressed the labor unions, nailed a floor under wages, hammered a ceiling over work-hours, and prohibited the employment of children. He encouraged the cities to build model tenements, and inaugurated stupendous rural reclamation schemes. He patched up the banking system, built dykes to restrain stock speculation, reorganized the credit structure, and revalued the dollar. He castigated the "economic royalists," pleaded for the "forgotten man," inveighed against "horse-and-buggy" methods, and gave new luster to the "democratic way of life." He cajoled the Legislature, scared the Judiciary, moved the center of power from Wall Street to Washington, and restored the word "Presidency" to its original meaning—namely, "front seat." He soaked the rich, he fed the poor, he challenged the mighty,

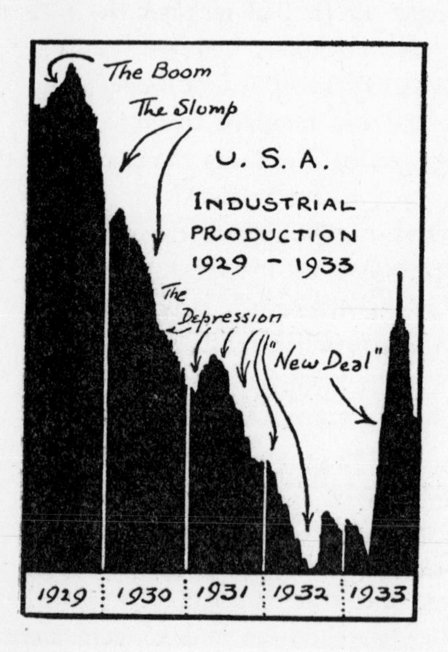

he cheered the downtrodden. He connived and contrived and set the whole nation in a whirl. And in the end he managed to check the Depression.

But that was all he managed to do. President Roosevelt never succeeded in achieving the general well-being which he had said would come with the New Deal. He failed even to restore the partial prosperity which had marked the late lamented New Era. In the circumstances, however, nothing else was to be expected. Even had he been less hindered by opposition from the right, and less troubled by impatience on the left, he would still have failed. For from the beginning to the end he was not quite sure where he wanted to go, let alone just how he was to get there. He liked to think that he had a plan, and kept insisting that all his stratagems were carefully considered parts of "a connected, logical whole." Actually, however, he was improvising most of the time. Skilled navigator that he was, he knew he had to tack with the wind. His vessel, he realized, was no mere raft like that which Stalin commanded. It was a tall clipper, heavily freighted, and carrying passengers who screamed at every lurch. That made Mr. Roosevelt's task exceedingly difficult.

Here was his problem. On the one hand he wanted to revive capitalism; on the other, and at the same time, he wanted to reform it. To accomplish the first he had to give the businessmen fresh confidence, and to accomplish the second he necessarily had to deprive them of that confidence. As a result, whatever he did with his right hand he had to undo with his left. So how could he plan?

The New Deal was at best a rough draft, or rather a series of rough drafts no two of which were quite consistent. Necessarily, therefore, there had to be confusion. For evidence one need merely look at what the New Deal was forced to do to aid agriculture. Essentially the farmers were the purest of all capitalists since they had never learnt to combine among themselves and reduce production when prices were low. Consequently, the Depression had hit them harder than any other capitalists. They had been literally knocked out, and the government could see only one way to set them on their feet again. That way, apparently, was to teach them how to become corrupt. The government had to show them that if they produced less, they would be able to profit more. So the farmers were actually paid not to grow all they could of wheat, cotton, and certain other "over-produced" crops. They were actually paid to slaughter their brood-animals. A New Deal sworn to create abundance went out of its way to enforce scarcity.

The stratagem was monstrous, and yet apparently unavoidable. Most of the other capitalist countries had had to resort to it in one form or another. Brazil was destroying millions of pounds of coffee each year in order to keep up the price in the world market. Ceylon was intentionally allowing many tea-plantations to go to seed, and Borneo was deliberately letting the jungle smother the rubber groves.

It was mad, and people knew it was mad. Yet they could see no better way to extricate themselves from the blind alley into which they had somehow blundered. Consider, for example, what was done in Europe. Desperate to relieve her unemployment problem, Holland put thousands of men to work planting wheat in lands reclaimed from the Zuyder Zee. But when these new fields began to bear, more wheat was harvested than the market could absorb. What to do? Donate the surplus to the poor, and let them turn it into bread? No, that would wreck the current price of wheat. So instead the surplus was dumped in Denmark, where there was a demand for cheap hog-fodder. But no sooner was that done than a new problem arose. The Danish pigs, having no respect for economics, took advantage of their improved diet to grow inordinately fat and fecund. Before long Denmark found herself with more pigs on her hands than could possibly be sold at a profit. Again what to do? Bring the price of pigs so low that even the poorest might have bacon for breakfast? Certainly not! That would ruin the established market. So instead the pork was turned into fertilizer, and then dumped in Holland to be spread on the new wheatfields that had been reclaimed in the Zuyder Zee! . . .

If the New Deal failed, it was because America, like every other capitalist land, was still wedded to an old error. People there continued to believe that a system born into a world cramped by scarcity was fit for a world swollen with abundance. The capitalist system had been good in its day. Not perfect, but definitely good. Now, however, its day was passing—perhaps even quite past. Yet most people continued to behave as though it were still present. They continued to climb over stiles which had long since been chopped up for kindling wood. They persisted in scrambling over high walls which had long ago crumbled into dust. They were blind. Most people were blind. Their eyes were still adjusted to the darkness which had reigned in former times. Now that they found themselves in the noonday glare, they were slow to discover that they need no longer grope.

But they would learn—eventually. Some had already begun to learn. The New Deal proved that. Despite all its limitations, despite all its confusions and evasions, the New Deal offered irrefutable proof that some people had begun to learn. For that phenomenon was not confined to the United States. It showed up in one form or another in many lands. A few have already been mentioned—Britain, France, Scandinavia, Spain—and there were others. For example, there was Palestine, where small but immensely impressive feats of progress were achieved during this period. Then there was Mexico, there was Chile, above all there was China. In each of those countries, and many more which might be named, a will asserted itself now to make the Machine fulfil its promise.

Yes, in many lands many people were beginning to realize at last why there was hunger in the midst of plenty, and strife where there was room only for peace. It was because psychology had failed to keep up with technology, because the ways of thought had lagged too far behind the needs of life. And the realization was leading to action. Rulers were being elected, or at least accepted, who were obviously bent on getting things done—and good things, progressive things. They were men who, though they might move slowly, were determined to move ahead. This was happening in many lands.

But not in all.

XXXVI. UNMADE IN GERMANY

OT in all lands was there that will to forge ahead along the path of peace and progress. Not in Germany, for example. There quite the opposite became true, and it is not hard to understand why. In Germany too many people had come to identify peace with shame and progress with despair.

Consider what those people had had to endure since the War. First the humiliation of defeat, then the ordeal of political revolution, then the drawn-out agony of financial chaos, then the sharp fever of artificial prosperity, finally the full horror of the Depression. It was too much. To be sure, the Russians had suffered worse; but they, after all, were Russians. The Germans were a more sensitive folk, at least to slights; also they were less inured to bleak misery. They were a proud people who had been schooled by arrogant rulers. They had a high culture and had been taught they deserved the highest place among the nations of the earth. Instead they felt themselves reduced almost to the lowest.

So they were disgruntled. Even before the War they had been disgruntled, and insofar as they had had any choice in the matter, that was why they had entered it. They had hoped to lay hold of an empire befittingly grand for a nation so great as they believed their own to be. But they had lost, and the smart of failure had left them sorer than before. Moreover, the soreness kept waxing, for their victorious rivals persisted in rubbing salt into their wounds. Many Germans had shown a willingness to rise above their defeat in battle. They had admitted the error of the Kaiser's bloody course, and had set up a new government sworn to seek prosperity by pursuing peace. It was a strenuously democratic government headed by men ardent for a better order in the world. Had that government been given a fair chance, it might have succeeded.

But it was not given a fair chance. Certain other nations, especially France, were afraid to give it a chance, and this encouraged more and more Germans to refuse to do so. From the outset there had been much internal opposition to the new government. The old monarchists had opposed it because it was republican, and the former militarists because it was pacifist. The big industrialists had opposed it because it was too socialistic, and the more radical workers because it was not socialistic enough. And these hostile elements grew increasingly belligerent as the years passed. Every evil born of the War, and every hardship entailed by the Peace, was blamed on the struggling regime. It was blamed because an inflation ruined the lower middle class and enriched a horde of classless profiteers. It was blamed because many German youths began to despise the martial spirit, and because many German maidens took to bobbing their hair. It was blamed for the growth of modern art and birth-control and nudism and unemployment. Also it was blamed because it tolerated Jews.

Nevertheless the government managed to survive for a while. Indeed, after 1924 it almost thrived. That was because the worst features of the Treaty of Versailles had finally been mitigated, and more and more foreign capital had begun to flow into the land. Mention has already been made of the many billions that were loaned to Germany, and though most of the money had to be handed out again as "reparations," the rest remained in the country to finance a boom. It was a fairly considerable boom while it lasted.

But then came 1929. No more building of new factories. There was no money for that—and less need. The factories that had already been built could not find markets for their goods. Construction ceased, production waned, and unemployment grew fearfully. Even the young men, they who were always the last to be fired, even they lost their jobs now. By 1930 nearly half the young men in the country were looking for work. And when it became clear to them that no work was to be found, they began to look for trouble.

Every other capitalist country was swept by the scythe of Depression, but in most of them there was sufficient stored wealth to blunt the stroke. The little shopkeepers and their kind could live off what they had tucked away in buried socks; the utterly destitute could turn to their governments for doles. In Germany, however, nearly all the socks had been emptied during the inflation ten years earlier. Moreover, the government was completely broke. Other countries could devalue their currencies, and thus needle their foreign trade. Germany did not dare. She was too fearful of reeling into another inflation. So she struggled to keep standing—and the scythe cut off her head.

Then Hitler took over.

Herr Adolf Hitler was Germany's vengeance on the world, and it was a tragic vengeance, for he was a tragic character. He had been born into a household that crawled with hate, for his father, a petty customs official in an Austrian bordertown, had been literally and otherwise a bastard. The man had drunk heavily, married inveterately, and bullied all whom he dared. He had died in his cups in 1903, leaving a sick widow, a small pension, and numerous children of whom Adolf was the youngest. The boy was not prepossessing. He had sullen eyes, fidgety hands, and a moody passion for idling. His bent seemed to be toward painting, and when he was seventeen he went to Vienna in the hope of winning a scholarship at the Art Academy there. But his application was rejected—he had more genius than talent—and he was forced into casual labor. That made his spleen run over. He had to become a vagrant, living off scraps and sleeping in flop-houses: one more country-boy who had failed to make good in the city. For eight years he had to exist thus, homeless, nameless, and choking with spleen. Finally, when he was twenty-five, the War broke out and he found relief.

The War brought him relief because it gave him something to live for. No longer was he a lonely one lost in a void. Once he joined the army, he had a place to sleep, a uniform to wear, a job to do, and a gun with which to do it. He *belonged.* After so many years of aimless drifting, that was a very sweet boon.

But then the War ended. The cause for which he had fought went down to defeat, and he was left once more a nobody possessing nothing and belonging nowhere. He could not stand it. Four years of war had stiffened his spine and left a twitch in his trigger-finger. Instead of succumbing to despair, he became a demagogue.

The stricken country had begun to breed political parties much as a carcass breeds worms, so it was not difficult for Hitler to find a platform. In Munich he attached himself to a group of seedy cranks and noisy bar-flies who had organized what they called the "German Workers Party." Almost at once he became their leader, for though he seemed to know even less than some of the others, he was able to express himself more vehemently. His ideas were as vague as his grammar was faulty; his gesticulations were as graceless as his voice was harsh. But there was a deep and queer fury in the young man, and when he arose to speak it leaped out and inflamed all who listened. Soon there were hundreds who flocked to hear him, soon tens of hundreds. Most of them were impoverished and frustrate folk, and they flocked to hear him for the best of reasons. They could huddle for warmth around the blaze of his spirit, and get drunk on the raw liquor of his words.

Hitler knew what those people wanted, for that same want had been in himself. They wanted to be told it was not their own fault that they were failures. They wanted to believe it was all because they had been cheated, robbed, betrayed. And they wanted to be assured that this treachery would not go unavenged. More than anything else they craved a warrant that they would yet be able to rise up and prove their prowess.

So Hitler gave them that warrant. He told them that enemies within their own midst had conspired against them, that Jews, Jesuits, Marxists, Freemasons, all sorts of dark un-German forces, had plotted to bring them low. And he swore that if they, the "true" Germans, would only put their trust in him, if they would but let him take complete charge, he would annihilate those enemies and raise Germany to its proper place in the sun. He would make the nation so mighty that all others would tremble in its presence. He would prove to the whole world that "true" Germans were the greatest people on earth.

And his listeners believed him. They believed because they wanted to believe, and also because they could see that he himself believed. So they did put their trust in him, more and more of them did that, and eventually he was actually able to wrest the authority he craved. It took time, of course. At first the majority of the Germans were inclined to laugh at "Handsome Adolf." He was slight and sallow, and when on his guard looked rather like an assistant floor-walker who still hoped for promotion. He wore a preposterous moustache, let a mop of hair fall over his brow, and usually had dandruff on his coat-collar. He did not drink or smoke or eat meat; and from all reports he had never been married or anything. Some believed he was a homosexual, but others said he was too abnormal even for that. Most educated Germans were quite embarrassed that such a creature should be able to attract any following at all.

Nevertheless he was allowed to carry on. The government, being liberal, felt it had no right to suppress him. It merely prayed that the public would not give him support. And so long as jobs were fairly plentiful, so long as times were relatively good, most of the public did not give him support. On the contrary, it looked on the man as a maniac.

But then came the Depression. Now Hitler was able to win millions of followers. He might be a madman, but most Germans were being driven mad, so they could not help looking to him as a leader. Sane men had governed Germany for more than ten years now, and what had they accomplished?

Adolf Hitler claimed to be directing a revolution; actually he was being swept along by a revulsion. In part it was a revulsion against the kind of government that had ruled Germany since the War; but basically it was something far graver. Basically, as we shall see, it was a revulsion against the whole trend of civilization since the Eighteenth Century. That trend had been toward a broader use of reason and a wider grant of freedom. People had believed that science could solve every earthly problem, and that democracy would destroy every social ill. They had believed that they needed merely to continue doing as they had done, constantly inventing more and better machines, constantly yielding more and greater liberties, constantly printing more and braver books, constantly producing more and readier comforts, and inevitably the whole world would become a Paradise.

But the Depression put an end to all that—at least in Germany. After 1929 the bulk of the people there began almost to loathe the faith they had formerly cherished. They felt it was a false faith, a lie as gross as the paunch on a profiteer. As early as 1918 millions of Germans had already begun to doubt that faith; but they had closed their eyes and clamped their jaws and struggled to swallow their suspicions. Now, however, they knew. The Depression had thrust an iron claw down their throats, and now they were retching up all that had so long roiled inside them.

Yet had that been the whole of the story, the worst might not have ensued. The Depression would have passed, taking the nausea with it, and the Germans would have begun to accept the old faith all over again. They would have learnt once more to believe in the possibility of progress. That, as we have seen, was what did happen in other lands. But in Germany the revulsion was too intense. It left the people so sickened that many of them would not hear of any "new deals." They wanted to have done with the game itself. They no longer had any desire for what the world called progress. They wanted to retreat. They wanted to go back to the sort of life they imagined their ancestors had lived, a life simple and earthy, harsh and heroic, slow as the seasons, stark as the thunder-clouds, bloody as the slaughter-pits.

So they took to shouting, "Heil Hitler!"

XXXVII. TOTAL-ARYANISM

HE Germans succumbed to Hitler for the same reason that the Americans elected Roosevelt, and the Russians accepted Stalin: they believed he could save them. Hitler, too, had a program, and it seemed to appeal to the Germans precisely because it was the opposite of both Roosevelt's and Stalin's. The latter two, though profoundly dissimilar, had at least one thing in common: they were headed in the same direction. Both aimed to make the Machine fulfil its promise; both sought to make life more abundant and urbane; both were obviously progressive. But Hitler's program?—that was just as obviously *re*gressive. In most respects it was comparable to the program which Mussolini had already initiated in Italy, the chief difference being that Hitler seemed bent on regressing with greater thoroughness and speed. He came of a people who were peculiarly gifted for thoroughness, and his own frenetic nature made him a demon for speed. Besides—and this may well have been the most telling factor—he was sincere. Hitler, unlike Mussolini, was no mere careerist. Regression to him was more than an expedient. It was a matter of principle.

Hitler believed that mankind had gone astray. Ever since the dawn of modern times the race had been painfully struggling to develop its intellectual faculties and curb its passions. It had been laboring with all its might to be "rational." The prevailing philosophy had scorned fanaticism and bigotry, and had insisted that people must think things through, see both sides of the question—in short, be "scientific." And most people who were at all educated had actually tried to follow that prescription, or had at least known that they *ought* to try. But not Hitler. To him the whole idea of rationalism seemed perverse. He was a mystic, and insisted that intuition was a far surer guide to truth than cogitation. The fact that this made him appear an eccentric merely proved to him how grievously mankind had been misled. It revealed how much damage had been done because the schools had set out to "enlighten" the young rather than indoctrinate them. "Education," declared Hitler, "ought to be confined to broad and general convictions . . . drummed into the minds and hearts of the people by incessant repetition."

Hitler believed that truth was essentially non-rational, even irrational, and for that reason if no other he simply could not help being regressive. Irrationalism was the cornerstone which the builders of the modern world had most contemptuously rejected. They had seen what evil effects it had had in the past: how it had enforced scarcity, cemented ignorance, buttressed despotism, and blocked progress. These, however, were precisely the effects which Hitler most ardently desired. He did not consider them evil at all. On the contrary, from where he stood, high on a mountain of supermania, they looked good. So he set out to achieve them.

His first task, therefore, was necessarily one of destruction. He had to demolish the entire ideological framework that sustained modern civilization. He had to assail not alone rationality, but also liberty, equality, fraternity, urbanity, and every other ideal of the Liberal Age. And that was just what he did do. Right from the start he inveighed against liberty. Most people, he insisted, did not want it anyway. They were inherently slavish, and wanted nothing but discipline. Moreover, said he, it was not merely foolish but criminal to try to make them over. People had no valid right to individual freedom since in reality they had no individual being. Only that to which they belonged, their herd, their nation, their State, that alone had real individuality. Therefore that alone might call its soul its own; the State alone could properly claim the privilege of doing as it pleased. Moreover, to exercise that privilege the State was in duty bound to deny it to all citizens. The State must absolutely control everything said or done or even thought within its domain. It must be "totalitarian"—and not just temporarily, as the stupid Bolsheviks said, but forever.

And what was true of liberty was equally true of equality. Hitler was all against it. People were not all of one kind biologically, so why should they be of one class socially? Females, for example, were obviously less strong than males. Did it not follow, therefore, that they deserved fewer privileges? The feminist trend of modern times seemed to Hitler a "sin against Nature." Women, he believed, were fit at best only to mate with men, never to compete with them. Therefore he insisted that they ought to be put back where they had always belonged—in the kitchen cooking, or in bed bearing children.

Moreover, the men themselves were not all of equal capacity, so even among them there ought to be no equal rights. A few were obviously born to lead, and the rest as obviously to follow. The male population of each state ought therefore to be sorted out and arranged in levels. A "natural" society was one built like a pyramid, with power grading down from the wilful Dictator on the pinnacle to the witless horde at the base. To achieve that, of course, the old aristocratic principle must be revived, but made to function in a new way now—or rather in the oldest way of all. Rank must be decided not on the basis of wealth or breeding, but solely on each man's innate capacity for leadership. Moreover, this capacity must first be recognized from above, and only then acknowledged from below. None could be elected to exercise authority; all must be appointed. Even the Dictator must be appointed—by himself.

Moreover, the same arrangement must be established among the various races, for these too were obviously not of one quality. Some were inherently superior, and others as inherently inferior. Consequently it was "unnatural" to talk of world-fraternity. Hitler was convinced that the Brotherhood of Man was nothing but a diabolical lie invented by Jews and disseminated by Bolsheviks in order to "corrupt the blood of their betters." Just what he meant by "blood" was more than a little vague—he was anti-semantic as well as anti-Semitic—but nevertheless he used the word constantly. "Blood," he insisted, was the one important criterion of nationality. Therefore there must be no mingling, no mixing, no crossing the boundaries set by differences of "blood." The fact that science had failed to discover any such differences meant nothing to Hitler. He was a confirmed irrationalist, so he had small respect for science. All he cared about was the "dictates of the Eternal Will," and these informed him that brotherhood was proper solely within the herd.

Did that mean that outside the herd there must always be hostility? Certainly, said Hitler. "The obligation in accordance with the Eternal Will that dominates this universe [is] to promote the victory of the better and stronger races, and to demand the submission of the worse and weaker." Therefore any race that wished to fulfil its divine obligation would necessarily have to gird for battle. Realizing that its welfare was dependent primarily on warfare, it would have to assign the bulk of its industry to the production of effective slaughter-goods, and devote most of its education to the training of efficient slaughterers. And not just for a time. No, forever.

That, of course, would entail hardship; but, said Hitler, so much the better. The more hardship a race inflicted on itself, the tougher it became, and hence the more capable of wresting power. And that, after all, was the object most to be desired in life. A race worthy to be called noble did not want comfort. It wanted Power. To what end? So that it might be able to conquer all other races. And after it had conquered them—might it then relax and seek comfort? Oh, no! If it ever did that it would become soft, and *be* conquered. Therefore whatever made for ease, all amenity and urbanity, all grace and charm and creature convenience, all that must be forgotten. The most virtuous use that could be made of machines was to produce the weapons that would destroy machines. The only excuse for cities was that they were the arsenals producing the means to demolish cities. If that meant that ultimately the world would be rid of machines and empty of cities, well and good. Perhaps only in such a world, one bare and primeval, could the good life be restored. Only in a world stark of comfort could life again become *stark* in the German sense: that is, "strong." Then man would once more be able to live as had his ancestors: harshly, dangerously, like the beasts. Existence would be sweet again with the bitterness of pain, and warm with the terror of death. Man could come back into his own—and his own would be the wilderness.

Such, by implication if not admission, was the program which Hitler offered his people—and the world. What it entailed was clear in every paragraph. It was an assault on all that mankind had been consciously striving for since at least the Eighteenth Century. It was an assault on all the bastions of the spirit that had been built with so great toil in modern times. It was against reason, liberty, equality, fraternity, peace, progress, and the pursuit of happiness. More: in its admiration for the berserk, and its lust to revert to the bucolic, it was fundamentally against the Machine. Consequently, it aimed to frustrate all that the political revolutions in America and France and Russia had preached, and undo all that the Industrial Revolution throughout the world had begun to achieve. In substance it was a panicky scream for total counter-revolution.

To be sure, Hitler himself did not say it was that. Quite

possibly he did not even know it. In any event, what he did say was so confused and confusing that it was long before the world got the point. Even many of Hitler's most devoted followers failed to see where he was bound to drag them. The more foolish among them did not try to see, and the rest did not dare to look. Yet his conduct even while still a slum-scouring agitator should have made the truth all too plain. If in no other way, he surely betrayed himself by the curious ferocity with which he inveighed against the Jews.

Whatever else the Jews may have been, first and foremost they were a symbol. They more than any other group on earth bespoke the modern spirit, for to that spirit they owed their very life. Not their existence, of course—that dated from ancient days—but their life as free humans. Such life virtually ceased for them in the medieval era, and it was not renewed again until the dawn of modern times. And that was why they were such devotees of the modern spirit. In a certain sense they were that spirit incarnate—with all its faults as well as virtues.

To benighted folk the Jews had always appeared to be a sinister element, and in one small sense this impression was correct. The Latin *sinister* means "left," and there is no denying that the Jews were inordinately prone to be leftish. There was a reason. At the time of the French Revolution it was solely the radicals seated on the left benches of the Estates-General who urged the emancipation of the Jews. And this remained true in France and everywhere else from then on. Always and everywhere it was the forces on the left that spoke up for the Jew. Naturally so, for those forces believed in progress, and they recognized that the Jew was peculiarly adapted to help that cause. Nor was this solely because Jews knew that reaction brought them persecution. The Gypsies knew that too, yet they never became agents of progress. The American Negroes knew it, so did the Hindu untouchables, yet those elements and countless others that stood to gain under the auspices of progress nevertheless remained stubbornly conservative. The decisive factor in the case of the Jew seems to have been that he was conditioned for progress by his natural habitat. Progress was primarily a product of the city, and the Jew was primarily a city creature.

That explains his spectacular advance in the Machine Age. Industrialism, it must be remembered, arose in the cities, so the Jew was able to rise with it. He was already at home in the cities, and had been at home in them for at least a thousand years. Ever since the Dark Ages, when the law had forbidden him to own land, he had had no other way to live than as a trafficker in goods or gold. Consequently, when the Machine arrived he was all prepared to climb aboard. Industrialism required capital, and he was the man to advance it; industrialism produced wares, and he was the man to sell them; industrialism agglomerated workers, and he was the man to help them organize. He could read and write, and he could count; he had the cunning born of persecution and the daring born of desperation. Therefore he was at an advantage now. All the talents bred in him by forty generations of urban life were able to flourish with the triumph of urban enterprise.

The Jew became the arch-capitalist, the arch-socialist, and also the arch-intellectual. For the city did more than bring forth factories and slums. It spawned universities, academies, conservatories, libraries. Consequently the Jew was able to move in on these, too. It was no accident that he became a leader in the arts and the learned professions. Now that the Machine had come into the world, there was more time and money to devote to cultural pursuits; and ninety-nine out of every hundred Jews—at least in the West—lived right around the places where that devotion was most hotly pursued. It was as natural for the Jews to become prize scholars as it was for the sea-girt Swedes to become prime sailors.

And that helps to account for the queer violence of Hitler's hostility to the Jews. He preached anti-Semitism for more than mere demagogic reasons. He genuinely believed that in fighting Israel he was, as he himself put it, "working in the spirit of the Almighty Creator." For to him the Almighty Creator was in a quite literal sense a pagan god—that is, a deity of the *pagus*, the "countryside." And Israel had become the living symbol of the city. Therefore Hitler had no choice. The restoration of the primeval way of life necessarily entailed the destruction of the culture bred in cities, and that in turn absolutely required the obliteration of any influence wielded by Jews. The man who had once been denied a scholarship in Vienna may have been deranged; but he was consistent.

All that, however, was largely lost on the world—until too late. When Hitler came to power in Germany in 1933, most people imagined that he would turn out to be at most another Mussolini. The latter had been frothing much the same reactionary doctrines for fully a decade already. Had he not repeatedly called liberty a "putrid carcass," and equality a "weakling's filthy dream"? Had he not roared from a hundred balconies that war alone can make a people "great"? Yet thus far Mussolini had apparently managed to do very little harm. Some people were inclined to argue that he had even done some good. Had he not made the Italian trains run on time?

But there was a difference. Though Fascism too was an

attempt to reverse the trend of civilization, it carried little of the threat inherent in Nazism. That was because Italy was relatively a backward country. (Note how few Jews it contained.) Though Mussolini too had set out to turn the clock back, he had been able at most to move the hands. He had been impotent to tamper with the works, because in Italy the works did not amount to much. But in Germany they were colossal. Even Britain did not have as good an industrial plant, and only the United States had a better one. With Hitler in command of Germany, the tide of progress was *really* in danger of being turned.

The major force behind that tide had been the Machine, and now Hitler was in a position to throw the Machine itself into reverse. He was in a position to put horse-power behind his drive for world power. James Watt had labored for years to contrive a little steam-engine capable of emptying a coal mine of water. Hitler needed merely to throw a switch, and a whole nation of engines stood ready to flood the world with blood.

The world, however, failed to see that. It stared but it did not see—until too late.

By then the switch had already been thrown.

XXXVIII. CAME THE COUNTER-REVOLUTION

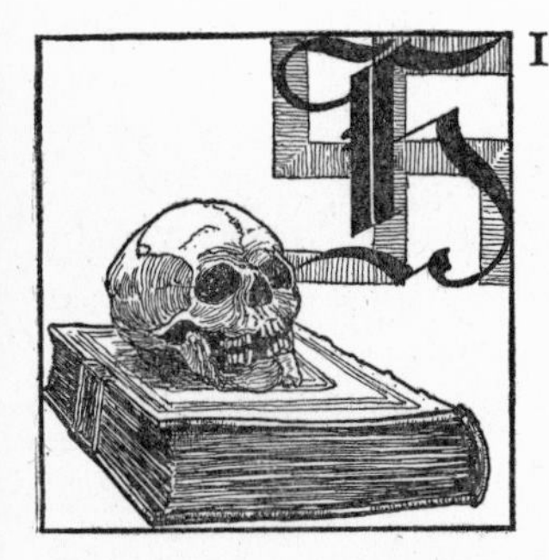

HITLER set out to turn the course of civilization, and at first there seemed to be neither the means nor the will to stop him. The elements that should have offered resistance from the start were too divided among themselves, and—what was worse—too confused within themselves. On the one hand there were the liberal capitalists, on the other the radical socialists, and had the two combined in time, they might have broken

Hitler's legs before he could take his first step. But they did not combine. How could they, seeing that both dreaded him less than they distrusted each other? True, there was much talk for a while about establishing a "united front" against him, but it was merely talk. All it created was a façade behind which each of the nominal allies connived with the actual enemy. The rulers of Britain and France secretly hoped to see Hitler march on Russia, and for that reason if no other they did nothing to keep him from arming. They even helped him. At the eleventh hour, however, the rulers of Russia agreed to supply him with food and fuel if he would march instead against Britain and France. That gave Hitler his chance. Soon he was marching all over Europe.

And conquering.

It was the Napoleonic story over again, but with one hair-raising difference. *This time the conqueror was a reactionary.* When Napoleon invaded Poland, he decreed the abolition of serfdom; when Hitler overran that land he introduced forced labor. Wherever Napoleon encountered ghetto walls, he tore them down; wherever Hitler saw a chance he put them up. These were typical contrasts, and they reflect more than a mere intellectual disparity between two men. Basically they reveal the spiritual cleavage between two eras. Napoleon had been the champion of a revolution, and his success was due in large part to the fact that in his day the world had been ready for revolution. If Hitler could enjoy a similar success a hundred and thirty years later, it was obviously because by then the world had become just as ready for revulsion.

And there lies the crux of this whole story. If hundreds of millions of people were willing to give in to Hitler, it was because at heart they had already given out. They had—

momentarily—lost faith in their own way of life. So much had gone wrong with it that they had begun to think the way itself might not be right. Hitler was therefore more an effect than a cause. He did not initiate the revulsion against progress; he merely implemented it. *He was not the wound but the gangrene.*

The main force making for progress had been the Machine, and one must remember that the Machine had always been resented in certain quarters. The duller lords had resented it, and so had the prouder peasants and craftsmen. The more precious poets had resented it, and so had any number of moody philosophers. And certain of these had known how to articulate their resentment. Highly gifted men—for example Wagner, Thoreau, Schopenhauer, Nietzsche, Spengler, Chesterton—these as well as scores of misanthropic hacks had worked themselves into an ivory-towering rage against industrialism. And the literature born of that rage had had considerable influence. Even had it been less brilliant and more logical it would still have had some effect, for it voiced a feeling that lurked in the hearts of most people.

Most people, it must be realized, had never really taken to the Machine; they had merely put up with it. They had accepted it with reluctance, even with repugnance, much as an impoverished maiden might accept a suitor who was rich but looked ugly and stern. The fault lay with themselves, of course. They did not try to understand the Machine. It was something new in life, and to enjoy it to the full, indeed to enjoy it at all, the human race had to develop a new way of living. Morals and politics, manners and economics, all these had to be made over completely. Common thought had to become more rational, private enterprise more orderly, and collective effort more universal in its scope. Liberty, equality, and fraternity had to become *actual* and world-wide.

But most people failed to realize that. Fundamentally they were like the peasant in the runaway locomotive who cannot comprehend why it will not start when he says "Giddap!"—or stop when he shouts "Whoa!"

That was why industrialism caused such chaos when it came roaring into the world, why it flung up so much horror and spewed forth so much filth. To be sure, these evils were somewhat alleviated with time; but not fast enough, and never adequately. Progress was indeed achieved, but more by default than intention. Mankind never really marched toward betterment; it *backed* into it. So the Black Life persisted. Even after a hundred and fifty years it was still virulent wherever it had been able to take root.

Nor was that the worst. Even had amelioration come more swiftly and surely, most people might still have nursed a grudge against the Machine. That was because the Machine enforced the growth of an order which they found hard on their nerves. It created a life that seemed to be all push, all go, go, go! The lights were too bright, the noises too loud, the tempo too swift and febrile. Almost all existence was made urban—even in the remote countryside it was at least sub-urban—and most people had a difficult time adjusting themselves to the change. At bottom they were still what their ancestors had been: peasants. During thousands of years they had lived one kind of life, and here they were being asked to learn to live another almost overnight. They just couldn't do it. They were told to rush, and they didn't want to rush. Not all the time, at least. In the past they had rushed only when there was killing to be done, or some other fine hot passion to indulge. The rest of the time they had idled. And that was still their desire. Most of the time they wanted to move slowly—like the sun, like the seasons, like the growing things in the earth.

This constant rushing around made them tired. Not physically tired; they could have stood that. No, mentally tired. The ordinary man had more time on his hands now, yet he seemed to find less leisure. There were too many things to want, too many strangers to face, too many problems to worry about. Nearly every aspiration of this new way of life was a strain on the ordinary man. The strain may have been unconscious, and a small price to pay for what it bought, but that did not make it any the less tiring.

Take liberty, for example: that was very tiring. Instead of allowing a man to sit back and wait for orders, it told him he must up and think for himself. Where once he had been able to lean on the crutch of tradition or authority, now he had to stand on his own feet. Wasn't that tiring?

Or take equality. According to that principle, a man no longer had a right to be content with the lot to which he had been born. He had to improve it, make it as good as the best, or write himself down a failure. And it was even worse for a woman. Where once she had been forbidden to think herself the equal of a man, now she was scorned if she thought anything else. Moreover, she was expected not alone to think that but to prove it. She had to earn her own living, insist on her own freedom, and expect a seat in a crowded subway only if she fought for it. Could anything have been more tiring than that?

Or take this obligation of indiscriminate fraternity. Whether a man liked it or not, he just had to accept it now. The Machine had so churned up the population that it was almost impossible any longer to live exclusively with one's own kind. Strangers were all over the place. One had to learn to get along not alone with people who came from foreign lands, but even with those who never left them. That was perhaps the most tiring demand of all.

The convenient buffer of distance had been all but destroyed by the Machine. The iron fingers of industrialism had fastened themselves around the planet and crushed it all into one tiny pellet. No advanced country could exist unto itself any longer, for none could provide for all its needs. Even so enormous a country as the United States was unable to do that. It might be able to get along without Swiss cheese, Scotch whiskey, Cayenne pepper, and Westphalian ham. But what about Sumatran rubber, Bolivian tungsten, Canadian nickel, or Malayan tin? Without these, and a hundred other imported commodities, American industry was ready for the junk-pile. And that was truer still of all other countries. The whole world had become one small settlement in which all men were next-door neighbors. But most of them did not care to have so many neighbors. They had been willing enough to *talk* about the ideal of the Brotherhood of Man, but now they were called on to practice it. That hurt.

There was a great deal in this machine-powered civilization that hurt. Bright professors and liberal preachers might say it was a salutary hurt, but that did not help much. Only one thing helped, and that was the thought of what could be gained at the price of the pain. For this civilization certainly offered compensations for the strain it imposed on mankind. At any rate, it *had* offered them. It had produced more physical convenience, more cultural enlightenment, more democracy, decency, urbanity, and prosperity than had ever existed on earth before. Thanks to industrialism, the general well-being had advanced farther in five generations than in any fifty preceding ones.

And so long as that advance continued, there was relatively little complaint. Now and again some sweet-souled poet might whimper that machinery was blighting the earth, or some bear-tempered philosopher might roar that city life was corrupting the race; but the population as a whole had paid little heed. Most people had refused to turn against the Machine—so long as it had kept clanking. They had been content to put up with urban life—so long as it had continued to give them a chance to rise. If they suffered a certain amount of nervous strain, they had stood for it much as a glutton stands for the heartburn after a good meal.

That was why industrial civilization had been able to advance so spectacularly for at least a century and a half. People had tolerated it because they had believed it could fulfil its promises. They had *seen* it fulfil them—at least partially. They had seen opportunities expand, and amenities increase, and generosity grow more common on every side. And this had engendered a widespread buoyancy, an almost universal optimism. Everywhere there had been the feeling that day by day in every way the world was getting better and better.

But then there was a sickening jolt. It came just when optimism seemed most in order, for by that date all the basic problems of technology had been virtually solved. The Machine was no longer the hideous, rattling monster it had been in early times. It had outgrown its infancy, outgrown even its adolescence. Now it was almost a mature thing, clean, swift, and beautifully efficient. Gone was the need to pack its cogs with human flesh, gone the need to oil its wheels with human sweat. The Machine was becoming very nearly automatic, and man was free at last to advance as never before. At last the means were within his grasp to banish want forever, and with it the cause of most of the woe that had plagued him since the beginning of time. Now he had a chance *really* to get ahead.

But he lost it. Just as he began to get into a stride, the earth suddenly quaked, and he stumbled. The great World War set the whole earth quaking, and man fell flat on his face. That should have served as a warning; but it did not. Once the War ended, and man could find his feet again, he brushed himself off and started to run on just as blindly as before. And even more wildly. Capitalism was allowed to grow increasingly monopolistic, and nationalism more and more rabid. So only one thing could ensue—and it did. Came the Depression, and man fell a second time. The very heavens seemed to crumble now, the earth's foundations fled, and man fell so hard this time that he could not so quickly find his feet again. In some lands it looked as though he would never find them.

Whereupon panic broke loose. Hundreds of millions of people became distraught and desperate. The worst afflicted were of course the young, those who had grown up since the War, for they felt they had been betrayed. Where, they asked, were the promises that their elders had so often made them, where the jobs to take, the ladders to climb, the fortunes to lay hold of? Where were the opportunities that were supposed to knock on their door? Where, for that matter, was the door? It had been carried off by the landlord or chopped down for kindling wood. It had vanished together with almost everything else that had once provided at least seeming security. Faith had vanished. Hope had vanished. Only a little doled-out charity remained, and even that seemed about to vanish. Was it any wonder, therefore, that so many young ones turned desperate? The sins of their parents had been visited on them too heavily. All the imperfections of the past had piled up on them, all the blunders caused by haste, all the crimes bred by greed, and—this was the worst—all the stupidities born of mental sloth. Who then can blame those young ones if they grew violent?

Rage seemed to be the only emotion befitting that generation, black rage against all that its forebears had done or dreamed. What had been latent from the very beginning had a chance to become overt and overwhelming now. Demagogues arose everywhere to preach open revolt against the whole scheme of liberal civilization. They took wild words out of Hitler's mouth—just as he had taken them out of Mussolini's—and damned every influence that had helped create the modern way of life. And great multitudes flocked to listen and cheer. They were sick of that way of life, sick and tired of it because they felt it had failed them. Whatever had been good about it had not been good enough. So now they were ready to believe it had been all bad.

And it was this that enabled Hitler to march and conquer. His battles were half-won even before he began to march, for those who might have halted him had *at first* hardly half a mind to try.

But only *at first*. Then they caught hold of themselves; late, but not too late, they turned and made a stand. Luckily the spirit of counter-revolution, though widespread, had never become universal. There were people left in the world who had not ceased to believe in the possibility of progress, people who were convinced that the real wave of the future could never be a backwash to the past. In every land there were some people like that, and in some lands there were many. And that was what saved the day.

Only for a while—but what an evil while!—were the forces

of reaction able to sweep all before them. They had the bigger tanks and the newer bombers and the fiercer will—then. The believers in progress had allowed themselves to be caught off their guard. They had argued while the others armed; they had relied on reason while the others primed their guns. But they woke up in time. Just in time they woke up to the fate awaiting them unless they made a stand. They saw then that more was at stake than the mastery of certain lands, or the primacy of a certain people. A way of life was at stake.

It had always been a faulty way, but by contrast with that which now threatened to take its place, it looked very nearly perfect. Those who had not yet abandoned it began to recall all the good things it had already yielded: the plenitude, the cleanness, the health and comfort and everyday decency. They recalled how it had wiped out the curse of slavery, lessened the blight of poverty, released women from their subservience to men, and men from their thraldom to lords. They bethought themselves of all it had done to foster science, and of the prodigies it had accomplished through the spread of education. They remembered suddenly how it had begun to give a new quality to life, a new richness and roundness and meaning. And thereupon a fire flooded their bones, and they made ready (at last!) really to fight.

It was a calamitous thing, they knew, to have to fight for civilization. Fighting for it would necessarily leave it maimed. But, they reasoned, better a maimed civilization than a dead one.

So they girded themselves and fought.

And they won. They had by far the greater resources, so it was inevitable that they should win—in the end. But that end was only the beginning. After the war came the peace, and this time, having learnt their lesson, men sought to make it truly a sound and lasting peace. They were not content merely to redraw the map; they set out to remake the world. For they knew then how drastically it needed to be remade, how desperately it needed to be rebuilt stone by stone from the very foundations. They realized at last why so much had gone wrong in the past. It was because so little effort had ever been made to set things right. Six generations had failed to perceive that the Machine was a new thing under the sun, and that, if it was to serve them as it could and should, they must create a new earth.

But then came that seventh generation, and it knew better.

Or did it?

THE END

INDEX